Guide to Food Storage

Follow this guide for food storage, and you can be sure that what's in your freezer, refrigerator, and pantry is fresh-tasting and ready to use in recipes.

In the Freezer (at -10° to 0° F)

DAIRY

Cheese, hard	6 months
Cheese, soft	6 months
Egg substitute, unopened	1 year
Egg whites	1 year
Egg yolks	1 year
Ice cream, sherbet	1 month

FRUITS AND VEGETABLES

Commercially frozen fruits	1 year
Commercially frozen vegetables	8 to 12 months

MEATS, POULTRY, AND SEAFOOD

Beef, Lamb, Pork, and Veal

Chops, uncooked	4 to 6 months
Ground and stew meat, uncooked	3 to 4 months
Ham, fully cooked, half	1 to 2 months
Roasts, uncooked	4 to 12 months
Steaks, uncooked	6 to 12 months

Poultry

All cuts, cooked	4 months
Boneless or bone-in pieces, uncooked	9 months

Seafood

Fish, fatty, uncooked	2 to 3 months
Fish, lean, uncooked	6 months

In the Refrigerator (at 34° to 40° F)

DAIRY

Butter	1 to 3 months
Buttermilk	1 to 2 weeks
Cheese, hard, wedge, opened	6 months
Cheese, semihard, block, opened	3 to 4 weeks
Cream cheese, fat-free, light, and ⅓-less-fat	2 weeks
Egg substitute, opened	3 days
Fresh eggs in shell	3 to 5 weeks

MEATS, POULTRY, AND SEAFOOD

Beef, Lamb, Pork, and Veal

Ground and stew meat, uncooked	1 to 2 days
Roasts, uncooked	3 to 5 days
Steaks and chops, uncooked	3 to 5 days

Chicken, Turkey, and Seafood

All cuts, uncooked	1 to 2 days

FRUITS AND VEGETABLES

Apples, beets, cabbage, carrots, celery, citrus fruits, eggplant, and parsnips	2 to 3 weeks
Apricots, asparagus, berries, cauliflower, cucumbers, mushrooms, okra, peaches, pears, peas, peppers, plums, salad greens, and summer squash	2 to 4 days
Corn, husked	1 day

In the Pantry (keep these at room temperature for 6 to 12 months)

BAKING AND COOKING STAPLES

- Baking powder
- Biscuit and baking mixes
- Broth, canned
- Cooking spray
- Honey
- Mayonnaise, fat-free, low-fat, and light (unopened)
- Milk, canned evaporated fat-free
- Milk, nonfat dry powder
- Mustard, prepared (unopened)
- Oils, olive and vegetable
- Pasta, dried
- Peanut butter
- Rice, instant and regular
- Salad dressings, bottled (unopened)
- Seasoning sauces, bottled
- Tuna, canned

FRUITS, LEGUMES, AND VEGETABLES

- Fruits, canned
- Legumes (beans, lentils, peas), dried or canned
- Tomato products, canned
- Vegetables, canned

WeightWatchers®

ultimate
five star
recipes

Oxmoor
House®

©2012 by Time Home Entertainment Inc.
135 West 50th Street, New York, NY 10020

ISBN 13: 978-0-8487-3638-5
ISBN 10: 0-8487-3638-9
Library of Congress Control Number: 2012934119
Printed in the United States of America
First printing 2012

Be sure to check with your health-care provider before making any changes in your diet.

WEIGHT WATCHERS and *PointsPlus* are the registered trademarks of Weight Watchers International, Inc. Trademarks are used under license by Time Home Entertainment Inc.

Oxmoor House
VP, Publishing Director: Jim Childs
Creative Director: Felicity Keane
Brand Manager: Michelle Turner Aycock
Senior Editor: Heather Averett
Managing Editor: Rebecca Benton

Weight Watchers® Ultimate Five Star Recipes
Editor: Shaun Chavis
Project Editor: Emily Chappell
Assistant Designer: Allison Sperando Potter
Director, Test Kitchen: Elizabeth Tyler Austin
Assistant Directors, Test Kitchen: Julie Christopher, Julie Gunter
Test Kitchen Professionals: Wendy Ball, R.D.; Allison E. Cox; Jessica Cox, R.D.; Victoria E. Cox;
  Margaret Monroe Dickey; Alyson Moreland Haynes; Stefanie Maloney; Callie Nash;
  Catherine Crowell Steele; Leah Van Deren
Photography Director: Jim Bathie
Senior Photo Stylist: Kay E. Clarke
Associate Photo Stylist: Katherine Eckert Coyne
Assistant Photo Stylist: Mary Louise Menendez
Production Manager: Theresa Beste-Farley

Contributors
Editor: Caroline Dunn
Designer: Cathy Robbins
Copy Editor: Carmine Loper
Proofreader: Norma Butterworth-McKittrick, Jacqueline Giovanelli
Indexer: Mary Ann Laurens
Test Kitchen Professionals: Tamara Goldis, Erica Hopper,
  Kathleen Royal Phillips
Interns: Erin Bishop, Mackenzie Cogle, Laura Hoxworth,
  Alicia Lavender, Anna Pollock, Ashley White

Cover: BBQ Chicken Pizza (page 144)

To order additional publications, call
1-800-765-6400.
For more books to enrich your life, visit
oxmoorhouse.com

To search, savor, and share
thousands of recipes, visit
myrecipes.com

Contents

Introduction

Secrets of Five-Star Recipes 4

    Want to Learn More about Weight Watchers? 4

About the Recipes 6

Recipes

Appetizers & Beverages 7

Breakfast 27

Soups & Sandwiches 59

Salads 79

Main Dishes 101

Side Dishes 151

Breads 161

Desserts 169

Index 189

Secrets of Five-Star Recipes

Good ingredients—and knowing how to use them—are the keys to dishes that are delicious enough to earn the highest ratings from our Test Kitchen staff (and raves from your family).

High-flavor ingredients are especially important in healthy cooking: You can use them to cook food with great taste and texture that is so enjoyable, it's easy to forget that it's light. With some creativity and clever techniques, you can enjoy food that is creamy, crunchy, crispy, spicy, and sweet—while still living your healthy lifestyle to the fullest. Here are some of the ingredients we use in this collection to make recipes worth five stars.

Greek yogurt, also known as Greek-style yogurt or strained yogurt, has a thicker texture than regular yogurt. Traditionally, it is made by straining regular yogurt through muslin or cheesecloth to let the whey drain away. The resulting thick texture makes it a perfect ingredient to add a creamy, rich texture to parfaits, dips, sauces, and more. Like regular yogurt, it is also made with bacteria that may be good for your digestive health.

> **Lemony Dill-Feta Dip, page 8**
> **Herbed Potato Pancake with Smoked Salmon, page 31**
> **Yogurt Parfaits with Mixed Berries, Honey, and Mint, page 56**

Soy sauce is made from fermented soybeans, salt, and wheat or barley. It is more than just a condiment to dash on food at a Chinese restaurant: Used as an ingredient, soy sauce can add a rich depth of flavor to salad dressings, soups, stews, and marinades. Dark soy sauce tends to be more flavorful than light soy sauce. Because soy sauce is high in sodium, use regular varieties in small amounts, or use lower-sodium versions. If you are sensitive to gluten, try tamari, soy sauce made only with soybeans.

> **Turkey Pot Stickers with Spicy Dipping Sauce, page 21**
> **Lime-Marinated Grilled Sea Bass, page 106**
> **Hot Peppered Pork, page 142**
> **Apricot-Glazed Chicken, page 144**

Want to Learn More about *Weight Watchers?*

Weight Watchers is a recognized leader in weight management that has been helping people successfully lose weight for more than 45 years. At *Weight Watchers,* weight management is a partnership that combines our knowledge with your efforts. Our weight-loss plan reflects sound and up-to-date scientific research. You'll find an integrated approach that offers good eating choices, healthy habits, a supportive environment, and exercise. For more information about the *Weight Watchers* program and a meeting nearest you, call 1-800-651-6000 or visit online at **www.weightwatchers.com**

Capers are the buds from a Mediterranean shrub of the same name. They are pickled and have an intense, sharp flavor. Find them in a jar packed in brine or in salt, and be sure to rinse away excess salt before using them. Often used in Greek and Italian cooking—in Sicilian cuisine, they're used to balance sweetness from fruits like currants or raisins to create a sweet-salty sensation—they pair nicely with lemons, fresh herbs, onions, vegetables, and seafood.

Goat Cheese–Green Olive Tapenade Crostini, page 14
Smoked Salmon Croustades, page 18
Italian Vegetable Caponata, page 23
Cheese-Stuffed Swordfish, page 108

Nuts are a great way to add crunch, flavor, and texture to pastries, appetizers, salads, pastas, rice pilafs, and main dishes. Though they're high in fat—use them sparingly!—they contain heart-healthy fats and are packed with protein and fiber. Try macadamia nuts, pecans, almonds, walnuts, pine nuts, and hazelnuts: Toast them first for the best flavor.

Hot Quinoa Cereal with Blueberries and Pecans, page 56
Pesto Pasta with Roasted Tomatoes and Walnuts, page 103
Orzo with Basil, Orange, and Pine Nuts, page 158
Pecan Pie Squares, page 186

Turbinado sugar, also sold as raw sugar, has a slight molasses flavor. It is made from evaporated cane juice and is formed in larger crystals than table sugar that hold their shape during baking. Sprinkled on top of fruit, a scone, muffin, cookie, cobbler, tart crust, or other pastry, it adds a golden sparkle and crunch that can turn an everyday food into a special, five-star treat.

Broiled Grapefruit, page 58

Citrus juice not only adds brightness to dishes, the acidity can enhance saltiness (so you can use a little less salt in recipes) and balance sweet and spicy flavors. Squeeze your own fresh juice for the best flavor. For fresh citrus zest, use unsprayed, unwaxed organic fruit, and use only the colored part of the skin, which contains the intense essential oils that add flavor and wonderful aroma. (Avoid using the white part just beneath the surface of the skin, the pith—it's bitter.) Try some different citrus fruits, such as sweeter, floral-scented Meyer lemons, raspberry-like blood oranges, and pink-fleshed Cara Cara oranges; or other forms such as candied zests and preserved lemons.

Chilled Mango Soup, page 60
Minted Pea Salad, page 84
Nectarine and Berry Crumble, page 173
Lemon Cheesecake, page 181

Wine and spirits such as orange liqueur, vodka, brandy, and rum are a great way to add natural flavor to savory and sweet dishes. Wine can add acidity to a recipe, and it can also be used to create a lip-smacking pan sauce. Reducing a wine or spirit—allowing it to simmer and evaporate until it becomes a thicker liquid—concentrates and enhances flavor. (In this process, some, but not all, of the alcohol will evaporate.) Liqueurs can also add flavor to baked goods. In frozen treats, liqueurs add flavor, and because alcohol doesn't totally freeze, it can be used to create a velvety texture.

Warm Beef Salad with Figs, page 87
Garlic Shrimp with Spinach and Vermicelli, page 130
Melon Sorbet, page 170

Specialty oils such as dark sesame oil, walnut oil, hazelnut oil, pistachio oil, and avocado oil aren't heated and used for cooking: They're too expensive, and much of their flavor would be lost. Instead, use them to add an extra punch of intense flavor and a lustrous feeling of indulgence in your mouth. Unlike butter or animal fats, these specialty oils contain more heart-healthy fats. Use them to make flavorful salad dressings, add just a few drops to food right before serving, or use them as dipping oils.

Turkey Pot Stickers with Spicy Dipping Sauce, page 21
Moo Shu Pork Wraps, page 76
Chunky Asian Slaw, page 99

About the Recipes

Weight Watchers® *Ultimate Five Star Recipes* gives you the nutrition facts you need to stay on track. Every recipe in this book has been evaluated by our Test Kitchen staff and received our highest endorsement. Each recipe also includes a **PointsPlus**® value. For more information on Weight Watchers, see page 4.

Each recipe has a list of nutrients—including calories, fat, saturated fat, protein, carbohydrates, dietary fiber, cholesterol, iron, sodium, and calcium—as well as a serving size and the number of servings. This information makes it easy for you to use the recipes for any weight-loss program that you choose to follow. Measurements are abbreviated g (grams) and mg (milligrams). Nutritional values used in our calculations come from either The Food Processor, Version 8.9 (ESHA Research), or are provided by food manufacturers.

Numbers are based on these assumptions:
• Unless otherwise indicated, meat, poultry, and fish always refer to skinned, boned, and cooked servings.
• When we give a range for an ingredient (3 to 3½ cups flour, for instance), we calculate using the lesser amount.
• Some alcohol calories evaporate during heating; the analysis reflects this.
• Only the amount of marinade absorbed by the food is used in calculations.
• Garnishes and optional ingredients are not included in an analysis.

Safety Note: Cooking spray should never be used near direct heat. Always remove a pan from heat before spraying it with cooking spray.

A Note on Diabetic Exchanges: You may notice that the nutrient analysis for each recipe does not include Diabetic Exchanges. Most dietitians and diabetes educators are now teaching people with diabetes to count total carbohydrates at each meal and snack, rather than counting exchanges. Counting carbohydrates gives people with diabetes more flexibility in their food choices and seems to be an effective way to manage blood glucose.

PointsPlus values
PointsPlus uses the latest scientific research to create a program that goes far beyond traditional calorie counting to give people the edge they need to lose weight and keep it off in a fundamentally healthier way. The program is designed to educate and encourage people to make choices that focus on foods that create a sense of satisfaction and are more healthful. *PointsPlus* values are calculated for foods based on their protein, fiber, fat, and carbohydrate content. This *PointsPlus* formula takes into account how these nutrients are processed by the body and helps you select foods that are both nutritious and satisfying! For more about the *PointsPlus* Program, visit WeightWatchers.com.

Appetizers & Beverages

PointsPlus value per serving: 0
White Bean Dip | page 8
Lemonade-Mint Iced Tea | page 12

PointsPlus value per serving: 1
Lemony Dill-Feta Dip | page 8
Strawberry-Mango Salsa | page 10
Chicken-Pesto Spread | page 10
Sparkling Cranberry-Citrus Green Tea | page 14
Smoked Salmon Croustades | page 18

PointsPlus value per serving: 2
Roasted Red Pepper and Chipotle Hummus | page 9
Bacon-Chile-Cheese Crescents | page 11
Red Pepper Pesto Crostini | page 12
Goat Cheese–Green Olive Tapenade Crostini | page 14
Crostini with Manchego and Honeyed
    Orange Relish | page 15
Pear and Swiss Triangles | page 16
Spanakopita Bites | page 16
Marinated Goat Cheese | page 17

Black Pepper and Sesame–Crusted Tuna Rounds | page 19
Turkey Pot Stickers with Spicy Dipping Sauce | page 21
Black Bean Cakes | page 22
Italian Vegetable Caponata | page 23
Pomegranate-Ginger Fizz | page 24

PointsPlus value per serving: 3
Honey-Drizzled Cherry, Goat Cheese, and Pistachio
    Crostini | page 13
Spicy Pork Sliders with Sweet
    Chipotle-Peach Sauce | page 20
Strawberry-Cherry Slush | page 26
Hot Spiced Chocolate | page 26

PointsPlus value per serving: 4
Strawberry–Piña Colada Milk Shakes | page 25
Fruity White Sangria | page 25

PointsPlus value per serving: 5
Barbados Punch | page 24

White Bean Dip

Menu
PointsPlus value
per serving: 3

White Bean Dip

1 ounce fat-free bagel chips
PointsPlus value
per serving: 3

Game Plan

1. Drain and rinse beans.

2. Combine ingredients as directed.

3. Serve chilled with bagel chips.

prep: 10 minutes • **chill:** 1 hour   *PointsPlus* value per serving: 0

Serve with fat-free bagel chips or raw vegetables.

  1 (15.8-ounce) can Great Northern beans, rinsed and drained
  2 teaspoons minced fresh thyme or ½ teaspoon dried thyme
  2 teaspoons balsamic or red wine vinegar
  1 teaspoon olive oil
  ½ teaspoon dry mustard
  ½ teaspoon freshly ground black pepper
  ¼ teaspoon salt
  2 tablespoons minced fresh parsley

1. Combine first 7 ingredients in a medium bowl. Mash until mixture is smooth using a potato masher; stir in parsley. Transfer to a small serving bowl; cover and chill at least 1 hour. **Yield:** 1¼ cups (serving size: 1 tablespoon).

Per serving: CALORIES 15; FAT 0.3g (sat 0g, mono 0.2g, poly 0g); PROTEIN 0.8g; CARB 2.1g; FIBER 0.8g; CHOL 0mg; IRON 0.2mg; SODIUM 55mg; CALC 6mg

Lemony Dill-Feta Dip

Menu
PointsPlus value
per serving: 1

Lemony Dill-Feta Dip

1 cup mixed celery, carrots, broccoli, and cherry tomatoes
PointsPlus value
per serving: 0

Game Plan

1. Rinse and chop vegetables and dill.

2. Grate lemon rind.

3. Combine dip ingredients in food processor, and serve with vegetables.

prep: 7 minutes   *PointsPlus* value per serving: 1

This Greek-inspired dip is also great as a spread for sandwiches or lamb burgers.

  1 garlic clove
  2 (3.5-ounce) packages reduced-fat feta cheese
  ⅓ cup plain fat-free Greek yogurt
  ⅓ cup light sour cream
  1 tablespoon chopped fresh dill
  1 teaspoon grated fresh lemon rind
  ⅛ teaspoon salt
  ¼ teaspoon freshly ground black pepper
Fresh-cut vegetables (optional)

1. With food processor on, drop garlic through food chute; process until minced. Add cheese and next 6 ingredients; pulse 3 times or until smooth. Serve with fresh-cut vegetables, if desired. **Yield:** 13 servings (serving size: about 2 tablespoons).

Per serving: CALORIES 43; FAT 2.5g (sat 1.7g, mono 0.5g, poly 0.1g); PROTEIN 4.1g; CARB 1.2g; FIBER 0.3g; CHOL 7mg; IRON 0mg; SODIUM 238mg; CALC 62mg

Roasted Red Pepper and Chipotle Hummus

prep: 7 minutes   *PointsPlus* value per serving: 2

The chipotle chile lends a subtle smokiness to this flavorful version of hummus. Serve with raw vegetables or baked pita chips for dipping, or spread on a sandwich for a tasty departure from mayonnaise.

1   (16-ounce) can chickpeas (garbanzo beans), rinsed and drained
½   cup bottled roasted red bell peppers
¼   cup fat-free sour cream
1   tablespoon fresh lime juice
1   garlic clove
1   chipotle chile
⅛   teaspoon salt
1   tablespoon extra-virgin olive oil

1. Place first 7 ingredients in a food processor; process until smooth. With processor on, slowly pour oil through food chute; process until well blended. **Yield:** 1¾ cups (serving size: ¼ cup).

Per serving: CALORIES 82; FAT 2.5g (sat 0.3g, mono 1.7g, poly 0.4g); PROTEIN 2.8g; CARB 12.2g; FIBER 2g; CHOL 1mg; IRON 0.6mg; SODIUM 172mg; CALC 32mg

Menu
PointsPlus value per serving: 2

Roasted Red Pepper and Chipotle Hummus

1 cup mixed vegetables
PointsPlus value per serving: 0

Game Plan

1. Rinse and drain chickpeas.

2. Rinse, drain, and cut vegetables.

3. Combine hummus ingredients, and process, adding oil slowly.

Strawberry-Mango Salsa

prep: 10 minutes • **other:** 10 minutes   *PointsPlus* value per serving: 1

This colorful salsa scoops up nicely with baked cinnamon-sugar pita chips, but it can also brighten up grilled fish or chicken.

    1   cup chopped strawberries
    1   ripe mango, peeled and diced
    ¾   cup finely chopped orange, yellow, or red bell pepper
    2   tablespoons chopped fresh mint
    1   teaspoon grated fresh orange rind
    2   tablespoons fresh orange juice
    1½   teaspoons sugar
    ⅛   teaspoon crushed red pepper

1. Combine all ingredients in a medium bowl. Let stand at least 10 minutes before serving, or cover and chill until ready to serve. **Yield:** 9 servings (serving size: ¼ cup).

Per serving: CALORIES 27; FAT 0.2g (sat 0g, mono 0g, poly 0.1g); PROTEIN 0.4g; CARB 6.9g; FIBER 1g; CHOL 0mg; IRON 0.2mg; SODIUM 1mg; CALC 7mg

Menu
PointsPlus value
per serving: 5

Strawberry-Mango Salsa

1 ounce baked
cinnamon-sugar pita chips
PointsPlus value
per serving: 4

Game Plan

1. Rinse, drain, and prepare fruits and vegetables.

2. Combine salsa ingredients, and chill.

Chicken-Pesto Spread

prep: 8 minutes   *PointsPlus* value per serving: 1

Enhance the flavor of this spread by using breast meat from a rotisserie chicken. Serve with crostini or whole-wheat crackers.

    ½   cup light mayonnaise, divided
    ¾   cup (1-inch) cubed cooked chicken breast
    ½   cup fresh basil leaves
    1   tablespoon pine nuts, toasted
    ¼   teaspoon salt
    ⅛   teaspoon freshly ground black pepper

1. Place 2 tablespoons mayonnaise and remaining ingredients a food processor; process 2 minutes or until smooth. Transfer mixture to a small bowl; fold in remaining 6 tablespoons mayonnaise. Cover and chill until ready to serve. **Yield:** 16 servings (serving size: 1 tablespoon).

Per serving: CALORIES 40; FAT 3.1g (sat 0.6g, mono 0.8g, poly 1.6g); PROTEIN 2.2g; CARB 0.6g; FIBER 0g; CHOL 8mg; IRON 0.1mg; SODIUM 102mg; CALC 4mg

Menu
PointsPlus value
per serving: 5

Chicken-Pesto Spread

1 ounce whole-wheat crackers
PointsPlus value
per serving: 4

Game Plan

1. Cook and cube chicken.

2. Combine spread ingredients in food processor.

3. Chill and serve with whole-wheat crackers.

Bacon-Chile-Cheese Crescents

prep: 7 minutes • **cook:** 13 minutes

PointsPlus value per serving: 2

A lightened chile rellenos mixture fills these tiny crescents.

⅓   cup (3 ounces) block-style ⅓-less-fat cream cheese, softened
¼   cup chopped green chiles, drained
4   center-cut 40%-less-fat bacon slices, cooked and crumbled
1   (8-ounce) can reduced-fat refrigerated crescent dinner roll dough
Butter-flavored cooking spray
1   teaspoon sesame seeds (optional)

1. Preheat oven to 375°.

2. Combine cream cheese, green chiles, and bacon in a small bowl.

3. Separate dough into triangles; cut each triangle in half, creating 16 triangles. Spread cheese mixture evenly on triangles. Roll up each triangle, starting at wide end. Place crescents, point sides down, on an ungreased baking sheet. Curve each into a crescent shape. Coat tops with cooking spray; sprinkle evenly with sesame seeds, if desired.

4. Bake at 375° for 13 minutes or until browned. Serve hot. **Yield:** 16 servings (serving size: 1 crescent).

Per serving: CALORIES 65; FAT 3.9g (sat 1.8g, mono 1.3g, poly 0.3g); PROTEIN 1.9g; CARB 6.4g; FIBER 0.1g; CHOL 6mg; IRON 0.4mg; SODIUM 165mg; CALC 9mg

Menu
PointsPlus value per serving: 3

Bacon-Chile-Cheese Crescents

1 cup celery slices
PointsPlus value per serving: 0

2 tablespoons fat-free ranch dressing
PointsPlus value per serving: 1

Game Plan

1. While oven preheats:
• Prepare filling.

2. Assemble crescent triangles.

3. While crescent triangles are baking:
• Rinse, drain, and slice celery.

Menu

PointsPlus value
per serving: 2

Red Pepper Pesto Crostini

Lemonade-Mint Iced Tea
PointsPlus value
per serving: 0

Game Plan

1. Combine pesto ingredients in blender, and process.

2. While mixture chills:
• Toast French bread.
• Prepare tea.

3. Top toast with cream cheese and pesto.

Red Pepper Pesto Crostini

prep: 5 minutes • **other:** 1 hour   *PointsPlus* value per serving: 2

Roasted red peppers give this nontraditional pesto a smoky yet sweet flavor. For a tart flavor balance, try serving with a refreshing glass of Lemonade-Mint Iced Tea.

    1   cup coarsely chopped drained bottled roasted red bell peppers (about 2 peppers)
    3   tablespoons grated fresh Parmesan cheese
    1   tablespoon sliced almonds, toasted
    2   teaspoons no-salt-added tomato paste
    1   garlic clove, chopped
    3   ounces fat-free cream cheese
   16   (½-inch-thick) slices diagonally cut French bread, toasted

1. Place first 5 ingredients in a blender; cover and process until smooth, stopping once to scrape down sides. Cover and chill at least 1 hour. Spread cream cheese evenly on toast slices; top each with 1 tablespoon pesto. **Yield:** 16 servings (serving size: 1 crostino).

Per serving: CALORIES 83; FAT 1.1g (sat 0.4g, mono 0.3g, poly 0.3g); PROTEIN 4.3g; CARB 14g; FIBER 0.7g; CHOL 1.6mg; IRON 0.9mg; SODIUM 213mg; CALC 50mg

Lemonade-Mint Iced Tea

prep: 10 minutes • **other:** 7 minutes   *PointsPlus* value per serving: 0

    8   cups water, divided
   12   regular-sized mint-flavored tea bags
   1½   tablespoons sugar-free lemon-flavored soft drink mix
        Ice cubes
        Mint sprigs (optional)

1. Bring 4 cups water to a boil in a saucepan. Remove from heat; add tea bags. Cover and steep 7 minutes. Remove and discard tea bags.
2. Pour tea into a large pitcher; add soft drink mix and remaining 4 cups water, stirring well. Serve over ice. Garnish with mint, if desired. **Yield:** 8 cups (serving size: 1 cup).

Per serving: CALORIES 3; FAT 0g (sat 0g, mono 0g, poly 0g); PROTEIN 0g; CARB 0g; FIBER 0g; CHOL 0mg; IRON 0mg; SODIUM 0mg; CALC 0mg

Honey-Drizzled Cherry, Goat Cheese, and Pistachio Crostini

prep: 7 minutes • **cook:** 5 minutes   *PointsPlus* value per serving: 3

A cherry pitter is indispensable when preparing fresh cherries in season, but you can easily prepare this appetizer any time of year using thawed frozen cherries.

4	ounces goat cheese, softened
½	teaspoon grated fresh orange rind
¼	teaspoon salt
¼	teaspoon freshly ground black pepper
12	(½-inch-thick) slices diagonally cut French bread baguette, toasted
1	cup chopped pitted cherries
¼	cup chopped pistachios
2	tablespoons honey

1. Combine first 4 ingredients in a small bowl. Spread goat cheese mixture evenly on 1 side of each toast slice. Top evenly with cherries and pistachios. Drizzle evenly with honey. **Yield:** 12 servings (serving size: 1 crostino).

Per serving: CALORIES 103; FAT 3.2g (sat 1.5g, mono 1.1g, poly 0.4g); PROTEIN 4g; CARB 15g; FIBER 1g; CHOL 4mg; IRON 0.9mg; SODIUM 189mg; CALC 18mg

Menu
PointsPlus value
per serving: 3

Honey-Drizzled Cherry, Goat Cheese, and Pistachio Crostini

Lemonade-Mint Iced Tea
(page 12)
PointsPlus value
per serving: 0

Game Plan

1. While bread is toasting:
- Prepare tea.
- Pit cherries.

2. Prepare goat cheese mixture.

3. Assemble crostini.

Menu

PointsPlus value
per serving: 3

Goat Cheese–Green Olive
Tapenade Crostini

Sparkling
Cranberry-Citrus Green Tea
PointsPlus value
per serving: 1

Game Plan

1. While bread is toasting
• Prepare tea.

2. Combine tapenade
ingredients in food
processor.

3. Assemble crostini.

Goat Cheese–Green Olive Tapenade Crostini

prep: 10 minutes   *PointsPlus* value per serving: 2

Green olives and orange rind give this tapenade a decidedly fresh twist that earned a top rating in our Test Kitchen.

  1 cup pitted green olives
  2 tablespoons fresh flat-leaf parsley leaves
  1 tablespoon capers, drained
  1 teaspoon grated fresh orange rind
  ¼ teaspoon freshly ground black pepper
  1 tablespoon olive oil
  8 ounces goat cheese, softened
 32 (¼-inch-thick) slices diagonally cut French bread baguette, toasted

1. Place first 5 ingredients in a food processor; pulse 4 times or until coarsely chopped. Add olive oil, and pulse 5 times or until finely chopped.
2. Spread about 1½ teaspoons goat cheese over each baguette slice, and top each with about 1½ teaspoons tapenade. **Yield:** 32 servings (serving size: 1 crostino).

Per serving: CALORIES 57; FAT 2.7g (sat 1.1g, mono 1.2g, poly 0.3g); PROTEIN 2.4g; CARB 5.8g; FIBER 0.3g; CHOL 3.3mg; IRON 0.5mg; SODIUM 155mg; CALC 15mg

Sparkling Cranberry-Citrus Green Tea

prep: 4 minutes   *PointsPlus* value per serving: 1

This is a pretty—and refreshing—way to dress up green tea.

  1 orange, halved
 1½ cups bottled diet green tea with citrus flavor, chilled
 1½ cups orange sparkling water, chilled
  1 cup cranberry juice, chilled

1. Squeeze juice from 1 orange half to measure 2 tablespoons. Combine orange juice, tea, sparkling water, and cranberry juice in a pitcher. Cut remaining orange half into 8 thin slices. Pour tea into 4 glasses. Garnish each serving with orange slices. **Yield:** 4 servings (serving size: 1 cup tea and 2 orange slices).

Per serving: CALORIES 48; FAT 0g (sat 0g, mono 0g, poly 0g); PROTEIN 0.3g; CARB 11.3g; FIBER 0.8g; CHOL 0mg; IRON 0.1mg; SODIUM 43mg; CALC 25mg

Crostini with Manchego and Honeyed Orange Relish

prep: 20 minutes • **cook:** 8 minutes   *PointsPlus* value per serving: 2

Manchego cheese is a sheep's milk cheese made in Spain. It has a creamy texture with a taste similar to feta cheese.

16	(½-inch-thick) slices diagonally cut French bread baguette
½	cup (2 ounces) shredded Manchego cheese
½	teaspoon freshly ground black pepper
1¼	cups navel orange sections, chopped (about 2 large)
2	tablespoons minced shallots (1 medium)
2	tablespoons water
2	tablespoons honey
1½	tablespoons fresh lime juice
1	tablespoon chopped fresh basil
⅛	teaspoon ground red pepper

1. Preheat oven to 450°.

2. Place baguette slices on a large baking sheet; sprinkle slices evenly with cheese and black pepper. Bake at 450° for 4 minutes or until cheese melts and baguette is lightly toasted.

3. Combine orange and next 3 ingredients in a small saucepan; bring to a boil. Remove pan from heat. Remove solids from cooking liquid using a slotted spoon; place in a small bowl. Stir lime juice, basil, and ground red pepper into orange mixture.

4. Top each toasted baguette slice with about 1 tablespoon orange relish. **Yield:** 16 servings (serving size: 1 crostino).

Per serving: CALORIES 64; FAT 1.5g (sat 0.9g, mono 0g, poly 0.1g); PROTEIN 2.4g; CARB 10.8g; FIBER 0.7g; CHOL 4mg; IRON 0.5mg; SODIUM 91mg; CALC 59mg

Menu

PointsPlus value
per serving: 4

Crostini with Manchego and Honeyed Orange Relish

Pomegranate-Ginger Fizz (page 24)
PointsPlus value
per serving: 2

Game Plan

1. While oven preheats:
- Slice baguette.
- Chop oranges.
- Mince shallots.
- Juice lime.

2. While bread toasts:
- Prepare Pomegranate-Ginger Fizz.
- Prepare orange relish.

3. Assemble crostini.

Pear and Swiss Triangles

prep: 5 minutes • **cook:** 12 minutes   *PointsPlus* value per serving: 2

Menu
PointsPlus value
per serving: 6

Pear and Swiss Triangles

Fruity White Sangria (page 25)
PointsPlus value
per serving: 4

Game Plan

1. While skillet heats:
• Trim bread
• Rinse and slice pear.
• Prepare sangria.

2. Assemble and cook
sandwiches.

3. Cut sandwiches and serve.

This simple appetizer is a sweet, mini-grilled cheese sandwich that showcases the decadent combination of pear and cheese.

  8 (1-ounce) slices white-wheat bread
  ¼ cup pear preserves
  4 (¾-ounce) slices light Jarlsberg cheese
  1 Anjou pear, thinly sliced
Cooking spray

1. Trim crusts from bread. Spread 1 tablespoon preserves over each of 4 bread slices. Top each with 1 cheese slice. Place pear slices evenly over cheese. Top with remaining bread slices. Coat both sides of sandwiches with cooking spray.
2. Heat a large nonstick skillet over medium heat. Add 2 sandwiches to pan. Cover with a sheet of foil; top with a heavy skillet. Cook 3 minutes or until lightly browned. Turn sandwiches over; replace foil and skillet. Cook 3 minutes or until golden. Repeat procedure with remaining sandwiches. Cut each sandwich diagonally into 4 triangles. Serve immediately. **Yield:** 8 servings (serving size: 2 triangles).

Per serving: CALORIES 91; FAT 2g (sat 0.9g, mono 0.3g, poly 0.3g); PROTEIN 5.7g; CARB 14.8g; FIBER 2.4g; CHOL 5mg; IRON 1.3mg; SODIUM 136mg; CALC 206mg

Spanakopita Bites

prep: 7 minutes • **other:** 10 minutes   *PointsPlus* value per serving: 2

Menu
PointsPlus value
per serving: 2

Spanakopita Bites

**1 cup mixed grapes, sliced
pear, and apple**
PointsPlus value
per serving: 0

Game Plan

1. While oven preheats:
• Rinse, drain, and
slice fruit.
• Squeeze spinach dry.

2. Prepare filling.

3. Bake until shells are
browned.

These are good served warm and even better at room temperature.

  2 (1.9-ounce) packages mini phyllo shells
  1 (10-ounce) package frozen chopped spinach, thawed, drained, and squeezed dry
  1 (4-ounce) package crumbled feta cheese with lemon, garlic, and oregano
  ½ cup egg substitute
  ½ teaspoon freshly ground black pepper

1. Preheat oven to 375°.
2. Place phyllo shells on a large rimmed baking sheet. Combine spinach and remaining ingredients in a medium bowl. Spoon filling evenly into shells.
3. Bake at 375° for 10 minutes or until filling is set (shells will be lightly browned). **Yield:** 15 servings (serving size: 2 spanakopita bites).

Per serving: CALORIES 59; FAT 2.9g (sat 0.9g, mono 1.1g, poly 0.4g); PROTEIN 3.4g; CARB 5.9g; FIBER 0.4g; CHOL 6mg; IRON 0.5mg; SODIUM 172mg; CALC 40mg

pictured on page 33

Marinated Goat Cheese

prep: 14 minutes • **other:** 4 hours and 10 minutes

PointsPlus value per serving: 2

Italy offers a tremendous variety of cheeses made from all types of milk, including sheep, goat, and buffalo. Goat cheese has a delightfully tangy flavor that is well complemented by the fresh herbs in this robust marinade. The cheese becomes more flavorful the longer it marinates.

⅓ cup chopped sun-dried tomatoes (about 12 tomatoes), packed without oil
¼ cup olive oil
2 tablespoons chopped fresh rosemary
1 tablespoon chopped fresh basil
2 teaspoons grated fresh lemon rind
½ teaspoon crushed red pepper
½ teaspoon freshly ground black pepper
3 garlic cloves, minced
2 (4-ounce) packages goat cheese, each cut into 10 slices
20 (¼-inch-thick) slices diagonally cut Italian or French bread baguette

1. Combine tomatoes and oil in a small bowl; let stand 10 minutes. Add rosemary and next 5 ingredients; stir well.
2. Place cheese slices in an 8-inch square baking dish; pour marinade over cheese. Cover and marinate at least 4 hours. Serve with baguette slices. **Yield:** 20 servings (serving size: 1 cheese slice and 1 baguette slice).

Per serving: CALORIES 61; FAT 3.9g (sat 1.9g, mono 1.6g, poly 0.3g); PROTEIN 2.9g; CARB 3.9g; FIBER 0.3g; CHOL 5mg; IRON 0.5mg; SODIUM 95mg; CALC 21mg

---

Menu
PointsPlus value
per serving: 2

Marinated Goat Cheese

1 cup mixed vegetables
PointsPlus value
per serving: 0

Game Plan

1. Prepare marinade.

2. While cheese marinates:
• Rinse, drain, and cut mixed vegetables.

Menu

PointsPlus value
per serving: 3

Smoked Salmon Croustades

**1 cup sliced celery with
2 tablespoons fat-free chive
vegetable dip**
PointsPlus value
per serving: 2

Game Plan

1. Rinse and chop dill and
celery.

2. Chop onion.

3. Prepare cream cheese
mixture, adding salmon.

4. Assemble croustades.

Smoked Salmon Croustades

prep: 22 minutes   *PointsPlus* value per serving: 1

Tiny, wafer-thin, crisp shells provide the perfect texture contrast to the creamy salmon filling in this easy appetizer. You can find the shells on the gourmet cracker aisle at your supermarket.

  1 (8-ounce) block ⅓-less-fat cream cheese, softened
  1 lemon
  2 tablespoons fat-free milk
  1 (4-ounce) package smoked salmon, coarsely chopped
  ¼ cup coarsely chopped red onion
  1 tablespoon chopped fresh dill
  1 tablespoon drained capers
  2 (1.4-ounce) packages baked mini croustades
Dill sprigs (optional)

1. Place cream cheese in a bowl; beat with a mixer at medium speed until smooth. Grate rind and squeeze juice from lemon to measure 1 teaspoon rind and 1 table-spoon juice. Add lemon rind, lemon juice, and milk to cream cheese; beat until well blended.

2. Stir in salmon and next 3 ingredients. Spoon 1 rounded teaspoonful of salmon mixture into each of 48 croustades. Garnish with dill sprigs, if desired. **Yield:** 24 servings (serving size: 2 croustades).

Per serving: CALORIES 47; FAT 3.2g (sat 1.4g, mono 0.1g, poly 0.1g); PROTEIN 2.4g; CARB 2.8g; FIBER 0.1g; CHOL 10mg; IRON 0.1mg; SODIUM 152mg; CALC 9mg

Black Pepper and Sesame–Crusted Tuna Rounds

prep: 4 minutes • **cook:** 4 minutes   *PointsPlus* value per serving: 2

Ahi tuna is a flavorful, nutrient-rich food that is high in omega-3 fatty acids and lean protein. Paired with cracked black peppercorns, sesame seeds, and wasabi sauce, this appetizer is loaded with flavor. For best tasting results, purchase fresh sushi-quality tuna because the tuna is just seared briefly and served rare. For a dramatic presentation, we used a mixture of sesame seeds and black sesame seeds.

¼ cup sesame seeds (or a mixture of sesame seeds and black sesame seeds)
2 teaspoons cracked black pepper
2 (6-ounce) tuna steaks (1-inch thick), halved lengthwise
Cooking spray
40 rice crackers
3 tablespoons plus 1 teaspoon wasabi sauce
Chopped fresh chives (optional)

1. Combine sesame seeds and pepper in a shallow dish. Dredge tuna in sesame seed mixture, turning to coat all sides.

2. Heat a medium nonstick skillet over medium-high heat. Coat pan with cooking spray. Add tuna; cook 30 seconds to 1 minute on each side of all 4 sides. Place tuna on a cutting board. Cut each piece of tuna crosswise into 10 slices.

3. Place 1 slice of tuna on each rice cracker, and top each with ¼ teaspoon wasabi sauce. Sprinkle evenly with chives, if desired. **Yield:** 20 servings (serving size: 2 topped crackers).

Per serving: CALORIES 73; FAT 3.5g (sat 0.5g, mono 1.5g, poly 1.1g); PROTEIN 6.1g; CARB 3.9g; FIBER 0.3g; CHOL 9mg; IRON 0.4mg; SODIUM 41mg; CALC 11mg

Menu
PointsPlus value
per serving: 3

Black Pepper and Sesame–Crusted Tuna Rounds

½ cup lightly steamed asparagus spears with 2 tablespoons lemon tahini dip
PointsPlus value
per serving: 1

Game Plan

1. While skillet is heating:
• Steam asparagus.
• Dredge tuna in sesame seed mixture.

2. Cook tuna, and serve on rice crackers.

3. Serve asparagus with lemon tahini dip.

Menu

PointsPlus value
per serving: 3

**Spicy Pork Sliders with
Sweet Chipotle-Peach Sauce**

**Lemonade-Mint Iced Tea
(page 12)**
PointsPlus value
per serving: 0

Game Plan

1. While oven preheats:
• Boil and steep tea.
• Combine pork and spices.

2. While pork bakes:
• Prepare fruit spread.

3. Assemble sliders, and
serve with tea.

Spicy Pork Sliders with Sweet Chipotle-Peach Sauce

prep: 7 minutes • **cook:** 24 minutes • **other:** 5 minutes

PointsPlus value per serving: 3

The small, flavorful dinner rolls used in this recipe can be found on the bread aisle of most supermarkets.

1 teaspoon chili powder
½ teaspoon ground cumin
¼ teaspoon ground cinnamon
¼ teaspoon salt
¼ teaspoon freshly ground black pepper
1 (1-pound) pork tenderloin, trimmed
Cooking spray
¼ cup peach fruit spread
1 chipotle chile, canned in adobo sauce, chopped
½ teaspoon adobo sauce
2 tablespoons light mayonnaise
1½ teaspoons honey mustard
12 (0.4-ounce) dinner rolls

1. Preheat oven to 425°.
2. Combine first 5 ingredients in a small bowl; rub evenly over pork.
3. Heat a large nonstick skillet over medium-high heat. Coat pan with cooking spray. Add pork; cook 2 minutes on each side or until browned. Transfer pork to a foil-lined jelly-roll pan. Bake at 425° for 19 minutes or until a thermometer registers 155°. Let pork stand 5 minutes or until thermometer reaches 160° (medium). Slice tenderloin into 24 pieces.
4. While pork cooks, place fruit spread in a microwave-safe bowl. Microwave at HIGH 20 to 30 seconds or until spread melts slightly. Stir in chipotle chile and next 3 ingredients. Refrigerate until ready to serve. Serve pork on rolls with sauce. **Yield:** 12 servings (serving size: 2 slices pork, 1 roll, and about 1½ teaspoons sauce).

Per serving: CALORIES 105; FAT 3.4g (sat 0.9g, mono 0.7g, poly 0.1g); PROTEIN 8.8g; CARB 9.6g; FIBER 0.2g; CHOL 25mg; IRON 0.8mg; SODIUM 168mg; CALC 24mg

Turkey Pot Stickers with Spicy Dipping Sauce

prep: 8 minutes • **cook:** 6 minutes   *PointsPlus* value per serving: 2

Round, wonton-like gyoza skins are sold in Asian markets. If you can't find them, you can substitute wonton wrappers.

    1   garlic clove, peeled
    1   (1-inch) piece peeled fresh ginger
    4   teaspoons lower-sodium soy sauce, divided
   ½   pound lean ground turkey breast
    1   green onion, quartered
    1   teaspoon dark sesame oil
  16   gyoza skins
        Cooking spray
    6   tablespoons water, divided
   ¼   cup rice vinegar
    2   teaspoons brown sugar
   ¼   teaspoon crushed red pepper

1. Drop garlic through food chute with food processor on; process until minced. Drop ginger through food chute, and process until minced. Add 1 teaspoon soy sauce and next 3 ingredients; pulse until onion is finely chopped.

2. Working with 1 gyoza wrapper at a time (cover remaining wrappers with a damp towel to keep them from drying), spoon about 1 teaspoon turkey mixture into center of wrapper. Moisten edges of wrapper with water; gently lift edges over filling, and crimp to seal. Repeat procedure with remaining wrappers and filling.

3. Heat a large nonstick skillet over medium-high heat. Coat pan with cooking spray; add pot stickers. Cook 4 minutes or until browned, turning occasionally. Add ¼ cup water to pan. Cover and steam 2 minutes or until tender.

4. While pot stickers steam, combine remaining 1 tablespoon soy sauce, remaining 2 tablespoons water, vinegar, brown sugar, and red pepper in a small bowl, stirring with a whisk. Serve sauce with pot stickers. Yield: 8 servings (serving size: 2 pot stickers and 1 tablespoon sauce).

Per serving: CALORIES 76; FAT 1.1g (sat 0.2g, mono 0g, poly 0g); PROTEIN 8g; CARB 8g; FIBER 0.4g; CHOL 13mg; IRON 0.7mg; SODIUM 185mg; CALC 9mg

Menu
PointsPlus value per serving: 3

Turkey Pot Stickers with Spicy Dipping Sauce

Sparkling Cranberry-Citrus Green Tea (page 14)
PointsPlus value per serving: 1

Game Plan

1. While tea is steeping:
  • Peel garlic and ginger.
  • Prepare pot sticker filling.

2. Wrap filling in gyoza skins.

3. While pot stickers steam:
  • Prepare dipping sauce.

Menu

PointsPlus value
per serving: 2

Black Bean Cakes

1 cup presliced carrots and
celery sticks
PointsPlus value
per serving: 0

Game Plan

1. While skillet is heating:
  • Drain black beans.
  • Mince garlic.

2. Prepare black beans balls,
and roll in breadcrumb
mixture.

3. Cook patties, and serve.

Black Bean Cakes

prep: 12 minutes • **cook:** 4 minutes   *PointsPlus* value per serving: 2

These bean cakes are a fun and quick way to add spice to any meal or party. Try adding fresh chopped cilantro as a topping for a bright look and taste.

    1   (15-ounce) can black beans, rinsed and drained
    2   tablespoons no-salt-added tomato paste
    2   garlic cloves, minced
 1½   teaspoons ground cumin, divided
   ¼   teaspoon salt
    2   tablespoons dry breadcrumbs
   ½   teaspoon freshly ground black pepper
Olive oil–flavored cooking spray
    2   teaspoons olive oil
   ¼   cup salsa
   ¼   cup fat-free sour cream
Chopped fresh cilantro (optional)

1. Combine first 3 ingredients, ½ teaspoon cumin, and salt in a large bowl; mash with a fork. Divide mixture evenly into 8 balls.

2. Combine breadcrumbs, pepper, and remaining 1 teaspoon cumin in a shallow dish. Roll balls in crumb mixture. Shape into ½-inch-thick patties.

3. Coat a large nonstick skillet with cooking spray; add oil. Place over medium-high heat until hot. Add patties; cook 2 minutes on each side or until lightly browned. Serve with salsa and sour cream, and garnish with cilantro, if desired. Serve immediately. **Yield:** 8 servings (serving size: 1 bean cake, 1½ teaspoons salsa, and 1½ teaspoons sour cream).

Per serving: CALORIES 62; FAT 1.5g (sat 0.2g, mono 0.8g, poly 0.1g); PROTEIN 3g; CARB 9.7g; FIBER 2.4g; CHOL 1mg; IRON 0.9mg; SODIUM 195mg; CALC 35mg

Italian Vegetable Caponata

prep: 17 minutes • **cook:** 43 minutes   *PointsPlus* value per serving: 2

The salty, acidic flavors of vinegar, tomatoes, capers, and kalamata olives harmonize with brown sugar and sweet raisins, creating a sweet-and-sour taste that's often found in Sicilian cooking. Though most often served at room temperature, caponata is also good served warm or chilled.

1	large fennel bulb with stalks (about 1 pound)
1	tablespoon olive oil
1	large eggplant (about 1½ pounds), cubed
1	cup cubed zucchini (about 1 small)
½	cup chopped celery (1 stalk)
½	cup chopped onion (½ small)
4	garlic cloves, minced
1	(14½-ounce) can petite-cut diced tomatoes, undrained
⅓	cup golden raisins
¼	cup coarsely chopped pitted kalamata olives
1	tablespoon light brown sugar
1	teaspoon drained capers, coarsely chopped
¼	teaspoon freshly ground black pepper
1	tablespoon balsamic vinegar

1. Remove and discard fennel stalks. Trim tough outer leaves from fennel bulb. Cut bulb in half through base. Cut out a small pyramid-shaped core from each half; discard. Place cored fennel cut sides down; slice crosswise into 4 thick slices. Cut slices into cubes. Set aside.

2. Heat oil in a Dutch oven over medium-high heat. Add fennel, eggplant, and next 4 ingredients; sauté 10 minutes. Add tomatoes and next 5 ingredients; bring to a boil. Cover, reduce heat, and simmer 15 minutes, stirring occasionally. Uncover and cook 13 minutes or until most of liquid evaporates. Remove from heat; stir in balsamic vinegar. **Yield:** 10 servings (serving size: ½ cup).

Per serving: CALORIES 93; FAT 2.6g (sat 0.3g, mono 1.7g, poly 0.3g); PROTEIN 2.1g; CARB 16.6g; FIBER 4.7g; CHOL 0mg; IRON 1mg; SODIUM 181mg; CALC 49mg

---

Menu
PointsPlus value
per serving: 4

Italian Vegetable Caponata

1 ounce baked pita chips
PointsPlus value
per serving: 2

Game Plan

1. While Dutch oven heats:
 • Rinse, drain, and cut fennel.
 • Chop celery, onion, and olives; mince garlic.

2. Sauté vegetables.

3. Add tomatoes, raisins, and remaining ingredients.

4. Finish with balsamic vinegar before serving.

Barbados Punch

Menu
PointsPlus value
per serving: 5

Barbados Punch

½ cup pineapple slices
PointsPlus value
per serving: 0

Game Plan

1. Trim and cube pineapple and any additional garnish.

2. Blend punch ingredients, and add ice.

3. Serve drink chilled.

prep: 8 minutes   *PointsPlus* value per serving: 5

This version of Barbados Punch contains just a touch of spiced rum, but it is big on fruit flavor—perfect as a refreshing summer drink.

  2 cups low-calorie tropical vegetable–fruit juice blend, chilled
  ¾ cup spiced rum
  ½ cup fresh lime juice
  3 tablespoons sugar
  4 cups ice cubes
  Fresh pineapple wedges (optional)
  Lime slices (optional)

1. Place first 4 ingredients in a blender; process until blended. With blender on, add ice cubes, 1 at a time; process until smooth and thick. Pour into 5 wine glasses. Garnish with pineapple wedges and lime slices, if desired. **Yield:** 5 servings (serving size: 1 cup).

Per serving: CALORIES 117; FAT 0g (sat 0g, mono 0g, poly 0g); PROTEIN 0.1g; CARB 10.8g; FIBER 0.1g; CHOL 0mg; IRON 0mg; SODIUM 15mg; CALC 4mg

Pomegranate-Ginger Fizz

Menu
PointsPlus value
per serving: 4

Pomegranate-Ginger Fizz

Crostini with Manchego
and Honeyed Orange Relish
(page 15)
PointsPlus value
per serving: 2

Game Plan
1. While oven preheats:
  • Slice baguette.
  • Chop oranges.
  • Mince shallots.
  • Juice lime.
2. While bread toasts:
  • Prepare Pomegranate-Ginger Fizz.
  • Prepare orange mixture.

3. Assemble crostini.

prep: 8 minutes   *PointsPlus* value per serving: 2

This impressive, colorful drink is full of flavor and antioxidants.

  ¼ cup fresh mint leaves
  1 lime, cut lengthwise into 4 wedges
  2 cups crushed ice
  2 cups nonalcoholic ginger beer
  1 cup pomegranate juice

1. Divide mint evenly among 4 glasses. Squeeze 1 lime wedge into each glass. Press mint with the back of a spoon to crush. Add ½ cup crushed ice to each glass. Pour ½ cup ginger beer and ¼ cup pomegranate juice over ice in each glass; stir. **Yield:** 4 servings (serving size: ¾ cup).

Per serving: CALORIES 105; FAT 0g (sat 0g, mono 0g, poly 0g); PROTEIN 0.3g; CARB 19.7g; FIBER 0.6g; CHOL 0mg; IRON 0.2mg; SODIUM 8mg; CALC 14mg

Strawberry–Piña Colada Milk Shakes

prep: 5 minutes   *PointsPlus* value per serving: 4

Serve this tropical treat with a salty side snack to enhance the flavor of both.

2½ cups vanilla fat-free ice cream
1 cup frozen unsweetened strawberries
1 (6-ounce) can unsweetened pineapple juice
½ cup light coconut milk
¼ teaspoon rum extract

1. Place all ingredients in a blender. Process until smooth, stopping once to scrape down sides. Pour evenly into 4 glasses; serve immediately. **Yield:** 4 servings (serving size: 1 cup).

Per serving: CALORIES 170; FAT 2g (sat 1.7g, mono 0.1g, poly 0g); PROTEIN 4.5g; CARB 36g; FIBER 4.6g; CHOL 0mg; IRON 0.4mg; SODIUM 70mg; CALC 137mg

Menu
PointsPlus value per serving: 6

Strawberry–Piña Colada Milk Shakes

3 ounces fat-free pretzel twists
PointsPlus value per serving: 2

Game Plan

1. Blend milk shake ingredients until smooth.

2. Serve drink cold with pretzel twists.

Fruity White Sangria

prep: 10 minutes   *PointsPlus* value per serving: 4

This traditional Spanish cocktail highlights summer's bounty. If peaches aren't in season, use thawed frozen peach slices.

1 (750-milliliter) bottle riesling or other slightly sweet white wine, chilled
2 cups sliced peeled peaches (about 2 large)
1 cup seedless green grapes, halved
½ cup raspberries
¼ cup thawed lemonade concentrate
2 cups sugar-free ginger ale

1. Combine first 5 ingredients in a large pitcher. Stir in ginger ale just before serving. **Yield:** 8 servings (serving size: 1 cup).

Per serving: CALORIES 123; FAT 0.1g (sat 0g, mono 0g, poly 0g); PROTEIN 0.6g; CARB 16g; FIBER 1.2g; CHOL 0mg; IRON 0.2mg; SODIUM 18mg; CALC 7mg

Menu
PointsPlus value per serving: 6

Fruity White Sangria

Pear and Swiss Triangles (page 16)
PointsPlus value per serving: 2

Game Plan

1. While skillet heats:
- Trim bread.
- Rinse and slice pear.
- Prepare sangria.

2. Assemble and cook sandwiches.

3. Cut sandwiches, and serve.

pictured on page 34

Strawberry-Cherry Slush

prep: 5 minutes

PointsPlus value per serving: 3

1⅓ cups frozen pitted dark sweet cherries
1 cup frozen strawberries
1 cup cherry-flavored lemon-lime soda, chilled
2 tablespoons sugar
2 tablespoons thawed frozen reduced-calorie whipped topping
1 tablespoon fresh lemon juice

1. Place all ingredients in a blender; cover and process until smooth, stopping twice to scrape down sides. Pour into tall chilled glasses. **Yield:** 3 servings (serving size: ¾ cup).

Per serving: CALORIES 128; FAT 0.3g (sat 0.3g, mono 0g, poly 0g); PROTEIN 0.8g; CARB 31.8g; FIBER 2.3g; CHOL 0mg; IRON 0.4mg; SODIUM 2mg; CALC 7mg

Hot Spiced Chocolate

prep: 17 minutes

PointsPlus value per serving: 3

Ginger flavor shines in this warm chocolate treat. You can use fat-free milk if that's what you have on hand.

4 cups 1% low-fat milk
3 tablespoons chopped crystallized ginger
8 whole cloves
2 (3-inch) cinnamon sticks, broken in half
⅓ cup fat-free chocolate syrup

1. Combine first 4 ingredients in a medium saucepan. Bring to a boil; reduce heat, and simmer 12 minutes. Remove from heat.
2. Strain milk mixture through a sieve over a bowl, discarding spices. Return milk to saucepan. Stir in chocolate syrup. Cook over low heat just until thoroughly heated. Serve hot. **Yield:** 6 servings (serving size: about ¾ cup).

Per serving: CALORIES 125; FAT 1.8g (sat 1.1g, mono 0.5g, poly 0.1g); PROTEIN 5.8g; CARB 21.3g; FIBER 0.8g; CHOL 7mg; IRON 0.3mg; SODIUM 93mg; CALC 209mg

Breakfast

PointsPlus value per serving: 1
Cream Cheese Sauce | page 49
Dark Cherry Sauce | page 50

PointsPlus value per serving: 2
Spiced Bacon | page 57
Broiled Grapefruit | page 58

PointsPlus value per serving: 3
Buttermilk Pancakes | page 32
Pear and Grape Salad | page 58

PointsPlus value per serving: 4
Blueberry-Yogurt Muffins | page 29
Herbed Potato Pancake with Smoked Salmon | page 31
Baked Eggs with Tomatoes and Artichokes | page 53
Leek and Asparagus Frittata | page 54
Yogurt Parfaits with Mixed Berries, Honey, and
    Mint | page 56

PointsPlus value per serving: 5
Orange Biscuits | page 28
Banana-Oatmeal Bread | page 30
Carrot Cake Pancakes with Cream Cheese Sauce | page 49
Chocolate Waffles with Dark Cherry Sauce | page 50
Pecan Waffles | page 51

PointsPlus value per serving: 7
Garden Omelet with Goat Cheese | page 52
Bacon and Egg Sandwiches with Basil
    Mayonnaise | page 55

PointsPlus value per serving: 9
Hot Quinoa Cereal with Blueberries and Pecans | page 56
Raisin and Almond Oatmeal | page 57

pictured on page 35

Orange Biscuits

prep: 24 minutes • **cook:** 14 minutes • **other:** 5 minutes

PointsPlus value per serving: 5

These tender, citrus-glazed biscuits received our Test Kitchen's highest rating.

Menu
PointsPlus value
per serving: 6

Orange Biscuits

**1 slice (1 ounce) warmed
Canadian bacon**
PointsPlus value
per serving: 1

Game Plan

1. Prepare biscuit mixture.

2. While biscuits bake:
  • Prepare glaze.
  • Heat Canadian bacon
    according to package
    directions.

13.5 ounces all-purpose flour (about 3 cups)
  3 tablespoons granulated sugar
  4 teaspoons baking powder
  1 teaspoon baking soda
  ¾ teaspoon salt
  ⅓ cup chilled butter, cut into small pieces
  1½ tablespoons grated fresh orange rind, divided
  1⅓ cups low-fat buttermilk
  3 tablespoons fresh orange juice, divided
     Cooking spray
  ¾ cup powdered sugar

1. Preheat oven to 425°.
2. Lightly spoon flour into dry measuring cups; level with a knife. Combine flour and next 4 ingredients in a large bowl; cut in butter with a pastry blender or 2 knives until mixture resembles coarse meal. Stir in 1 tablespoon orange rind.
3. Combine buttermilk and 2 tablespoons orange juice; add to flour mixture, stirring just until moist.
4. Turn dough out onto a lightly floured surface; knead lightly 4 times. Pat dough to ¾-inch thickness; cut with a 2½-inch biscuit cutter. Place biscuits on a baking sheet coated with cooking spray; lightly coat tops with cooking spray.
5. Bake at 425° for 14 minutes or until lightly browned.
6. While biscuits bake, combine powdered sugar, remaining 1½ teaspoons orange rind, and remaining 1 tablespoon orange juice. Let biscuits cool 5 minutes on a wire rack; drizzle glaze evenly over biscuits. **Yield:** 13 servings (serving size: 1 biscuit).

Per serving: CALORIES 202; FAT 5.6g (sat 3.2g, mono 1.5g, poly 0.3g); PROTEIN 4g; CARB 34g; FIBER 0.9g; CHOL 14mg; IRON 1.5mg; SODIUM 404mg; CALC 137mg

pictured on page 36

Blueberry-Yogurt Muffins

prep: 8 minutes • **cook:** 18 minutes • **other:** 10 minutes

PointsPlus value per serving: 4

These muffins are about as satisfying and versatile as a food can be. They harmonize perfectly with coffee and the morning paper, with a salad for a light lunch, or with milk as a snack anytime.

  9 ounces all-purpose flour (about 2 cups)
  ⅓ cup sugar
  1 teaspoon baking powder
  1 teaspoon baking soda
  ¼ teaspoon salt
  ¼ cup orange juice
  2 tablespoons canola oil
  1 teaspoon vanilla extract
  1 large egg, lightly beaten
  1 (8-ounce) carton vanilla low-fat yogurt
  1 cup fresh or frozen blueberries, thawed
     Cooking spray
  1 tablespoon sugar

1. Preheat oven to 400°.

2. Lightly spoon flour into dry measuring cups; level with a knife. Combine flour and next 4 ingredients in a large bowl; make a well in center of mixture. Combine orange juice and next 4 ingredients; add to flour mixture, stirring just until moist. Gently fold in blueberries.

3. Spoon batter evenly into 12 muffin cups lightly coated with cooking spray; sprinkle 1 tablespoon sugar evenly over batter. Bake at 400° for 18 minutes or until a wooden pick inserted in center comes out clean. Remove from pans immediately; cool on a wire rack. **Yield:** 12 servings (serving size: 1 muffin).

Per serving: CALORIES 159; FAT 3.2g (sat 0.6g, mono 0.8g, poly 1.7g); PROTEIN 3.5g; CARB 29.1g; FIBER 0.9g; CHOL 19mg; IRON 1.1mg; SODIUM 218mg; CALC 40mg

Menu
PointsPlus value per serving: 6

Blueberry-Yogurt Muffins

1 orange
PointsPlus value per serving: 0

1 cup fat-free milk
PointsPlus value per serving: 2

Game Plan

1. While oven preheats:
  • Prepare muffin mixture.

2. While muffins bake:
  • Peel and section orange.

pictured on page 37

Banana-Oatmeal Bread

prep: 6 minutes • **cook:** 1 hour and 10 minutes • **other:** 10 minutes

PointsPlus value per serving: 5

We took banana bread to the next yummy level with the addition of chewy oats, brown sugar, and a hint of cinnamon. Serve warm for breakfast, or pack a slice with your lunch for an afternoon snack.

Menu
PointsPlus value
per serving: 6

Banana-Oatmeal Bread

2 slices extra-lean
turkey bacon
PointsPlus value
per serving: 1

Game Plan

1. While oven preheats:
  • Prepare banana bread
  mixture.

2. While bread cooks:
  • Heat turkey bacon
  according to package
  instructions.

 1 cup packed brown sugar
 7 tablespoons canola oil
 2 large egg whites
 1 large egg
 1 cup old-fashioned rolled oats
 1⅓ cups mashed ripe banana (about 2 large)
 ½ cup fat-free milk
 9 ounces all-purpose flour (about 2 cups)
 1 tablespoon baking powder
 ½ teaspoon baking soda
 ½ teaspoon salt
 ½ teaspoon ground cinnamon
 Cooking spray

1. Preheat oven to 350°.

2. Combine first 4 ingredients in a large bowl; beat with a mixer at medium speed until blended. Combine oats, banana, and milk; add to sugar mixture, beating well.

3. Lightly spoon flour into dry measuring cups; level with a knife. Combine flour, baking powder, baking soda, salt, and cinnamon; stir with a whisk. Add to sugar mixture; beat just until moist.

4. Spoon batter into a 9 x 5–inch loaf pan coated with cooking spray. Bake at 350° for 1 hour and 10 minutes or until a wooden pick inserted in center comes out clean. Cool 10 minutes in pan on a wire rack; remove loaf from pan. Cool completely on wire rack. **Yield:** 18 servings (serving size: 1 slice).

Per serving: CALORIES 186; FAT 6.3g (sat 1g, mono 1.6g, poly 3.7g); PROTEIN 3.2g; CARB 30.3g; FIBER 1.3g; CHOL 12mg; IRON 1mg; SODIUM 209mg; CALC 41mg

Herbed Potato Pancake with Smoked Salmon

prep: 5 minutes • **cook:** 14 minutes

PointsPlus value per serving: 4

This recipe is simple and satisfying, yet elegant enough for a Sunday brunch.

- 1 (20-ounce) package refrigerated shredded hash brown potatoes
- 2 tablespoons chopped fresh dill
- ½ teaspoon freshly ground black pepper, divided
- ¼ teaspoon salt
- Cooking spray
- 4 ounces smoked salmon, torn into pieces
- 1 (6-ounce) carton plain fat-free Greek yogurt
- Chopped fresh dill (optional)

1. Heat a 12-inch nonstick skillet over medium heat 2 minutes or until very hot.

2. While pan heats, combine potatoes, 2 tablespoons dill, ¼ teaspoon pepper, and salt in a medium bowl. Coat pan with cooking spray. Add potato mixture to pan; cook, uncovered, 6 to 7 minutes or until bottom is browned (do not stir).

3. Coat potato mixture with cooking spray. Place a large round platter over potato mixture. Carefully invert potato pancake onto platter, and slide back into skillet, browned side up. Cook, uncovered, 6 to 7 minutes or until potato is tender (do not stir). Return potato pancake to platter; sprinkle with remaining ¼ teaspoon pepper. Cut pancake into 4 wedges. Top wedges evenly with salmon pieces and yogurt. Garnish with additional dill, if desired. **Yield:** 4 servings (serving size: 1 potato wedge, 1 ounce salmon, and about 2 tablespoons yogurt).

Per serving: CALORIES 184; FAT 1.2g (sat 0.3g, mono 0.6g, poly 0.3g); PROTEIN 10.8g; CARB 31g; FIBER 3.7g; CHOL 7mg; IRON 1.6mg; SODIUM 486mg; CALC 33mg

Menu
PointsPlus value per serving: 5

Herbed Potato Pancake with Smoked Salmon

½ cup orange juice
PointsPlus value per serving: 1

Game Plan

1. While skillet heats:
- Prepare potato mixture.

2. Prepare pancakes as directed.

3. Top pancakes with yogurt and salmon.

pictured on page 38

Buttermilk Pancakes

prep: 8 minutes • **cook:** 5 minutes per batch   *PointsPlus* value per serving: 3

Nothing can surpass the welcoming aroma of pancakes hot off the griddle. We've given you the *PointsPlus* value per pancake to help you plan your serving size. One tablespoon maple syrup has a *PointsPlus* value of 1.

4.5 ounces all-purpose flour (about 1 cup)
  2 tablespoons sugar
  1 teaspoon baking powder
  ½ teaspoon baking soda
  1 cup low-fat buttermilk
  1 tablespoon canola oil
  1 large egg, lightly beaten
     Cooking spray
     Maple syrup (optional)

1. Lightly spoon flour into a dry measuring cup; level with a knife. Combine flour, sugar, baking powder, and baking soda in a large bowl; stir with a whisk. Combine buttermilk, oil, and egg; add to flour mixture, stirring until batter is smooth.
2. Pour about ¼ cup batter per pancake onto a hot nonstick griddle or nonstick skillet coated with cooking spray. Cook 2 to 3 minutes or until tops are covered with bubbles and edges look cooked. Carefully turn pancakes over; cook 2 to 3 minutes or until bottoms are lightly browned. Serve with maple syrup, if desired. Yield: 9 servings (serving size: 1 pancake).

Per serving: CALORIES 94; FAT 2.5g (sat 0.6g, mono 0.6g, poly 1.1g); PROTEIN 3g; CARB 15g; FIBER 0.4g; CHOL 25mg; IRON 0.7mg; SODIUM 129mg; CALC 50mg

---

Menu
PointsPlus value per serving: 4

Buttermilk Pancakes

1 tablespoon maple syrup
PointsPlus value per serving: 1

1 cup fresh blueberries
PointsPlus value per serving: 0

Game Plan

1. Prepare pancake mixture.

2. While pancakes are cooking:
  • Warm maple syrup.

Marinated Goat Cheese | page 17

Strawberry-Cherry Slush | page 26

Orange Biscuits | page 28

Blueberry-Yogurt Muffins | page 29

Banana-Oatmeal Bread | page 30

Buttermilk Pancakes |
page 32

Thai Pumpkin Soup | page 64

Hot Balsamic Slaw Dogs | page 75

40

Provençal Tomato Bread Salad | page 86

Spicy Chicken Finger Salad | page 90

Warm Beef Salad with Figs | page 87

Smoked Turkey–Mango Salad | page 91

**Crab Cakes over Mixed Greens with
Lemon Dressing** | page 94

Linguine Verde | page 102

Caramelized Onion Pizza | page 105

Grilled Tilapia Tacos with Ranch Slaw | page 112

Carrot Cake Pancakes with Cream Cheese Sauce

prep: 13 minutes • **cook:** 7 minutes per batch   *PointsPlus* value per serving: 5

Sprinkle these pancakes with additional cinnamon, and then serve with fresh fruit and coffee for an unforgettable breakfast.

5.125 ounces all-purpose flour (about 1¼ cups)
   2   teaspoons baking powder
  1½   teaspoons ground cinnamon
   ½   teaspoon salt
   ¾   cup fat-free milk
   ⅓   cup packed brown sugar
   1   tablespoon canola oil
   2   large eggs, lightly beaten
   ½   cup finely grated carrot (about 1 large)
   ⅓   cup flaked sweetened coconut
       Cooking spray
       Cream Cheese Sauce

1. Lightly spoon flour into dry measuring cups; level with a knife. Combine flour and next 3 ingredients in a large bowl, stirring with a whisk.

2. Combine milk and next 3 ingredients; add to flour mixture, stirring until batter is smooth. Stir in carrot and coconut.

3. Pour about ¼ cup batter per pancake onto a hot nonstick griddle or nonstick skillet coated with cooking spray. Cook 4 minutes or until tops are covered with bubbles and edges look cooked. Carefully turn pancakes over; cook 3 minutes or until bottoms are lightly browned. Serve with Cream Cheese Sauce. **Yield:** 10 servings (serving size: 1 pancake and about 1 tablespoon Cream Cheese Sauce).

Per serving: CALORIES 172; FAT 4.2g (sat 1.7g, mono 1.6g, poly 0.7g); PROTEIN 4.2g; CARB 29.6g; FIBER 1.1g; CHOL 45mg; IRON 1.2mg; SODIUM 251mg; CALC 128mg

Cream Cheese Sauce

prep: 4 minutes   *PointsPlus* value per serving: 1

   ¾   cup powdered sugar
   ¼   cup (2 ounces) tub-style ⅓-less-fat cream cheese, softened
   1   tablespoon fat-free milk
   ½   teaspoon vanilla extract

1. Combine all ingredients in a small bowl, stirring with a whisk until smooth. **Yield:** 9 servings (serving size: 1 tablespoon).

Per serving: CALORIES 52; FAT 0.9g (sat 0.6g, mono 0.3g, poly 0g); PROTEIN 0.7g; CARB 10.5g; FIBER 0g; CHOL 3mg; IRON 0mg; SODIUM 30mg; CALC 22mg

---

Menu
PointsPlus value per serving: 6

Carrot Cake Pancakes

Cream Cheese Sauce
PointsPlus value per serving: 1

Game Plan

1. While cream cheese softens:
• Grate carrot.
• Heat griddle.

2. While pancakes are browning:
• Prepare Cream Cheese Sauce.

Menu

PointsPlus value
per serving: 7

**Chocolate Waffles
with Dark Cherry Sauce**

1 cup fat-free milk
PointsPlus value
per serving: 2

Game Plan

1. While Dark Cherry Sauce
cooks:
• Prepare chocolate waffle
mixture.

2. Cook waffles according to
manufacturer's directions.

3. Top waffles with sauce,
and serve.

Chocolate Waffles with Dark Cherry Sauce

prep: 7 minutes • **cook:** 15 minutes per batch   *PointsPlus* value per serving: 5

The waffles will be soft when you first remove them from the waffle iron, but they will quickly firm up upon standing. You can freeze the waffles and reheat them in a toaster oven to the desired crispness.

    1   cup low-fat baking mix
    1   tablespoon sugar
    ⅓   cup chocolate syrup
    ⅓   cup fat-free milk
    1½ tablespoons canola oil
    3   large egg whites
    Butter-flavored cooking spray
    Dark Cherry Sauce
    ½   cup frozen fat-free whipped topping, thawed

1. Combine baking mix and sugar in a medium bowl; stir with a whisk. Combine chocolate syrup, milk, and oil in a small bowl; stir with a whisk. Add chocolate mixture to baking mix mixture; stir just until moist.
2. Place egg whites in a medium bowl, and beat with a mixer at high speed until soft peaks form. Gently fold one-third of egg whites into batter. Fold remaining egg whites into batter.
3. Coat a waffle iron with cooking spray; preheat. Spoon ⅓ cup batter per waffle onto hot waffle iron, spreading batter to edges. Cook according to manufacturer's instructions until waffle iron stops steaming. Repeat procedure with remaining batter. Serve with Dark Cherry Sauce and whipped topping. **Yield:** 9 servings (serving size: 1 waffle, 2 tablespoons sauce, and about 1 tablespoon whipped topping).

Per serving: CALORIES 187; FAT 3.5g (sat 0.3g, mono 1.7g, poly 1.2g); PROTEIN 3.1g; CARB 35.8g; FIBER 1g; CHOL 0mg; IRON 0.6mg; SODIUM 174mg; CALC 68mg

Dark Cherry Sauce

prep: 1 minute • **cook:** 15 minutes   *PointsPlus* value per serving: 1

    1   (12-ounce) package frozen pitted dark sweet cherries
    ⅔   cup seedless red raspberry fruit spread

1. Bring cherries and fruit spread to a boil in a medium skillet over medium-high heat; reduce heat, and cook, uncovered, 15 minutes or until thick, stirring often. Remove from heat. Serve warm. **Yield:** 18 servings (serving size: 1 tablespoon).

Per serving: CALORIES 36; FAT 0g (sat 0g, mono 0g, poly 0g); PROTEIN 0.1g; CARB 8.6g; FIBER 0.4g; CHOL 0mg; IRON 0mg; SODIUM 0mg; CALC 3mg

Pecan Waffles

prep: 10 minutes • **cook:** 7 minutes per batch   *PointsPlus* value per serving: 5

To keep waffles warm and crisp after cooking, place them directly on a rack in a preheated 300° oven until time to serve.

5.125 ounces all-purpose flour (about 1¼ cups), divided
  ¾ cup pecan halves
  1 tablespoon sugar
  1½ teaspoons baking powder
  ¼ teaspoon baking soda
  ¼ teaspoon salt
  1¾ cups fat-free buttermilk
  ¼ cup butter, melted
  1 large egg yolk
  3 large egg whites
  Butter-flavored cooking spray
  ¾ cup sugar-free maple-flavored syrup

1. Lightly spoon flour into dry measuring cups; level with a knife. Process half of flour and pecans in a food processor 30 seconds or until pecans are finely ground.
2. Transfer flour mixture to a large bowl. Add remaining flour, sugar, and next 3 ingredients, stirring well with a whisk.
3. Combine buttermilk, butter, and egg yolk, stirring well with a whisk. Add to flour mixture, stirring well with a whisk.
4. Beat egg whites with a mixer at high speed until stiff peaks form (do not over-beat). Fold egg whites into batter.
5. Coat a waffle iron with cooking spray; preheat. Spoon about ⅓ cup batter per 4-inch waffle onto hot waffle iron, spreading batter to edges. Cook according to manufacturer's instructions until waffle iron stops steaming. Repeat procedure with remaining batter. Serve with syrup. **Yield:** 12 servings (serving size: 1 waffle and 1 tablespoon syrup).

Per serving: CALORIES 164; FAT 9.1g (sat 3g, mono 3.9g, poly 1.6g); PROTEIN 4.4g; CARB 18.6g; FIBER 1g; CHOL 28mg; IRON 0.8mg; SODIUM 254mg; CALC 66mg

Menu
PointsPlus value
per serving: 7

Pecan Waffles

1 tablespoon sugar-free maple syrup
PointsPlus value
per serving: 1

1 cup fat-free milk
PointsPlus value
per serving: 1

Game Plan

1. While waffle iron preheats:
  • Prepare waffle mixture.

2. While waffles cook:
  • Warm syrup.

Menu

PointsPlus value
per serving: 7

**Garden Omelet
with Goat Cheese**

1 cup red seedless grapes
PointsPlus value
per serving: 0

Game Plan

1. While spinach and herbs
cook:
• Whisk together eggs
and milk.

2. Prepare eggs.

3. Rinse and drain grapes.

Garden Omelet with Goat Cheese

prep: 9 minutes • **cook:** 11 minutes   *PointsPlus* value per serving: 7

As the egg mixture begins to cook in Step 2, gently lift the edges of the omelet with a spatula, and tilt the pan so any uncooked portion flows underneath.

 2   teaspoons olive oil
 ½   cup packed fresh baby spinach
 ½   cup chopped seeded tomato
 2   tablespoons finely chopped shallots
 ½   tablespoon chopped fresh basil
 ⅛   teaspoon salt
 ¼   teaspoon freshly ground black pepper
 ½   cup egg substitute
 2   tablespoons 1% low-fat milk
 1   tablespoon goat cheese, cut into small pieces

1. Heat oil in a large nonstick skillet over medium heat. Add spinach and next 5 ingredients. Cook 4 minutes, stirring frequently. Remove from pan, and keep warm.

2. Combine egg substitute and milk, stirring with a whisk. Pour egg mixture into pan. Cook over medium heat 5 minutes or until set.

3. Spoon spinach mixture over omelet. Sprinkle with goat cheese. Loosen omelet with a spatula; fold in half. Serve immediately. **Yield:** 1 serving (serving size: 1 omelet).

Per serving: CALORIES 277; FAT 17.9g (sat 5.2g, mono 8.8g, poly 3.4g); PROTEIN 19.7g; CARB 10.7g; FIBER 1.7g; CHOL 13.9mg; IRON 3.8mg; SODIUM 601mg; CALC 181mg

Baked Eggs with Tomatoes and Artichokes

prep: 4 minutes • **cook:** 13 minutes   *PointsPlus* value per serving: 4

Tomatoes and chives infuse garden-fresh flavor into this delightful rise-and-shine dish.

     2   teaspoons butter
     1   (1.6-ounce) slice multigrain bread, cut into 4 pieces
     4   canned artichoke bottoms
     1   plum tomato, cut into 4 thick slices
     ½   teaspoon chopped fresh chives, divided
     4   large eggs
     ¼   teaspoon salt
     ¼   teaspoon freshly ground black pepper

1. Preheat oven to 375°.
2. Rub ½ teaspoon butter on bottom and up sides of each of 4 (4-ounce) ramekins or custard cups.
3. Press 1 bread piece into each of 4 ramekins. Top bread pieces evenly with artichoke bottoms, tomato slices, and ¼ teaspoon chives. Break 1 egg on top of tomato mixture in each ramekin. Sprinkle each evenly with remaining ¼ teaspoon chives, salt, and pepper. Bake at 375° for 13 minutes or until desired degree of doneness. Serve immediately. **Yield:** 4 servings (serving size: 1 ramekin).

Per serving: CALORIES 132; FAT 8g (sat 2.8g, mono 2.4g, poly 1g); PROTEIN 8.1g; CARB 7.9g; FIBER 1.4g; CHOL 216mg; IRON 1.3mg; SODIUM 312mg; CALC 64mg

Menu
PointsPlus value
per serving: 4

**Baked Eggs with
Tomatoes and Artichokes**

1 cup cubed watermelon
PointsPlus value
per serving: 0

Game Plan

1. While oven preheats:
   • Prepare egg mixture
     in ramekins.

2. While eggs bake:
   • Cube watermelon.

Menu

PointsPlus value
per serving: 4

Leek and Asparagus Frittata

1 small grapefruit
PointsPlus value
per serving: 0

Game Plan

1. While broiler preheats:
- Rinse and slice vegetables.
- Slice and section grapefruit.
- Heat skillet.

2. Cook vegetable mixture, and add eggs.

3. Broil frittata.

Leek and Asparagus Frittata

prep: 7 minutes • **cook:** 8 minutes   *PointsPlus* value per serving: 4

Herbes de Provence is a blend of rosemary, marjoram, basil, bay leaves, thyme, and lavender and is commonly used in cuisine from the south of France. Look for it on the spice aisle at your supermarket.

1	tablespoon olive oil
1	cup sliced leek
1½	cups (1-inch) sliced asparagus
3	large egg whites
2	large eggs
1	teaspoon dried herbes de Provence
¼	teaspoon salt
⅛	teaspoon freshly ground black pepper
½	cup grated fresh Parmesan cheese, divided

1. Preheat broiler.

2. Heat oil in a large ovenproof skillet over medium-high heat. Add leek and asparagus to pan; sauté 3 minutes or until browned.

3. While leek mixture cooks, combine egg whites and the next 4 ingredients in a medium bowl, stirring with a whisk. Stir in ¼ cup cheese.

4. Reduce heat to low. Pour egg mixture over vegetable mixture. As mixture starts to cook, gently lift edges of frittata with a spatula, and tilt pan so uncooked portion flows underneath. Cook 2 to 3 minutes, and remove from heat. Sprinkle remaining ¼ cup cheese over frittata.

5. Broil frittata 2 minutes or until set and lightly browned. Cut into 4 wedges.

Yield: 4 servings (serving size: 1 wedge).

Per serving: CALORIES 140; FAT 9g (sat 3g, mono 4.3g, poly 1g); PROTEIN 10.8g; CARB 5g; FIBER 1.2g; CHOL 115mg; IRON 2.2mg; SODIUM 379mg; CALC 152mg

Bacon and Egg Sandwiches with Basil Mayonnaise

prep: 6 minutes • **cook:** 7 minutes   *PointsPlus* value per serving: 7

This recipe updates simple bacon and egg sandwiches by adding fresh basil and a juicy sliced tomato. Accompany the sandwiches with ripe melon cubes to complete the meal.

¼   cup light mayonnaise
2   tablespoons chopped fresh basil
½   teaspoon fresh lemon juice
4   precooked bacon slices
8   (1-ounce) slices 100% whole-wheat bread
Butter-flavored cooking spray
4   large eggs
⅛   teaspoon salt
¼   teaspoon freshly ground black pepper
1   small tomato, cut into 4 slices

1. Preheat broiler.

2. Combine mayonnaise, basil, and lemon juice in a small bowl, stirring with a whisk.

3. Heat bacon in microwave according to package directions; cut bacon slices in half. Place bread in a single layer on a large baking sheet. Broil 2 minutes on each side or until toasted.

4. Heat a large nonstick skillet over medium-high heat. Coat pan with cooking spray. Crack eggs over pan; sprinkle with salt and pepper. Cook eggs 3 minutes or until desired degree of doneness.

5. Spread basil mayonnaise evenly on toast; top each of 4 toast slices with 1 egg, 2 bacon halves, and 1 tomato slice. Top with remaining 4 slices of toast. Cut sandwiches in half diagonally. **Yield:** 4 servings (serving size: 1 sandwich).

Per serving: CALORIES 232; FAT 13.9g (sat 3g, mono 3.9g, poly 1.6g); PROTEIN 16.4g; CARB 23g; FIBER 10.5g; CHOL 221mg; IRON 4mg; SODIUM 640mg; CALC 336mg

Menu
PointsPlus value
per serving: 7

**Bacon and Egg Sandwiches
with Basil Mayonnaise**

1 cup presliced melon cubes
PointsPlus value
per serving: 0

Game Plan

1. While broiler preheats:
  • Prepare mayonnaise
    mixture.
  • Heat bacon.

2. While bread toasts:
  • Prepare eggs.

3. Assemble sandwiches.

Menu
PointsPlus value
per serving: 5

Yogurt Parfaits with
Mixed Berries, Honey,
and Mint

½ cup orange
or grapefruit juice
PointsPlus value
per serving: 1

Game Plan

1. Rinse and drain berries.

2. Assemble parfaits.

Yogurt Parfaits with Mixed Berries, Honey, and Mint

prep: 8 minutes   *PointsPlus* value per serving: 4

1½	cups vanilla fat-free Greek yogurt
2	tablespoons honey
1	cup blueberries
1	cup strawberries
2	tablespoons chopped fresh mint
½	cup low-fat granola without raisins

1. Combine yogurt and honey. Spoon about 3 tablespoons yogurt mixture into each of 4 parfait or wine glasses. Top with half of berries; sprinkle with half of mint and all of granola. Repeat layers, using remaining yogurt mixture, berries, and mint. **Yield:** 4 servings (serving size: 1 parfait).

Per serving: CALORIES 161; FAT 1g (sat 0.2g, mono 0g, poly 0.1g); PROTEIN 9.1g; CARB 30.7g; FIBER 2.7g; CHOL 0mg; IRON 1.1mg; SODIUM 63mg; CALC 77mg

Menu
PointsPlus value
per serving: 10

Hot Quinoa Cereal with
Blueberries and Pecans

½ cup orange juice
PointsPlus value
per serving: 1

Game Plan

1. Rinse and drain quinoa.

2. While quinoa cooks:
   • Rinse and drain berries.
   • Toast pecans.

3. Assemble cereal.

Hot Quinoa Cereal with Blueberries and Pecans

prep: 5 minutes • **cook:** 14 minutes   *PointsPlus* value per serving: 9

1	cup uncooked quinoa
2	cups water
¼	teaspoon salt
⅓	cup fat-free sweetened condensed milk
2	cups fresh blueberries
¼	cup chopped pecans, toasted

1. Place quinoa in a fine sieve; place sieve in a large bowl. Fill bowl with enough water to cover quinoa. Using your hands, rub grains together for 30 seconds; rinse and drain. Repeat procedure twice. Drain well.
2. Combine quinoa, 2 cups water, and salt in a medium saucepan; bring to a boil. Cover, reduce heat, and simmer 14 minutes or until liquid is almost absorbed. Stir in sweetened condensed milk. Remove from heat.
3. Spoon cereal evenly into 4 bowls. Top evenly with blueberries and pecans. **Yield:** 4 servings (serving size: about ¾ cup cereal, ½ cup blueberries, and 1 tablespoon chopped pecans).

Per serving: CALORIES 322; FAT 7.6g (sat 0.7g, mono 3.5g, poly 3g); PROTEIN 9.2g; CARB 56.5g; FIBER 4.4g; CHOL 3mg; IRON 3.1mg; SODIUM 185mg; CALC 95mg

Raisin and Almond Oatmeal

prep: 1 minute • **cook:** 2 minutes

PointsPlus value per serving: 9

Cinnamon-swirl oatmeal provides a flavorful starting point for this hearty, quick-and-easy breakfast. Add only three more ingredients, and the meal is ready!

- 2 (1.58-ounce) packets high-fiber cinnamon-swirl instant oatmeal
- ¼ cup golden raisins
- 1⅓ cups 1% low-fat milk
- 2 tablespoons chopped salted roasted almonds

1. Combine first 3 ingredients in a microwave-safe bowl. Microwave mixture at HIGH 2 to 3 minutes or until bubbly. Spoon oatmeal evenly into 2 bowls; sprinkle evenly with almonds. **Yield:** 2 servings (serving size: about ¾ cup oatmeal and 1 tablespoon almonds).

Per serving: CALORIES 345; FAT 8.1g (sat 1.9g, mono 4.4g, poly 1.6g); PROTEIN 11.9g; CARB 59.3g; FIBER 12g; CHOL 8mg; IRON 4.6mg; SODIUM 316mg; CALC 336mg

Menu
PointsPlus value per serving: 10

Raisin and Almond Oatmeal

½ cup orange or grapefruit juice
PointsPlus value per serving: 1

Game Plan

1. Microwave oatmeal, raisins, and milk.

2. Top with almonds.

Spiced Bacon

prep: 4 minutes • **cook:** 8 minutes

PointsPlus value per serving: 2

- 2 tablespoons dark brown sugar
- ¼ teaspoon ground cinnamon
- ⅛ teaspoon ground cloves
- ⅛ teaspoon ground red pepper
- 8 center-cut bacon slices
- Cooking spray

1. Combine first 4 ingredients. Rub sugar mixture over both sides of bacon. Heat a large nonstick skillet over medium heat. Coat pan with cooking spray. Cook bacon until crisp, turning occasionally. **Yield:** 4 servings (serving size: 2 slices).

Per serving: CALORIES 78, FAT 4.1g (sat 2g, mono 1.1g, poly 0g) PROTEIN 4g, CARB 7g, FIBER 0.1g, CHOL 15g, IRON 0.1mg, SODIUM 272mg, CALC 8mg

Menu
PointsPlus value per serving: 5

Spiced Bacon

1 whole-wheat English muffin
PointsPlus value per serving: 3

Game Plan

1. While skillet preheats:
 • Toast English muffin.

2. Prepare bacon.

Pear and Grape Salad

prep: 7 minutes

PointsPlus value per serving: 3

A sprinkle of blue cheese adds a hint of saltiness to this sweet combination of fruits.

2½   tablespoons balsamic vinegar
1   teaspoon olive oil
½   teaspoon sugar
Dash of pepper
1   red pear, cored and sliced
1   green pear, cored and sliced
1   cup red grapes, halved
2   tablespoons crumbled blue cheese
1   tablespoon toasted pecans

1. Combine first 4 ingredients in a small bowl, stirring with a whisk. Place pear slices and grapes in a bowl, and drizzle with dressing; toss gently to coat. Spoon salad onto a serving plate; sprinkle evenly with blue cheese and pecans. **Yield:** 4 servings (serving size: about ¾ cup salad).

Per serving: CALORIES 129; FAT 3.7g (sat 1.1g, mono 1.9g, poly 0.6g); PROTEIN 1.5g; CARB 24g; FIBER 3.3g; CHOL 3mg; IRON 0.3mg; SODIUM 67mg; CALC 41mg

Menu
PointsPlus value per serving: 4

Pear and Grape Salad

2 low-fat turkey bacon slices
PointsPlus value per serving: 1

Game Plan

1. Prepare turkey bacon according to package directions.

2. While pecans are toasting:
• Prepare dressing.
• Assemble salad ingredients.

3. Top salad with toasted pecans and cheese.

Broiled Grapefruit

prep: 2 minutes • **cook:** 7 minutes

PointsPlus value per serving: 2

2   medium-sized pink grapefruit
2   tablespoons turbinado sugar
¼   cup plain fat-free Greek yogurt

1. Preheat broiler.
2. Cut grapefruits in half crosswise. Place grapefruit halves on a baking sheet. Sprinkle each half with 1½ teaspoons sugar. Broil 7 minutes or until lightly browned and sugar melts. Serve each grapefruit half with 1 tablespoon yogurt. **Yield:** 4 servings (serving size: 1 grapefruit half).

Per serving: CALORIES 83; FAT 0g (sat 0g, mono 0g, poly 0g); PROTEIN 2.3g; CARB 20.1g; FIBER 2g; CHOL 0mg; IRON 0mg; SODIUM 5mg; CALC 50mg

Menu
PointsPlus value per serving: 6

Broiled Grapefruit

Leek and Asparagus Frittata (page 54)
PointsPlus value per serving: 4

Game Plan

1. While broiler preheats:
• Halve grapefruit, and sprinkle with sugar.
• Rinse and slice vegetables.

2. While grapefruit cooks:
• Cook vegetable mixture, and add eggs.

3. Broil frittata.

Soups & Sandwiches

PointsPlus value per serving: 1
Thai Pumpkin Soup | page 64
Tahini Sauce | page 73

PointsPlus value per serving: 2
Rustic Italian Tomato and Red Pepper Soup with Basil | page 63

PointsPlus value per serving: 3
Chilled Mango Soup | page 60
Spicy Shrimp Pico de Gallo | page 61
Blender Gazpacho | page 62
Southwestern Chicken and Rice Soup | page 69

PointsPlus value per serving: 4
Tuscan Squash and Bean Soup | page 65
Yellow Split Pea Soup with Spicy Sausage | page 66
Turkey Dogs with Fennel Slaw | page 75

PointsPlus value per serving: 5
Smoky Lentil Soup with Ham | page 64
Moo Shu Pork Wraps | page 76

PointsPlus value per serving: 6
Turkey Taco Soup | page 67
Hot Balsamic Slaw Dogs | page 75

PointsPlus value per serving: 7
Poblano-Chicken Chowder | page 68
Fried Egg and Avocado Bagel Sandwiches | page 70
Grilled Chicken Caesar Panini | page 74
Round Italian Sandwich | page 77

PointsPlus value per serving: 8
Cranberry-Chicken Sandwiches | page 74
Steak Sandwiches with Horseradish Mayonnaise | page 78

PointsPlus value per serving: 9
Avocado and Cucumber Soup with Spicy Shrimp Pico de Gallo | page 61
Catfish Sandwiches with Tartar Sauce | page 71
Falafel Sandwiches with Tahini Sauce | page 72
Portobello Paninis | page 73

Chilled Mango Soup

prep: 11 minutes • **other:** 2 hours   *PointsPlus* value per serving: 3

Garnished with fresh raspberries and kiwi, this creamy milk shake of a soup is perfect for a ladies' luncheon when served alongside a tossed green salad with grilled chicken.

1½ cups coarsely chopped peeled ripe mango (about 2 medium)
 1   cup pineapple-orange-banana juice
 ½   cup half-and-half
 ½   teaspoon grated fresh lime rind
 2   tablespoons fresh lime juice
 ½   cup diced peeled kiwi
15   raspberries

1. Place first 5 ingredients in a blender; process until smooth. Cover and chill 2 hours.

2. Ladle soup into bowls; top with kiwi and raspberries. **Yield:** 5 servings (serving size: ½ cup soup, about 1½ tablespoons kiwi, and 3 raspberries).

Per serving: CALORIES 130; FAT 2.8g (sat 1.7g, mono 0.9g, poly 0.1g); PROTEIN 2g; CARB 25.9g; FIBER 2.8g; CHOL 12mg; IRON 0.3mg; SODIUM 19mg; CALC 60mg

---

Menu
PointsPlus value per serving: 5

Chilled Mango Soup

1 cup mixed greens with 2 tablespoons fat-free balsamic vinaigrette
PointsPlus value per serving: 0

2 ounces grilled, shredded chicken
PointsPlus value per serving: 2

Game Plan

1. Peel and chop mango.
2. Process and chill soup.
3. Assemble salad, and serve with chilled soup.

Avocado and Cucumber Soup

prep: 10 minutes

PointsPlus value per serving: 9

This creamy soup is the perfect light meal for a hot summer evening, or chill your thermos and take it for lunch.

- 1 cup coarsely chopped English cucumber (½ large)
- 1 cup water
- ½ cup fresh cilantro leaves
- ½ cup nonfat buttermilk
- 3 tablespoons fresh lime juice
- ½ teaspoon salt
- 2 ripe peeled avocados, coarsely chopped

Spicy Shrimp Pico de Gallo

1. Place first 7 ingredients in a blender; process until smooth. Ladle soup evenly into bowls; top evenly with Spicy Shrimp Pico de Gallo. Yield: 4 servings (serving size: about ¾ cup soup and about ⅔ cup pico de gallo).

Per serving: CALORIES 229; FAT 14.6g (sat 2.3g, mono 9.3g, poly 1.9g); PROTEIN 15.1g; CARB 11.9g; FIBER 4.4g; CHOL 111mg; IRON 2.7mg; SODIUM 604mg; CALC 85mg

Menu

PointsPlus value per serving: 9

Avocado and Cucumber Soup

Spicy Shrimp Pico de Gallo
PointsPlus value per serving: 3

Game Plan

1. Wash and drain all vegetables.

2. Chop cucumber and avocado.

3. Prepare soup, and assemble spicy shrimp mixture.

Spicy Shrimp Pico de Gallo

prep: 6 minutes

PointsPlus value per serving: 3

- 1½ cups coarsely chopped cooked peeled shrimp (8 ounces)
- 1 cup refrigerated prechopped tomato, bell pepper, and onion mix
- 1 tablespoon fresh lime juice
- 1 tablespoon extra-virgin olive oil
- ¼ teaspoon salt
- ¼ teaspoon freshly ground black pepper
- 2 garlic cloves, minced
- 1 jalapeño pepper, seeded and minced

1. Combine all ingredients in a bowl. Yield: 2½ cups (serving size: about ⅔ cup).

Per serving: CALORIES 102; FAT 4.2g (sat 0.7g, mono 2.8g, poly 0.6g); PROTEIN 12.4g; CARB 3.4g; FIBER 0.7g; CHOL 111mg; IRON 1.9mg; SODIUM 274mg; CALC 32mg

Menu

PointsPlus value
per serving: 5

Blender Gazpacho

1 (1-ounce) slice toasted
ciabatta bread
PointsPlus value
per serving: 2

Game Plan

1. Rinse, drain, and chop
all vegetables.

2. Process and chill soup.

3. Just before serving, toast
or grill ciabatta bread.

Blender Gazpacho

prep: 17 minutes • **other:** 2 hours   *PointsPlus* value per serving: 3

This easy summer soup is a great way to add more veggies to your meal.

4	cups grape tomatoes
1	cup chopped seeded peeled cucumber
½	cup chopped yellow bell pepper
1½	cups low-sodium tomato juice
¼	cup chopped red onion
3	tablespoons chopped fresh parsley
1½	tablespoons olive oil
½	teaspoon grated fresh lemon rind
1½	tablespoons fresh lemon juice
1	tablespoon white balsamic vinegar
¼	teaspoon salt
¼	teaspoon freshly ground black pepper
4	thin cucumber slices (optional)

1. Place tomatoes and cucumber in a blender; process until vegetables are finely chopped. Add remaining ingredients except cucumber slices; process until well blended. Chill 2 hours.

2. Ladle soup into bowls; top with cucumber slices, if desired. **Yield:** 4 servings (serving size: 1 cup).

Per serving: CALORIES 112; FAT 5.4g (sat 0.8g, mono 4.1g, poly 0.5g); PROTEIN 2.3g; CARB 14.3g; FIBER 3.3g; CHOL 0mg; IRON 0.7mg; SODIUM 208mg; CALC 46mg

Rustic Italian Tomato and Red Pepper Soup with Basil

prep: 12 minutes • **cook:** 34 minutes • **other:** 10 minutes

PointsPlus value per serving: 2

Bell pepper, onion, and carrot make this soup heartier than a traditional tomato soup.

  Cooking spray
1 cup chopped red bell pepper
½ cup chopped onion
1 carrot, peeled and sliced (½ cup)
1 garlic clove, minced
1 (14-ounce) can fat-free, lower-sodium chicken broth
⅛ to ¼ teaspoon crushed red pepper
1 pound fresh tomatoes, chopped (about 2 medium)
3 tablespoons chopped fresh basil
2 teaspoons extra-virgin olive oil
¼ teaspoon salt

1. Heat a Dutch oven over medium-high heat. Coat pan with cooking spray. Add bell pepper, onion, and carrot; coat vegetables with cooking spray. Cook 4 minutes or until onion is translucent, stirring frequently. Add garlic, and cook 15 seconds, stirring constantly. Add broth and crushed red pepper. Bring to a boil; cover, reduce heat, and simmer 15 to 20 minutes or until carrot is very tender.
2. Add tomato to pan. Bring to a boil; cover, reduce heat, and simmer 5 minutes. Remove pan from heat. Stir in basil, oil, and salt; cover and let stand 10 minutes.
Yield: 4 servings (serving size: 1 cup).

Per serving: CALORIES 73; FAT 2.7g (sat 0.4g, mono 1.7g, poly 0.5g); PROTEIN 2.4g; CARB 10.9g; FIBER 3g; CHOL 0mg; IRON 0.6mg; SODIUM 309mg; CALC 29mg

---

Menu
PointsPlus value per serving: 4

Rustic Italian Tomato and Red Pepper Soup with Basil

1 (1-ounce) slice whole-wheat toast
PointsPlus value per serving: 1

1 ounce mozzarella cheese
PointsPlus value per serving: 1

Game Plan

1. While Dutch oven heats:
• Rinse, drain, and chop vegetables.

2. Sauté vegetables, and add broth.

3. During final simmer:
• Melt cheese on toast.

pictured on page 39

Thai Pumpkin Soup

prep: 6 minutes • **cook:** 8 minutes   *PointsPlus* value per serving: 1

2 tablespoons red curry paste
1 (13.5-ounce) can light coconut milk
1 cup water
1 (15-ounce) can pumpkin
2 tablespoons fish sauce
¼ cup chopped fresh cilantro (optional)
Lime wedges (optional)

1. Place curry paste in a medium saucepan. Add coconut milk, stirring with a whisk until smooth. Stir in 1 cup water and pumpkin; cook over medium heat 8 minutes or until thoroughly heated. Remove from heat; stir in fish sauce.
2. Ladle soup into bowls. If desired, top with chopped cilantro and serve with lime wedges. **Yield:** 6 servings (serving size: ¾ cup).

Per serving: CALORIES 38; FAT 0.9g (sat 0.8g, mono 0g, poly 0g); PROTEIN 1.3g; CARB 7g; FIBER 2.1g; CHOL 0mg; IRON 1mg; SODIUM 559mg; CALC 21mg

Menu
PointsPlus value
per serving: 5

Thai Pumpkin Soup

2 frozen vegetable spring rolls
PointsPlus value
per serving: 4

Game Plan

1. Thaw spring rolls according to package directions.

2. While oven preheats:
• Prepare soup.

3. While soup cooks:
• Bake spring rolls.

Smoky Lentil Soup with Ham

prep: 6 minutes • **cook:** 37 minutes   *PointsPlus* value per serving: 5

2 teaspoons canola oil
1½ cups chopped onion
½ cup chopped carrot
3¾ cups fat-free, lower-sodium chicken broth
¾ cup dried lentils
¾ teaspoon dried thyme
¼ teaspoon freshly ground black pepper
1 cup chopped low-sodium deli ham
¼ cup chopped fresh parsley

1. Heat oil in a large saucepan over medium-high heat. Add onion and carrot; cook 5 minutes or until golden brown, stirring frequently.
2. Add broth and next 3 ingredients; bring to a boil. Cover, reduce heat, and simmer 20 minutes. Add ham; return mixture to a simmer, and cook, uncovered, 8 to 10 minutes or until lentils are tender. Ladle soup into bowls, and top with parsley. **Yield:** 4 servings (serving size: 1 cup).

Per serving: CALORIES 222; FAT 3g (sat 0.2g, mono 1.5g, poly 0.7g); PROTEIN 18g; CARB 32.7g; FIBER 6.5g; CHOL 13mg; IRON 4.1mg; SODIUM 682mg; CALC 28mg

Menu
PointsPlus value
per serving: 7

Smoky Lentil Soup with Ham

1 (2-inch) square cornbread
PointsPlus value
per serving: 2

Game Plan

1. Rinse, drain, and chop vegetables.

2. Sauté vegetables, and add broth.

3. While soup simmers:
• Chop ham.
• Rinse and chop parsley.

4. Add ham, and simmer.

Tuscan Squash and Bean Soup

prep: 5 minutes • **cook:** 37 minutes *PointsPlus* value per serving: 4

Using grated hard cheese in combination with no-salt-added and regular beans keeps the sodium in check. In our testing, we used a 6-cheese Italian blend that includes Parmesan, Asiago, and Romano. If that's not available, Parmesan cheese works equally well.

 2 teaspoons olive oil
 2 cups chopped onion
1¼ cups chopped celery
 4 small yellow squash, halved lengthwise and sliced
 2 large garlic cloves, minced
 1 (15-ounce) can no-salt-added Great Northern beans, undrained
 1 (15-ounce) can Great Northern beans, rinsed and drained
 1 (14.5-ounce) can roasted garlic–flavored chicken broth
 ¼ teaspoon freshly ground black pepper
 2 teaspoons chopped fresh rosemary
 ⅔ cup (2½ ounces) grated 6-cheese Italian blend cheese
 2 tablespoons chopped fresh basil
 2 tablespoons fresh lemon juice

1. Heat oil in a Dutch oven over medium-high heat. Add onion and celery; sauté until tender. Add squash; cook 7 minutes, stirring occasionally. Add garlic, and sauté 30 seconds.

2. Stir in beans, broth, and pepper; bring to a boil. Cover, reduce heat, and simmer for 15 minutes. Stir in rosemary; simmer 5 minutes. Remove from heat; stir in cheese, basil, and lemon juice. **Yield:** 7 servings (serving size: 1 cup).

Per serving: CALORIES 170; FAT 3.4g (sat 1g, mono 1.1g, poly 0.2g); PROTEIN 10.8g; CARB 27.6g; FIBER 9g; CHOL 3.6mg; IRON 1.9mg; SODIUM 641mg; CALC 167mg

Menu
PointsPlus value
per serving: 5

**Tuscan Squash
and Bean Soup**

**1 (1-ounce) wheat
baguette slice**
PointsPlus value
per serving: 1

Game Plan

1. Rinse, drain, and chop vegetables.

2. Prepare soup.

Menu
PointsPlus value
per serving: 7

**Yellow Split Pea Soup
with Spicy Sausage**

**1 (1-ounce) slice French bread,
toasted and brushed with
1 teaspoon olive oil**
PointsPlus value
per serving: 3

Game Plan

1. While sausage is cooking in
Dutch oven:
• Rinse, drain, and chop
  vegetables.

2. Add vegetables, and cook.

3. Add other ingredients, and
simmer.

4. Toast bread, and brush with
olive oil just before serving.

Yellow Split Pea Soup with Spicy Sausage

prep: 10 minutes • **cook:** 1 hour and 12 minutes   *PointsPlus* value per serving: 4

Split peas are simply dried peas that are mechanically cut in half so that they will cook faster.

4	ounces hot turkey Italian sausage
1½	cups chopped onion
½	cup chopped celery
½	cup chopped carrot
1½	teaspoons olive oil
⅛	teaspoon crushed red pepper
2	garlic cloves, minced
3	cups fat-free, lower-sodium chicken broth
3	cups water
1½	cups yellow split peas

1. Remove casings from sausage. Cook sausage in a large Dutch oven over medium-high heat until browned, stirring to crumble. Add onion and next 4 ingredients; sauté 10 minutes or until vegetables are tender. Add garlic; cook 1 minute, stirring frequently. Stir in broth, 3 cups water, and peas. Bring to a boil. Partially cover, reduce heat, and simmer 45 minutes or until peas are tender. **Yield:** 7 servings (serving size: about 1 cup).

Per serving: CALORIES 196; FAT 3.4g (sat 0.5g, mono 0.7g, poly 0.2g); PROTEIN 12.1g; CARB 29.5g; FIBER 13g; CHOL 10mg; IRON 1.2mg; SODIUM 300mg; CALC 27mg

Turkey Taco Soup

prep: 1 minute • **cook:** 13 minutes   *PointsPlus* value per serving: 6

Try topping this spicy soup with diced avocado and a little lime juice for an interesting flavor twist.

Cooking spray
1   pound ground turkey breast
1   teaspoon salt-free Southwest chipotle seasoning
2   cups frozen seasoned corn and black beans
2   (14.5-ounce) cans fire-roasted diced tomatoes, undrained
1   avocado, diced (optional)
1   (4.5-ounce) package commercial tortilla strips
Fresh lime juice (optional)

1. Heat large nonstick skillet over medium-high heat. Coat pan with cooking spray. Add turkey and chipotle seasoning; cook 5 minutes or until turkey is browned, stirring to crumble.
2. Stir in corn mixture and tomatoes. Bring to a boil; cover, reduce heat, and simmer 5 minutes or until vegetables are tender. Top each serving with avocado, tortilla strips, and lime juice, if desired. **Yield:** 4 servings (serving size: about 1 cup).

Per serving: CALORIES 245; FAT 1.9g (sat 0.5g, mono 0g, poly 0g); PROTEIN 30.2g; CARB 23.9g; FIBER 3.9g; CHOL 46mg; IRON 2.7mg; SODIUM 676mg; CALC 32mg

Menu
PointsPlus value per serving: 8

Turkey Taco Soup

Diced avocado
PointsPlus value per serving: 2

Lime juice
PointsPlus value per serving: 0

Game Plan

1. Brown turkey.

2. Add vegetables.

3. While soup simmers:
  • Quarter and dice avocado.
  • Squeeze lime over diced avocado before serving.

Menu

PointsPlus value
per serving: 10

Poblano-Chicken Chowder

1 ounce baked tortilla chips
PointsPlus value
per serving: 3

Game Plan

1. While chicken cooks:
 • Rinse, drain, and chop
  vegetables.
 • Sauté onion and chile.

2. Assemble soup, and
simmer.

3. Serve with baked tortilla
chips.

Poblano-Chicken Chowder

prep: 22 minutes • **cook:** 1 hour and 24 minutes • **other:** 10 minutes

PointsPlus value per serving: 7

Some like it hot; some don't. For more heat, increase the amount of poblano chile to ¾ cup. For little or no heat, substitute an Anaheim or green bell pepper for the poblano.

1½ pounds chicken thighs, skinned
 3 cups water
 2 teaspoons olive oil
 ¾ cup chopped onion
 ½ cup diced seeded poblano chile
 1 pound small red potatoes, chopped
 2 cups fresh corn kernels
 ¾ teaspoon salt
 ¼ teaspoon freshly ground black pepper
 ¼ cup chopped fresh cilantro

1. Combine chicken and 3 cups water in a Dutch oven; bring to a boil. Cover, reduce heat, and simmer 45 minutes. Remove chicken from pan; cool 10 minutes. Remove chicken from bones; shred chicken. Discard bones. Reserve broth in pan.
2. Heat oil in a large nonstick skillet over medium-high heat. Add onion and poblano chile; sauté 5 minutes or until tender. Add onion mixture to broth; stir in chicken, potato, and next 3 ingredients. Bring to a boil; cover, reduce heat, and simmer 20 minutes or until potato is tender. Stir in cilantro. **Yield:** 6 servings (serving size: 1⅓ cups).

Per serving: CALORIES 256; FAT 8.9g (sat 2.2g, mono 3.8g, poly 2.1g); PROTEIN 19.3g; CARB 26.5g; FIBER 3.3g; CHOL 57mg; IRON 1.8mg; SODIUM 360mg; CALC 28mg

Southwestern Chicken and Rice Soup

prep: 5 minutes • **cook:** 25 minutes

PointsPlus value per serving: 3

Long-grain rice stays separated and fluffier during cooking, which makes it perfect for this soup. Cooking the rice in water with cumin will help integrate the flavors in the soup.

- 2 (14.5-ounce) cans fat-free, lower-sodium chicken broth
- 1 cup water
- 1 cup frozen onion, celery, and bell pepper seasoning blend
- ½ cup uncooked long-grain rice
- ¼ teaspoon ground cumin
- 1½ cups chopped cooked chicken breast
- 1 cup chopped seeded peeled tomato (about 1 large tomato)
- ½ cup frozen whole-kernel corn
- 1 (4.5-ounce) can chopped green chiles, undrained
- ¼ cup lime juice
- 2 tablespoons chopped fresh cilantro
- ¼ teaspoon salt

1. Bring broth and 1 cup water to a boil in a large saucepan. Stir in seasoning blend, rice, and cumin. Return to a boil. Cover, reduce heat, and simmer 15 minutes or until rice is tender.

2. Stir chicken and next 3 ingredients into rice mixture; bring to a boil. Remove mixture from heat; stir in lime juice, cilantro, and salt. **Yield:** 8 servings (serving size: 1 cup).

Per serving: CALORIES 109; FAT 1.1g (sat 0.3g, mono 0.4g, poly 0.3g); PROTEIN 11.1g; CARB 13.7g; FIBER 0.8g; CHOL 22mg; IRON 0.8mg; SODIUM 482mg; CALC 19mg

Menu

PointsPlus value per serving: 6

Southwestern Chicken and Rice Soup

1 ounce baked tortilla strips
PointsPlus value per serving: 3

Game Plan

1. While rice is simmering:
• Peel, seed, and chop tomato.

2. Assemble soup, and serve with tortilla strips.

Fried Egg and Avocado Bagel Sandwiches

Menu
PointsPlus value
per serving: 7

**Fried Egg and Avocado
Bagel Sandwiches**

1 small orange
PointsPlus value
per serving: 0

Game Plan

1. While skillet heats:
• Separate eggs.
• Toast bagels.

2. Cook egg whites,
and quarter them.

3. Assemble sandwiches.

prep: 11 minutes • **cook:** 4 minutes   *PointsPlus* value per serving: 7

Thin is in! Thin bagels let you trim the bread and pile on the fresh veggies.

Cooking spray
 1 teaspoon olive oil
 4 large egg whites
 ¼ teaspoon salt
 ¼ teaspoon freshly ground black pepper
 ½ cup light chive and onion tub-style cream cheese
 4 whole-wheat bagel thins, toasted
12 slices ripe peeled avocado (about 1 large)
 8 (¼-inch-thick) slices tomato (about 1 large)
 1 cup fresh baby spinach

1. Heat a large nonstick skillet over medium-high heat. Coat pan with cooking spray. Add oil. Add egg whites to skillet. Sprinkle evenly with salt and pepper. Cover, reduce heat to medium, and cook 3 minutes or just until set. Divide egg whites into 4 portions. Remove from skillet.

2. Spread 1 tablespoon cream cheese on each bagel half. Arrange 3 avocado slices over each bagel bottom. Top each with 2 tomato slices, 1 egg portion, and ¼ cup spinach; cover with bagel tops. **Yield:** 4 servings (serving size: 1 sandwich).

Per serving: CALORIES 285; FAT 11.8g (sat 4g, mono 5.5g, poly 1.3g); PROTEIN 12.8g; CARB 33.3g; FIBER 4.5g; CHOL 14mg; IRON 2.2mg; SODIUM 630mg; CALC 158mg

Catfish Sandwiches with Tartar Sauce

prep: 14 minutes • **cook:** 10 minutes   *PointsPlus* value per serving: 9

Relish can be sweet or savory. Be sure to choose a sweet pickle relish for the tartar sauce to balance the slight saltiness of the catfish.

½   cup fat-free mayonnaise
1   tablespoon sweet pickle relish
½   teaspoon garlic powder
1½   teaspoons fresh lemon juice
1   teaspoon Worcestershire sauce
⅓   cup yellow cornmeal
2   teaspoons salt-free Cajun seasoning
¼   teaspoon salt
4   (6-ounce) catfish fillets, cut in half
2   teaspoons canola oil
Cooking spray
4   (1.4-ounce) light wheat hamburger buns, toasted
4   green leaf lettuce leaves
4   (¼-inch-thick) slices tomato
4   lemon wedges

1. Combine first 5 ingredients in a small dish; set aside.

2. Combine cornmeal, Cajun seasoning, and salt in a shallow dish. Dredge fillet halves in cornmeal mixture, shaking off excess.

3. Heat a large nonstick skillet over medium-high heat. Add oil, swirling to coat. Add fish; cook 5 minutes. Coat fish with cooking spray; turn and cook 5 minutes or until fish flakes easily when tested with a fork or until desired degree of doneness.

4. Spread 1 tablespoon tartar sauce on each bun half. Top each bottom half with 1 lettuce leaf, 1 tomato slice, 2 fillet halves, and top half of bun. Serve with lemon wedges. **Yield:** 4 servings (serving size: 1 sandwich and 1 lemon wedge).

Per serving: CALORIES 318; FAT 9.2g (sat 1.6g, mono 3g, poly 2.2g); PROTEIN 33.2g; CARB 33.8g; FIBER 5.9g; CHOL 102mg; IRON 2.7mg; SODIUM 739mg; CALC 106mg

Menu
PointsPlus value
per serving: 9

**Catfish Sandwiches
with Tartar Sauce**

1 small orange
PointsPlus value
per serving: 0

Game Plan

1. Prepare tartar sauce and breading.

2. While skillet heats:
• Dredge fish.

3. While fish cooks:
• Toast buns.
• Assemble sandwiches.

Menu
PointsPlus value
per serving: 9

Falafel Sandwiches
with Tahini Sauce

Game Plan

1. Chop and sauté onion,
garlic, and spices.

2. Prepare chickpea mixture,
and chill.

3. While mixture chills:
• Prepare Tahini Sauce.

4. While skillet heats:
• Shape chickpea mixture
into patties.

5. Brown patties, and
assemble sandwiches.

Falafel Sandwiches with Tahini Sauce

prep: 8 minutes • **cook:** 28 minutes • **other:** 30 minutes

PointsPlus value per serving: 9

Highly seasoned chickpea patties are nestled in pita halves and drizzled with a sesame seed sauce. Pitas from a local bakery or Middle Eastern market will be fresher and easier to split than those found in the grocery store.

1½ tablespoons olive oil, divided
1 cup finely chopped onion (about 1 large)
3 garlic cloves, coarsely chopped
1 teaspoon ground cumin
½ teaspoon ground coriander
4 (1-ounce) slices white bread, torn into large pieces
2 tablespoons chopped fresh cilantro
¼ teaspoon salt
¼ teaspoon freshly ground black pepper
1 (16-ounce) can chickpeas (garbanzo beans), rinsed and drained
1 large egg
Tahini Sauce
Cooking spray
2 (6-inch) whole-wheat pitas, cut in half and split horizontally
4 romaine lettuce leaves
4 (¼-inch-thick) slices tomato
8 cucumber slices

1. Heat 1½ teaspoons oil in a large nonstick skillet over medium heat. Add onion, and sauté 4 minutes. Add garlic, and sauté 1 minute. Add cumin and coriander, and sauté 1 minute.
2. Place onion mixture, bread, and next 5 ingredients in a blender or food processor; pulse 5 to 6 times until mixture is coarsely ground. Cover and chill at least 30 minutes.
3. While chickpea mixture chills, prepare Tahini Sauce.
4. Shape chickpea mixture into 8 (½-inch-thick) patties on a sheet of wax paper (mixture will be sticky). Heat 1½ teaspoons oil in a large nonstick skillet coated with cooking spray over medium-high heat. Add 4 patties, and cook 5 minutes on each side or until lightly browned. Remove patties from pan; keep warm. Repeat procedure with remaining 1½ teaspoons oil and remaining 4 patties.
5. Line each pita half with 1 lettuce leaf, 1 tomato slice, and 2 cucumber slices. Fill each pita half with 2 falafel patties; drizzle 2 tablespoons Tahini Sauce over each pita half. **Yield:** 4 servings (serving size: 1 pita half).

Per serving: CALORIES 357; FAT 10.7g (sat 1.2g, mono 5.2g, poly 2.4g); PROTEIN 13.4g; CARB 55.1g; FIBER 8.2g; CHOL 53mg; IRON 3.7mg; SODIUM 753mg; CALC 99mg

Tahini Sauce

prep: 9 minutes

PointsPlus value per serving: 1

- ¼ cup tahini (roasted sesame seed paste)
- ¼ cup water
- 2 tablespoons chopped fresh parsley
- 2 tablespoons fresh lemon juice
- 1 teaspoon minced garlic
- ¼ teaspoon salt
- ⅛ teaspoon ground red pepper

1. Place all ingredients in a food processor; process until smooth. **Yield:** ½ cup (serving size: 1 tablespoon).

Per serving: CALORIES 46; FAT 4g (sat 0.6g, mono 1.5g, poly 1.8g); PROTEIN 1.4g; CARB 2.1g; FIBER 0.4g; CHOL 0mg; IRON 0.4mg; SODIUM 76mg; CALC 13mg

Portobello Panini

prep: 5 minutes • **cook:** 9 minutes

PointsPlus value per serving: 9

If you don't have a panini press, use a grill pan to cook both the mushrooms and the sandwiches. The optional bottled roasted red peppers are a colorful addition to this sandwich.

- 4 (4-inch) portobello caps
- Olive oil–flavored cooking spray
- ¼ teaspoon freshly ground black pepper
- 1 (4-ounce) package goat cheese with herbs
- 4 (3-ounce) ciabatta rolls, halved horizontally
- 1⅓ cups arugula
- 2 bottled roasted red bell peppers, sliced (optional)

1. Preheat panini grill.
2. Remove brown gills from the undersides of mushrooms using a spoon; discard gills. Coat mushrooms with cooking spray; sprinkle evenly with black pepper. Place mushrooms on panini grill; cook 3 minutes or until tender.
3. Spread goat cheese evenly on roll bottoms; top evenly with arugula, mushrooms, and, if desired, bell peppers, and cover with roll tops. Coat sandwiches with cooking spray, and place, 2 at a time, on panini grill; cook 3 minutes or until cheese melts and bread is toasted. Repeat with remaining 2 sandwiches. **Yield:** 4 servings (serving size: 1 sandwich).

Per serving: CALORIES 316; FAT 8.1g (sat 4.6g, mono 1.7g, poly 1g); PROTEIN 17.3g; CARB 47.9g; FIBER 3.2g; CHOL 10mg; IRON 0.6mg; SODIUM 619mg; CALC 38mg

Menu
PointsPlus value per serving: 10

Portobello Panini

¼ cup dried apple chips
PointsPlus value per serving: 1

Game Plan

1. While panini grill heats:
• Slice ciabatta rolls.
• Clean mushrooms.

2. Grill mushrooms.

Grilled Chicken Caesar Panini

Menu
PointsPlus value
per serving: 7

Grilled Chicken Caesar Panini

1 cup red seedless grapes
PointsPlus value
per serving: 0

Game Plan

1. While panini grill heats:
- Spread dressing on bread.
- Assemble sandwiches.

2. While sandwiches are grilling:
- Rinse and drain grapes.

prep: 4 minutes • **cook:** 8 minutes   *PointsPlus* value per serving: 7

- ¼ cup light Caesar dressing
- 8 (0.5-ounce) slices Italian bread
- 4 slices reduced-fat provolone cheese
- 2 cups shredded cooked chicken breast
- 1 cup baby arugula or baby spinach
- Olive oil–flavored cooking spray

1. Preheat panini grill.

2. Spread ½ tablespoon dressing evenly on each bread slice. Top each of 4 bread slices with 1 slice cheese, ½ cup chicken, ¼ cup arugula, and 1 bread slice. Coat sandwiches with cooking spray; place on panini grill, and cook 4 to 5 minutes or until golden brown. **Yield:** 4 servings (serving size: 1 sandwich).

Note: If you don't have a panini grill, place sandwiches in a large nonstick skillet over medium heat. Place a piece of foil over sandwiches; top with a heavy skillet. Cook 2 to 3 minutes on each side or until golden and cheese melts.

Per serving: CALORIES 285; FAT 8.8g (sat 3.6g, mono 2.7g, poly 1.5g); PROTEIN 30.3g; CARB 18.7g; FIBER 0.9g; CHOL 77mg; IRON 1.6mg; SODIUM 528mg; CALC 73mg

Cranberry-Chicken Sandwiches

Menu
PointsPlus value
per serving: 10

Cranberry-Chicken Sand-wiches

1 ounce baked chips
PointsPlus value
per serving: 2

Game Plan

1. While bread is toasting:
- Prepare cheese spread.
- Rinse and drain lettuce leaves

2. Assemble sandwiches.

prep: 14 minutes   *PointsPlus* value per serving: 8

We used only the breast meat from a deli rotisserie chicken for these sandwiches.

- ½ cup (4 ounces) tub-style light cream cheese
- ¼ cup cranberry chutney
- 2 tablespoons chopped pecans or walnuts, toasted
- 8 (0.8-ounce) slices light wheat bread, toasted
- 2 cups shredded cooked chicken breast (about 9 ounces)
- 4 Bibb lettuce leaves

1. Combine first 3 ingredients in a small bowl; stir well.

2. Spread cream cheese mixture evenly on each bread slice. Top each of 4 bread slices evenly with chicken and lettuce leaves. Top with remaining bread slices, coated sides down. **Yield:** 4 servings (serving size: 1 sandwich).

Per serving: CALORIES 311; FAT 9.4g (sat 3.5g, mono 3.4g, poly 1.4g); PROTEIN 28.4g; CARB 29.4g; FIBER 3.3g; CHOL 68mg; IRON 3.2mg; SODIUM 395mg; CALC 175mg

pictured on page 40

Hot Balsamic Slaw Dogs

prep: 5 minutes • **cook:** 8 minutes   *PointsPlus* value per serving: 6

 4 (1.6-ounce) light beef hot dogs
Cooking spray
 2 cups packaged coleslaw
 ¼ cup balsamic vinegar
 ¼ teaspoon freshly ground black pepper
 4 white-wheat hot dog buns
 1 teaspoon prepared mustard (optional)

1. Preheat grill to medium-high heat.
2. Place hot dogs on grill rack coated with cooking spray. Grill 8 to 10 minutes or until done.
3. While hot dogs cook, combine coleslaw and next 2 ingredients in a large non-stick skillet. Cook over medium-high heat until slaw begins to wilt and vinegar almost evaporates.
4. Spread buns evenly with mustard, if desired. Place hot dogs in buns; top evenly with slaw. Serve immediately. **Yield:** 4 servings (serving size: 1 sandwich).

Per serving: CALORIES 199; FAT 8.5g (sat 3g, mono 0g, poly 1g); PROTEIN 11.5g; CARB 25.1g; FIBER 4.9g; CHOL 20mg; IRON 3.6mg; SODIUM 711mg; CALC 265mg

> ## Menu
> ***PointsPlus* value per serving: 9**
>
> **Hot Balsamic Slaw Dogs**
>
> **½ cup vegetarian baked beans**
> ***PointsPlus* value per serving: 3**
>
> ## Game Plan
>
> **1.** While grill preheats:
> • Heat skillet.
>
> **2.** While hot dogs are grilling:
> • Prepare slaw.
> • Heat beans according to package directions.
>
> **3.** Assemble hot dogs.

Turkey Dogs with Fennel Slaw

prep: 5 minutes • **cook:** 8 minutes   *PointsPlus* value per serving: 4

You can make the slaw for these highly rated sandwiches ahead of time and store it in the refrigerator—it will only be better since the flavors have had extra time to meld.

 4 (1.75-ounce) 98% fat-free turkey hot dogs
 1 cup packaged coleslaw
 1 cup thinly sliced fennel
 ¼ cup thinly sliced red onion
 ¼ cup light coleslaw dressing
 1 tablespoon finely chopped fennel fronds
 1 tablespoon fresh lemon juice
 4 (0.7-ounce) white-wheat hot dog buns, toasted

1. Heat hot dogs according to package directions. Keep warm.
2. While hot dogs heat, combine coleslaw and next 5 ingredients. Place hot dogs in buns; top evenly with slaw. **Yield:** 4 servings (serving size: 1 sandwich).

Per serving: CALORIES 185; FAT 5.6g (sat 0.5g, mono 0g, poly 1g); PROTEIN 10.6g; CARB 30g; FIBER 5.3g; CHOL 27.5mg; IRON 3mg; SODIUM 865mg; CALC 270mg

> ## Menu
> ***PointsPlus* value per serving: 6**
>
> **Turkey Dogs with Fennel Slaw**
>
> **1 ounce baked chips**
> ***PointsPlus* value per serving: 2**
>
> ## Game Plan
>
> **1.** While hot dogs are heating:
> • Slice vegetables.
> • Prepare slaw.
> • Toast buns.
>
> **2.** Assemble hot dogs.

Menu

PointsPlus value
per serving: 8

Moo Shu Pork Wraps

½ cup steamed shelled
edamame
PointsPlus value
per serving: 3

Game Plan

1. Begin steaming edamame.

2. While skillet heats:
• Rinse and slice onions.

3. Prepare pork, mushrooms,
and eggs; wilt slaw.

4. Assemble pork wraps.

Moo Shu Pork Wraps

prep: 11 minutes • **cook:** 10 minutes • **other:** 5 minutes

PointsPlus value per serving: 5

Cooking spray
1 (¾-pound) pork tenderloin, trimmed and cut diagonally into
   ¼-inch-thick slices
¼ teaspoon freshly ground black pepper
1 (3½-ounce) package shiitake mushrooms
5 tablespoons water, divided
2 large eggs
⅛ teaspoon salt
3 cups packaged cabbage-and-carrot coleslaw
2 tablespoons lower-sodium soy sauce
2 teaspoons cornstarch
1 teaspoon dark sesame oil
2 tablespoons hoisin sauce
6 (6-inch) low-carb, high-fiber flour tortillas
3 tablespoons sliced green onions

1. Heat a large nonstick skillet over medium-high heat. Coat pan with cooking spray. Sprinkle pork with pepper. Add pork to pan, and cook 3 minutes or until pork is browned, stirring after 1 minute. Transfer pork to a plate; keep warm. Add mushrooms to pan; coat mushrooms with cooking spray, and cook 2 minutes without stirring. Stir in 2 tablespoons water, scraping pan to loosen browned bits; cook 1 minute or until liquid evaporates. Add mushrooms to pork; keep warm.
2. Combine eggs and salt, stirring with a whisk. Heat a small nonstick skillet over medium-high heat. Coat pan with cooking spray. Add egg mixture to pan, and cook 30 seconds or until scrambled, stirring constantly. Transfer scrambled egg to another plate.
3. Return large skillet to medium-high heat. Coat pan with cooking spray. Add coleslaw; cook 2 minutes or until slightly wilted, stirring frequently. Combine remaining 3 tablespoons water, soy sauce, cornstarch, and sesame oil in a small bowl, stirring with a whisk until smooth. Add soy sauce mixture to coleslaw. Stir in pork and mushrooms.
4. Spread hoisin sauce evenly on 1 side of each tortilla. Spoon pork mixture evenly over hoisin sauce; top evenly with scrambled egg and green onions. Fold tortilla over filling. **Yield:** 6 servings (serving size: 1 wrap).

Per serving: CALORIES 228; FAT 6.1g (sat 1.3g, mono 1.5g, poly 0.5g); PROTEIN 17g; CARB 23.4g; FIBER 2.9g; CHOL 97mg; IRON 2.7mg; SODIUM 594mg; CALC 90mg

Round Italian Sandwich

prep: 12 minutes • **other:** 1 hour   *PointsPlus* value per serving: 7

Arugula has a stronger, sometimes spicier flavor than spinach. It can sometimes have a peppery or mustard-like flavor.

  1 (6½-inch) round loaf sourdough bread (about 8 ounces)
  2 (1-ounce) slices provolone cheese
  2 slices (1-ounce) turkey salami
  1 slice (1-ounce) turkey ham
  2 small tomatoes, thinly sliced
  2 cups trimmed arugula or spinach
  2 tablespoons balsamic vinegar
  2 tablespoons grated fresh Parmesan cheese
  ½ teaspoon freshly ground black pepper

1. Slice bread horizontally into 3 equal layers, using an electric knife or serrated knife. Layer half each of provolone cheese, salami, ham, tomato, and arugula on bottom slice of bread. Sprinkle arugula with half each of balsamic vinegar, Parmesan cheese, and pepper; top with second bread slice. Repeat procedure with remaining provolone cheese, salami, ham, tomato, and arugula. Sprinkle arugula with remaining balsamic vinegar, Parmesan cheese, and pepper; top with remaining bread slice.

2. Wrap sandwich tightly in plastic wrap, and chill 1 hour. To serve, slice sandwich into 4 wedges. **Yield:** 4 servings (serving size: 1 wedge).

Per serving: CALORIES 277; FAT 7.8g (sat 4g, mono 2.1g, poly 1.1g); PROTEIN 15.9g; CARB 36g; FIBER 2.1g; CHOL 29mg; IRON 2.8mg; SODIUM 702mg; CALC 207mg

Menu
PointsPlus value
per serving: 7

Round Italian Sandwich

1 cup mixed cucumber slices, cherry tomatoes, and celery sticks
PointsPlus value
per serving: 0

Game Plan

1. Rinse, drain, and slice tomatoes, and trim arugula.

2. Assemble sandwich, and chill until ready to serve.

Menu
PointsPlus value
per serving: 8

Steak Sandwiches
with Horseradish Mayonnaise

1 small pear
PointsPlus value
per serving: 0

Game Plan

1. While skillet is heating:
- Season steak.
- Slice onion, and mince garlic.

2. While steak cooks:
- Prepare horseradish mayonnaise.

3. Assemble sandwiches.

Steak Sandwiches with Horseradish Mayonnaise

prep: 3 minutes • **cook:** 9 minutes   *PointsPlus* value per serving: 8

Prepared horseradish is made by preserving grated horseradish root in vinegar. It adds a pungent bite to the creamy sauce that smothers the juicy steak filling in this sandwich.

Cooking spray
¾ pound boneless sirloin steak, thinly sliced
¼ teaspoon salt
¼ teaspoon freshly ground black pepper
½ cup thinly sliced red onion
1 garlic clove, minced
1 tablespoon Worcestershire sauce
¼ cup light mayonnaise
3 tablespoons fat-free milk
1 tablespoon prepared horseradish
4 (4-ounce) onion hamburger buns

1. Heat a large nonstick skillet over medium-high heat. Coat pan with cooking spray. Sprinkle steak evenly with salt and pepper. Add steak to pan. Cook 4 minutes or until browned, stirring frequently. Add onion; cook 3 minutes or until onion is tender, stirring frequently. Add garlic; cook 1 minute, stirring constantly. Stir in Worcestershire sauce. Remove pan from heat; cover and keep warm.

2. While steak cooks, combine mayonnaise, milk, and horseradish, stirring with a whisk. Spoon beef mixture evenly onto bottoms of buns; drizzle evenly with horseradish mayonnaise. Top with bun tops. **Yield:** 4 servings (serving size: 1 sandwich).

Per serving: CALORIES 322; FAT 8.7g (sat 2.8g, mono 3g, poly 1.7g); PROTEIN 25g; CARB 36.5g; FIBER 1.4g; CHOL 50mg; IRON 3.2mg; SODIUM 674mg; CALC 211mg

Salads

PointsPlus value per serving: 1
Sweet Lemon-Jicama Slaw | page 99
Chunky Asian Slaw | page 99

PointsPlus value per serving: 2
Fresh Orange and Spring Greens Salad | page 80
Minted Pea Salad | page 84

PointsPlus value per serving: 3
Date and Goat Cheese Salad | page 81
Spring Greens with Sweet Lime Vinaigrette
    and Berries | page 83
Fresh Herb Insalata | page 84
Sun-Dried Tomato and Goat Cheese
    Salad | page 85
Green Bean, Roasted Beet, and Feta
    Salad | page 95
Marinated Bean Salad | page 96
Grilled Potato and Arugula Salad | page 98

PointsPlus value per serving: 4
Green Goddess Chicken Salad | page 89
Smoked Turkey–Mango Salad | page 91
German Potato Salad | page 97
Warm Gorgonzola Potato Salad | page 98
Bulgur and Pine Nut Salad | page 100

PointsPlus value per serving: 5
Fig, Arugula, and Mint Salad | page 81
Mixed Greens with Grapefruit, Hearts of Palm,
    Avocado, and Queso Fresco | page 82
Curry Chicken Salad | page 88
Spicy Thai Pork Salad | page 92

PointsPlus value per serving: 6
Provençal Tomato Bread Salad | page 86
Apple-Pecan Chicken Salad | page 89
Spicy Chicken Finger Salad | page 90
Grilled Tuna Salad with Avocado-Wasabi
    Dressing | page 93

PointsPlus value per serving: 7
Warm Beef Salad with Figs | page 87
Crab Cakes over Mixed Greens with Lemon
    Dressing | page 94

Menu
PointsPlus value
per serving: 5

**Fresh Orange and Spring
Greens Salad**

**1 (6-ounce) container fat-free
Greek yogurt**
PointsPlus value
per serving: 3

Game Plan

1. While almonds toast:
• Slice onions.

2. Grate, peel, and section
oranges.

3. Rinse greens.

4. Prepare dressing.

5. Assemble salad.

Fresh Orange and Spring Greens Salad

prep: 20 minutes   *PointsPlus* value per serving: 2

**To toast almonds, cook them in a small skillet over medium heat for
about 5 minutes. Be sure to stir constantly to prevent burning.**

    4   large navel oranges
    ¼   cup cider vinegar
    2   tablespoons "measures-like-sugar" calorie-free sweetener
    1   tablespoon canola oil
    ¼   teaspoon crushed red pepper
    ⅛   teaspoon salt
    ½   cup halved and thinly sliced red onion
    1   (5-ounce) package spring mix salad greens
    ¼   cup slivered almonds, toasted

1. Grate 2 teaspoons rind from 1 orange. Place rind in a large bowl. Peel and section
oranges over a medium bowl, collecting juice. Drain orange sections, reserving
sections and ¼ cup orange juice; save remaining juice for another use. Add reserved
juice, vinegar, and next 4 ingredients to rind, stirring well.
2. Add onion and greens to dressing; toss well. Add reserved orange sections, and
toss gently. Sprinkle with almonds. Serve immediately. **Yield:** 8 servings (serving
size: 1 cup salad and ½ tablespoon almonds).

Per serving: CALORIES 77; FAT 3.5g (sat 0.3g, mono 2.2g, poly 0.9g); PROTEIN 1.6g; CARB 11.4g; FIBER 2.5g; CHOL 0mg; IRON 0.4mg; SODIUM 44mg; CALC 41mg

Fig, Arugula, and Mint Salad

prep: 12 minutes   *PointsPlus* value per serving: 5

Arugula punctuates a tasty combination of blue cheese, honey, and figs with a spicy kick in this flavorful salad.

- 1½ tablespoons white balsamic vinegar
- 1 tablespoon olive oil
- 1 tablespoon honey
- ¼ teaspoon ground cumin
- ¼ teaspoon salt
- ¼ teaspoon freshly ground black pepper
- 4 cups loosely packed arugula
- ¼ cup fresh mint leaves
- 12 fresh figs, halved
- ¼ cup (1 ounce) crumbled blue cheese

1. Combine first 6 ingredients in a large bowl, stirring with a whisk. Add arugula and mint; toss well. Divide arugula mixture among plates. Top with fig halves, and sprinkle with blue cheese. **Yield:** 4 servings (serving size: 1 cup arugula mixture, 6 fig halves, and 1 tablespoon cheese).

Per serving: CALORIES 191; FAT 6g (sat 1.9g, mono 3.1g, poly 0.7g); PROTEIN 3.3g; CARB 35g; FIBER 4.9g; CHOL 5mg; IRON 1mg; SODIUM 182mg; CALC 128mg

---

Menu
PointsPlus value
per serving: 5

Fig, Arugula, and Mint Salad

1 cup mixed berries
PointsPlus value
per serving: 0

Game Plan

1. Rinse arugula, mint leaves, and berries.
2. Halve figs.
3. Assemble salad.

Date and Goat Cheese Salad

prep: 8 minutes   *PointsPlus* value per serving: 3

This is a quick salad, perfect as a starter course for entertaining.

- 1 (5-ounce) package spring mix salad greens
- ⅓ cup chopped pitted Medjool dates
- ¼ cup (1 ounce) crumbled goat cheese
- ¼ teaspoon salt
- ⅛ teaspoon freshly ground black pepper
- 3 tablespoons pomegranate vinaigrette
- ¼ cup slivered almonds, toasted (optional)

1. Combine first 5 ingredients in a large bowl. Add vinaigrette, tossing gently to coat. Divide salad among plates; sprinkle with toasted almonds, if desired. **Yield:** 4 servings (serving size: 1½ cups).

Per serving: CALORIES 107; FAT 4.7g (sat 2.1g, mono 1.4g, poly 0.9g); PROTEIN 3.4g; CARB 14.6g; FIBER 1.8g; CHOL 7mg; IRON 0.7mg; SODIUM 268mg; CALC 27mg

---

Menu
PointsPlus value
per serving: 4

Date and Goat Cheese Salad

1 (1-ounce) slice French bread, warmed
PointsPlus value
per serving: 1

Game Plan

1. While bread heats:
   • Toast almonds, if desired.
2. Assemble salad, and top with almonds, if desired.

Menu

PointsPlus value
per serving: 7

Mixed Greens with Grapefruit,
Hearts of Palm, Avocado, and
Queso Fresco

1 whole-wheat pita,
quartered and warmed
PointsPlus value
per serving: 2

Game Plan

1. While pita warms:
• Drain hearts of palm.
• Slice avocado.

2. Assemble salad, and serve
with warmed pita.

Mixed Greens with Grapefruit, Hearts of Palm, Avocado, and Queso Fresco

prep: 12 minutes   *PointsPlus* value per serving: 5

Queso fresco is a slightly salty Mexican cheese with a texture and taste similar to farmer cheese. Try a Latin market if you can't find it in your grocery store.

 1   tablespoon honey
 1   tablespoon jarred grapefruit juice
 2   teaspoons extra-virgin olive oil
 ⅛   teaspoon salt
 ¼   teaspoon freshly ground black pepper
 6   cups mixed baby salad greens
1½   cups sliced drained hearts of palm
 ¾   cup jarred red grapefruit sections
 1   small avocado, peeled and sliced
 ¼   cup (1 ounce) crumbled queso fresco

1. Combine first 5 ingredients, stirring with a whisk; add greens and next 3 ingredients, tossing gently. Divide salad among plates. Sprinkle each with cheese.
Yield: 4 servings (serving size: 1½ cups salad and 1 tablespoon cheese).

Per serving: CALORIES 114; FAT 6.6g (sat 1.5g, mono 3.8g, poly 0.7g); PROTEIN 3.9g; CARB 11.5g; FIBER 3.3g; CHOL 5mg; IRON 1.6mg; SODIUM 233mg; CALC 82mg

Spring Greens with Sweet Lime Vinaigrette and Berries

prep: 15 minutes

PointsPlus value per serving: 3

The classic flavors of strawberries and mint are updated with fresh lime for a refreshing salad that earned our Test Kitchen's highest rating.

 4 cups spring mix salad greens
 2 cups sliced strawberries
 ½ cup thinly sliced red onion
 ¼ cup chopped fresh mint
 1 teaspoon grated fresh lime rind
 ¼ cup fresh lime juice
 3 tablespoons sugar
 1 tablespoon canola oil
 ⅛ teaspoon crushed red pepper
 2 tablespoons sliced almonds, toasted

1. Place greens on a large platter; top with strawberries, onion, and mint.
2. Combine lime rind and next 4 ingredients in a small bowl, stirring with a whisk. Drizzle vinaigrette over salad; sprinkle with almonds. **Yield:** 6 servings (serving size: 1 cup salad, about 1 tablespoon dressing, and 1 teaspoon almonds).

Per serving: CALORIES 111; FAT 5.3g (sat 1.1g, mono 2.2g, poly 1g); PROTEIN 2.7g; CARB 15.3g; FIBER 2.6g; CHOL 4mg; IRON 0.7mg; SODIUM 34mg; CALC 66mg

Menu
PointsPlus value
per serving: 4

Spring Greens with Sweet Lime Vinaigrette and Berries

⅓ cup fat-free cottage cheese with mixed berries
PointsPlus value
per serving: 1

Game Plan

1. While almonds toast:
 • Rinse berries.
 • Rinse and chop mint.

2. Slice onion.

3. Grate and juice lime.

4. Prepare salad dressing and assemble salad.

5. Serve mixed berries over cottage cheese.

Fresh Herb Insalata

Menu
PointsPlus value
per serving: 5

Fresh Herb Insalata

1 (1-ounce) slice whole-wheat baguette, toasted with ½ ounce shaved Parmesan cheese
PointsPlus value per serving: 2

Game Plan

1. While bread and cheese toast:
• Rinse herbs.
• Mince shallots.
• Juice lemon.

2. Assemble salad.

3. Prepare dressing, and toss with salad.

prep: 9 minutes   *PointsPlus* value per serving: 3

Basil, mint, and parsley add fresh flavors to the more traditional salad mix of butter lettuce and radicchio. A sweet dressing made with honey helps balance the strong flavors from the greens.

  1 (7-ounce) bag butter lettuce and radicchio mix
  ½ cup fresh basil leaves
  ½ cup fresh mint leaves
  ½ cup fresh flat-leaf parsley leaves
  2 tablespoons fresh lemon juice
  2 tablespoons extra-virgin olive oil
  1 tablespoon honey
  1 tablespoon minced shallots
  ¼ teaspoon salt
  ¼ to ½ teaspoon freshly ground black pepper

1. Combine first 4 ingredients in a large bowl.
2. Combine lemon juice and next 5 ingredients in a small bowl, stirring well with a whisk. Pour over salad greens; toss well. Serve immediately. **Yield:** 4 servings (serving size: 2 cups).

Per serving: CALORIES 98; FAT 7.3g (sat 1g, mono 5.4g, poly 0.7g); PROTEIN 1.3g; CARB 8.3g; FIBER 1.2g; CHOL 0mg; IRON 1.3mg; SODIUM 158mg; CALC 43mg

Minted Pea Salad

Menu
PointsPlus value
per serving: 4

Minted Pea Salad

1 (1-ounce) slice warmed ciabatta bread
PointsPlus value per serving: 2

Game Plan

1. While bread heats:
• Rinse peas.
• Rinse and tear mint.
• Grate lemon rind, and juice lemon.

2. Assemble salad.

prep: 7 minutes   *PointsPlus* value per serving: 2

  4 cups frozen petite green peas
  ½ cup torn fresh mint leaves
  1 shallot, thinly sliced
  1 teaspoon grated fresh lemon rind
  1 teaspoon fresh lemon juice
  ⅛ teaspoon salt
  ⅛ teaspoon freshly ground black pepper

1. Place peas in a colander, and rinse under cool running water to thaw; drain well. Combine peas, mint leaves, and shallot in a medium bowl. Add lemon rind, lemon juice, salt, and pepper; toss gently to combine. **Yield:** 4 servings (serving size: 1 cup).

Per serving: CALORIES 110; FAT 0.6g (sat 0.1g, mono 0g, poly 0.3g); PROTEIN 7.3g; CARB 19.8g; FIBER 6.4g; CHOL 0mg; IRON 2.3mg; SODIUM 220mg; CALC 40mg

Sun-Dried Tomato and Goat Cheese Salad

prep: 10 minutes *PointsPlus* value per serving: 3

Look for mâche, or lamb's lettuce, in most whole-foods markets and some large supermarkets. If you can't find it, substitute baby spinach or arugula.

- 4 cups mâche, torn
- 2 cups chopped trimmed baby watercress leaves or large watercress
- 1 cup chopped yellow tomato
- ½ cup thinly sliced red onion
- ¼ cup (2 ounces) goat cheese, crumbled
- 2 tablespoons chopped drained oil-packed sun-dried tomato halves
- 1 tablespoon oil from sun-dried tomatoes
- 1 tablespoon red wine vinegar
- 1 teaspoon honey
- ½ teaspoon Dijon mustard
- ¼ teaspoon salt
- ¼ teaspoon freshly ground black pepper

1. Combine mâche and watercress in a large bowl. Add chopped tomato and next 3 ingredients; toss gently to mix.

2. Combine sun-dried tomato oil and next 3 ingredients in a small bowl, stirring with a whisk until blended. Stir in salt and pepper. Drizzle dressing over salad; toss gently to mix. **Yield:** 4 servings (serving size: 1¾ cups).

Per serving: CALORIES 108; FAT 7g (sat 2.6g, mono 3.5g, poly 0.5g); PROTEIN 5.1g; CARB 7.8g; FIBER 2.1g; CHOL 7mg; IRON 1.9mg; SODIUM 240mg; CALC 114mg

---

Menu
PointsPlus value per serving: 5

Sun-Dried Tomato and Goat Cheese Salad

5 rosemary flatbread crackers
PointsPlus value per serving: 2

Game Plan

1. Rinse greens, and chop tomato.

2. Assemble salad.

3. Prepare dressing, and drizzle over salad.

pictured on page 41

Provençal Tomato Bread Salad

prep: 20 minutes • **other:** 30 minutes   *PointsPlus* value per serving: 6

With crusty French bread, salty mozzarella cheese, and fresh herbs, this salad can stand alone as a meal or serve as a tasty addition to a larger meal.

Menu
PointsPlus value
per serving: 6

Provençal Tomato Bread Salad

Game Plan

1. Tear bread into pieces.

2. Rinse and chop tomatoes, cucumber, and basil; slice onion.

3. Assemble salad.

4. Prepare dressing, and serve.

8   ounces stale French bread, torn into bite-sized pieces
6   ounces part-skim mozzarella cheese, cut into ½-inch cubes
3   medium tomatoes, chopped
1   cup chopped cucumber (about 1 small)
½   cup chopped fresh basil
⅓   cup thinly sliced red onion, cut in half
⅓   cup sliced ripe olives
¼   cup tomato juice
2   tablespoons balsamic vinegar
1   tablespoon olive oil
½   teaspoon freshly ground black pepper
¼   teaspoon salt
2   large garlic cloves, minced
    Basil sprigs (optional)

1. Combine first 7 ingredients in a large bowl; toss gently.
2. Combine tomato juice and next 5 ingredients in a small jar; cover tightly, and shake vigorously. Pour over bread mixture, and toss gently. Cover and chill 30 minutes before serving. Garnish with basil sprigs, if desired. **Yield:** 7 servings (serving size: about 1½ cups).

Per serving: CALORIES 213; FAT 8.6g (sat 3.6g, mono 3.4g, poly 0.7g); PROTEIN 10.8g; CARB 24.4g; FIBER 1.8g; CHOL 17mg; IRON 2mg; SODIUM 536mg; CALC 217mg

pictured on page 43

Warm Beef Salad with Figs

prep: 14 minutes • **cook:** 13 minutes • **other:** 8 hours and 5 minutes

PointsPlus value per serving: 7

Figs are in season from summer until early fall. If fresh figs aren't in season, substitute dried figs, which are available year-round in most supermarkets.

2   tablespoons dry red wine
1   tablespoon minced fresh oregano
1   tablespoon minced fresh rosemary
1   tablespoon minced fresh marjoram
1   tablespoon minced fresh thyme
2   teaspoons olive oil
2   large garlic cloves, minced
12 ounces boneless round steak, trimmed (¾ inch thick)
¼   cup plain fat-free yogurt
2   tablespoons white wine vinegar
2   tablespoons honey mustard
2   tablespoons orange juice
Cooking spray
4   cups mixed baby salad greens
1   cup snow peas, trimmed and cut into very thin strips
8   large fresh or dried figs, sliced

1. Combine first 7 ingredients; rub herb mixture over both sides of steak. Place steak in a heavy-duty, zip-top plastic bag; seal bag. Marinate in refrigerator 8 hours or overnight.
2. Preheat broiler.
3. Combine yogurt, vinegar, mustard, and orange juice in a small bowl; stir well, and set aside.
4. Place steak on rack of a broiler pan coated with cooking spray. Broil 3 to 4 minutes on each side or until desired degree of doneness. Let stand 5 minutes; cut into thin strips. Arrange greens, snow peas, and figs on a platter; arrange steak evenly over greens mixture. Stir dressing, and drizzle over salad. **Yield:** 4 servings (serving size: ¼ of salad).

Per serving: CALORIES 274; FAT 7.5g (sat 2.4g, mono 3.2g, poly 0.4g); PROTEIN 22.8g; CARB 29.7g; FIBER 5.1g; CHOL 57mg; IRON 3.8mg; SODIUM 126mg; CALC 98mg

---

Menu

PointsPlus value
per serving: 8

Warm Beef Salad with Figs

1 (1-ounce) slice French bread, warmed
PointsPlus value
per serving: 1

Game Plan

1. Prepare steak, and let marinate.

2. While broiler preheats:
• Prepare dressing.

3. While steak cooks:
• Rinse and chop greens; slice snow peas.
• Slice figs.

4. While steak rests:
• Assemble salad.
• Toast French bread.

Menu
PointsPlus value
per serving: 9

Curry Chicken Salad

15 multi-seed crackers
PointsPlus value
per serving: 4

1 medium pear
PointsPlus value
per serving: 0

Game Plan

1. While almonds toast:
• Rinse and chop apple.
• Chop cooked chicken.

2. Assemble chicken salad.

3. Top with toasted, chopped
almonds.

Curry Chicken Salad

prep: 20 minutes • **other:** 1 hour   *PointsPlus* value per serving: 5

**Mixing mayonnaise and sour cream keeps this curry chicken salad
lighter than using mayonnaise alone. Serve with a side of crackers
and a piece of fruit for an easy-to-pack lunch.**

1½   cups chopped apple
 1   teaspoon fresh lemon juice
 3   cups chopped cooked chicken breast
 ¾   cup thinly sliced celery
 ¼   cup raisins
 ⅓   cup light mayonnaise
 ⅓   cup fat-free sour cream
 2   tablespoons minced fresh chives
 2   teaspoons sugar
 ½   teaspoon curry powder
 ¼   teaspoon salt
 2   tablespoons slivered almonds, toasted and chopped

1. Combine apple and lemon juice in a large bowl; toss well to coat apple. Add
chicken, celery, and raisins; toss well.
2. Combine mayonnaise and next 5 ingredients in a small bowl; pour over chicken
mixture, and toss well. Sprinkle with chopped almonds. Cover and chill at least
1 hour. **Yield:** 6 servings (serving size: about 1 cup).

Per serving: CALORIES 198; FAT 4.6g (sat 0.8g, mono 1.6g, poly 1.3g); PROTEIN 23.5g; CARB 15.1g; FIBER 1.2g; CHOL 62mg; IRON 1.1mg; SODIUM 288mg; CALC 54mg

Green Goddess Chicken Salad

prep: 8 minutes   *PointsPlus* value per serving: 4

Try using the remaining dressing as a dip for carrot sticks or other raw vegetables.

⅓   cup plain fat-free yogurt
3   tablespoons light mayonnaise
2   tablespoons white vinegar
2   tablespoons chopped fresh parsley
1   tablespoon chopped fresh dill
¼   teaspoon salt
¼   teaspoon freshly ground black pepper
1   (6-ounce) package five-lettuce blend
2   cups sliced cooked chicken
1   cup halved grape tomatoes

1. Place first 7 ingredients in a blender or food processor; pulse until smooth.
2. Remove dressing packet from salad blend; reserve for another use. Combine salad blend, chicken, and tomato in a large bowl. Pour half of dressing over salad, reserving remaining dressing for another use; toss gently to coat. Serve immediately. **Yield:** 4 servings (serving size: about 1⅓ cups).

Per serving: CALORIES 178; FAT 6.2g (sat 1.3g, mono 1.8g, poly 2.6g); PROTEIN 22.9g; CARB 5.3g; FIBER 0.6g; CHOL 64mg; IRON 1.3mg; SODIUM 313mg; CALC 56mg

Menu
PointsPlus value
per serving: 4

Green Goddess Chicken Salad

1 cup carrot sticks
PointsPlus value
per serving: 0

Game Plan

1. Rinse parsley and dill.

2. Prepare dressing.

3. Assemble salad.

Apple-Pecan Chicken Salad

prep: 9 minutes   *PointsPlus* value per serving: 6

8   cups chopped romaine lettuce (about 2 romaine hearts)
2   cups coarsely chopped Fuji apple (2 apples)
¼   cup sweetened dried cranberries
¼   cup pecan pieces, toasted
1   (6-ounce) package refrigerated grilled chicken strips
⅓   cup strawberry-balsamic vinaigrette
⅓   cup (1.3 ounces) crumbled blue cheese

1. Place first 5 ingredients in a large bowl. Add vinaigrette; toss well. Sprinkle salad with cheese. Serve immediately. **Yield:** 4 servings (serving size: 3 cups).

Per serving: CALORIES 227; FAT 9.7g (sat 3g, mono 3.7g, poly 1.6g); PROTEIN 14.2g; CARB 23.3g; FIBER 4.9g; CHOL 36mg; IRON 2.3mg; SODIUM 562mg; CALC 130mg

Menu
PointsPlus value
per serving: 8

Apple-Pecan Chicken Salad

5 toasted sesame crackers
PointsPlus value
per serving: 2

Game Plan

1. While pecans toast:
• Rinse and chop lettuce and apple.

2. Assemble salad.

pictured on page 42

Spicy Chicken Finger Salad

prep: 7 minutes • **cook:** 15 minutes   *PointsPlus* value per serving: 6

Adding hot sauce to a commercial ranch dressing spices up this chicken finger salad.

Menu

PointsPlus value
per serving: 6

Spicy Chicken Finger Salad

1 medium orange
PointsPlus value
per serving: 0

Game Plan

1. While oven preheats:
• Prepare coating.
• Coat chicken.

2. While chicken cooks:
• Rinse and tear lettuce.
• Rinse and chop celery.
• Slice onion.

3. Prepare dressing.

4. Assemble salad.

⅓ cup cornflake crumbs
2 teaspoons chili powder
½ teaspoon garlic powder
1 pound chicken breast tenders
Cooking spray
6 cups torn romaine lettuce
1 cup sliced celery
½ cup sliced red onion
⅓ cup fat-free ranch dressing
1½ teaspoons hot sauce
¼ cup (1 ounce) crumbled blue cheese

1. Preheat oven to 375°.

2. Combine first 3 ingredients in a heavy-duty zip-top plastic bag; add chicken. Seal bag, and shake until chicken is well coated.

3. Place chicken on a baking sheet coated with cooking spray. Bake at 375° for 15 minutes or until chicken is done.

4. Combine lettuce, celery, and onion. Combine dressing and hot sauce; pour over lettuce mixture, and toss well.

5. Place lettuce mixture on plates. Arrange chicken evenly over salads; sprinkle with cheese. **Yield:** 4 servings (serving size: about 2 cups salad mixture, about 4 ounces chicken, and 1 tablespoon cheese).

Per serving: CALORIES 238; FAT 4.8g (sat 2.1g, mono 1.1g, poly 0.6g); PROTEIN 30g; CARB 18.2g; FIBER 3.1g; CHOL 72mg; IRON 2.9mg; SODIUM 567mg; CALC 105mg

pictured on page 44

Smoked Turkey–Mango Salad

prep: 12 minutes   *PointsPlus* value per serving: 4

**Savoy cabbage is a mild cabbage with crinkled leaves. If you have
extra cabbage left after making the salad, keep it in the refrigerator
for up to four weeks, and use the versatile cabbage, cooked or raw,
in a variety of dishes.**

- 6 ounces smoked turkey breast, cut into very thin strips
- 4 cups thinly sliced Savoy cabbage
- 1 cup finely chopped peeled mango
- ½ cup chopped fresh cilantro
- ½ medium red onion, thinly sliced
- 3 tablespoons unsweetened grapefruit juice
- 2 tablespoons cider vinegar
- 1 tablespoon olive oil
- ½ teaspoon freshly ground black pepper
- ¼ teaspoon salt

1. Combine first 5 ingredients in a large bowl. Combine grapefruit juice and
next 4 ingredients in a small jar; cover tightly, and shake vigorously. Pour dressing
over salad, and toss gently. Serve immediately. **Yield:** 4 servings (serving size: about
1⅔ cups).

Per serving: CALORIES 138; FAT 4.4g (sat 0.5g, mono 2.5g, poly 0.4g); PROTEIN 13.2g; CARB 14.7g; FIBER 4g; CHOL 23mg; IRON 1.1mg; SODIUM 473mg; CALC 44mg

---

Menu
PointsPlus value
per serving: 6

Smoked Turkey–Mango Salad

1 whole-wheat pita, cut into
triangles and warmed
PointsPlus value
per serving: 2

Game Plan

1. While pita heats:
- Cut turkey.
- Rinse and slice cabbage, and chop cilantro.
- Slice onion.
- Chop mango.

2. Prepare dressing.

3. Assemble salad.

Spicy Thai Pork Salad

prep: 16 minutes • **cook:** 6 minutes   *PointsPlus* value per serving: 5

In a time crunch, try bagged preshredded lettuce and carrots.

  1   pound lean ground pork
  2   tablespoons sambal oelek (fresh ground chile paste)
  ¼   cup chopped fresh cilantro
 11   cups thinly sliced iceburg lettuce (1 head)
 1½   cups shredded carrot
  6   tablespoons thinly sliced radishes (4 medium)
  ¼   cup light sesame-ginger dressing

1. Cook pork in a medium nonstick skillet over medium-high heat 6 minutes or until browned, stirring to crumble. Remove pan from heat; drain pork well. Return pork to pan, and stir in chile paste and cilantro.

2. Combine lettuce and carrot in a large bowl. Divide lettuce mixture among plates; top with pork mixture, radishes, and dressing. **Yield:** 4 servings (serving size: 3 cups lettuce mixture, ¾ cup pork mixture, 1½ tablespoons radishes, and 1 tablespoon dressing).

Per serving: CALORIES 191; FAT 5.6g (sat 1.5g, mono 2g, poly 0.8g); PROTEIN 25.4g; CARB 11.4g; FIBER 2.7g; CHOL 67mg; IRON 1.7mg; SODIUM 419mg; CALC 39mg

---

Menu
PointsPlus value per serving: 5

Spicy Thai Pork Salad

1 medium orange
PointsPlus value per serving: 0

Game Plan

1. While pork cooks:
 • Rinse and chop cilantro, lettuce, and radishes.

2. Assemble salad.

Grilled Tuna Salad with Avocado-Wasabi Dressing

prep: 17 minutes • **cook:** 4 minutes   *PointsPlus* value per serving: 6

3   (6-ounce) tuna steaks (about 1½ inches thick)
¼   teaspoon salt
½   teaspoon freshly ground black pepper
Cooking spray
⅓   cup ranch-flavored yogurt dressing
3   tablespoons water
2   teaspoons fresh lime juice
2   teaspoons wasabi (Japanese horseradish)
1   avocado, peeled and coarsely chopped
1   (6.5-ounce) package green and red butter lettuce blend
3   tablespoons thinly sliced green onions
2   tablespoons thinly sliced radishes (about 2)

1. Preheat grill to medium-high heat.
2. Sprinkle tuna evenly with salt and pepper. Place tuna on grill rack coated with cooking spray. Grill 2 to 3 minutes on each side or until fish flakes easily when tested with a fork or until desired degree of doneness. Break steaks into chunks using 2 forks.
3. Combine dressing and next 4 ingredients in a blender or food processor; process until smooth.
4. Place lettuce on plates. Top with grilled tuna, green onions, and radishes. Drizzle dressing evenly over salads. **Yield:** 4 servings (serving size: 1½ cups lettuce, 3 ounces tuna, about 2 teaspoons green onions, 1½ teaspoons radishes, and 3 tablespoons dressing).

Per serving: CALORIES 268; FAT 10.6g (sat 2g, mono 4.5g, poly 2.5g); PROTEIN 31.8g; CARB 7.8g; FIBER 3.2g; CHOL 61mg; IRON 1.8mg; SODIUM 438mg; CALC 58mg

Menu
PointsPlus value
per serving: 6

**Grilled Tuna Salad with
Avocado-Wasabi Dressing**

1 medium orange
PointsPlus value
per serving: 0

Game Plan

1. While grill preheats:
  • Juice lime.

2. While tuna grills:
  • Rinse and slice onions
    and radishes.

3. Prepare dressing.

4. Assemble salad.

pictured on page 45

Crab Cakes over Mixed Greens with Lemon Dressing

Menu
PointsPlus value
per serving: 7

**Crab Cakes over Mixed Greens
with Lemon Dressing**

Game Plan

1. Grate lemon rind, and juice lemon.

2. Prepare dressing, and chill.

3. While dressing chills:
• Prepare and cook crab cake patties.

4. Plate crab cakes over greens.

prep: 10 minutes • **cook:** 18 minutes

PointsPlus value per serving: 7

These tender, tasty crab cakes—served on a bed of crisp greens and topped with a tangy dressing—received our Test Kitchen's highest rating.

    2 tablespoons Dijon mustard, divided
    3 tablespoons water
    ½ teaspoon grated fresh lemon rind
    3 tablespoons fresh lemon juice
    2 tablespoons olive oil
    1 tablespoon minced shallots
    ½ teaspoon sugar
    ¼ teaspoon salt
    ½ teaspoon freshly ground black pepper
    ¼ cup light mayonnaise
    3 tablespoons chopped green onions
    1 tablespoon Worcestershire sauce
    1 large egg, lightly beaten
 1¼ cups panko (Japanese breadcrumbs), divided
    1 pound lump crabmeat, drained and shell pieces removed
 Cooking spray
    4 teaspoons olive oil, divided
    1 (10-ounce) package spring mix salad greens

1. Combine 1 tablespoon Dijon mustard and next 8 ingredients in a medium bowl, stirring well with a whisk. Cover and chill.

2. Combine remaining 1 tablespoon Dijon mustard, mayonnaise, and next 3 ingredients in a large bowl, stirring with a whisk. Gently fold in ¼ cup panko and crabmeat. Shape mixture into 12 (½-inch-thick) patties. Dredge patties in remaining 1 cup panko. Coat both sides of patties with cooking spray.

3. Heat 2 teaspoons oil in a large nonstick skillet coated with cooking spray over medium heat. Add 6 patties, and cook 4 minutes on each side or until browned. Remove from pan; keep warm. Repeat procedure with remaining 2 teaspoons oil and patties. Serve crab cakes over greens; drizzle with dressing. **Yield:** 6 servings (serving size: 2 crab cakes, 1½ cups mixed greens, and 2 tablespoons dressing).

Per serving: CALORIES 255; FAT 12.4g (sat 2.1g, mono 6.7g, poly 3g); PROTEIN 16.5g; CARB 18.6g; FIBER 1.7g; CHOL 79mg; IRON 1mg; SODIUM 609mg; CALC 44mg

Green Bean, Roasted Beet, and Feta Salad

prep: 26 minutes • **cook:** 50 minutes • **other:** 20 minutes

PointsPlus value per serving: 3

To get a jump start on this recipe, prepare the beets and green beans up to a day in advance.

    5   medium beets (about 2 pounds), trimmed, peeled, and cut into
        ½-inch wedges
        Cooking spray
    5   teaspoons olive oil, divided
    1¼ pounds green beans, trimmed
    2   tablespoons thawed orange juice concentrate
    1   tablespoon white wine vinegar
    ⅛   teaspoon salt
    ⅛   teaspoon freshly ground black pepper
    1   head Bibb lettuce, separated into leaves
    ¼   cup sliced red onion
    ¼   cup (1 ounce) crumbled feta cheese

1. Preheat oven to 400°.
2. Place beets on a large rimmed baking sheet coated with cooking spray; drizzle with 2 teaspoons oil, and toss well. Bake at 400° for 50 minutes or until beets are tender and lightly browned, stirring once. Cool beets 20 minutes or until they reach room temperature.
3. While beets cook, cook beans in boiling water to cover 3 to 5 minutes or until crisp-tender. Drain; rinse with cold water. Drain.
4. Combine orange juice concentrate, remaining 1 tablespoon oil, vinegar, salt, and pepper in a small bowl, stirring well with a whisk.
5. Place lettuce on a large platter; top with green beans, beets, and onion slices. Drizzle with dressing, and sprinkle with feta cheese. **Yield:** 8 servings (serving size: 1 cup lettuce, about ¾ cup beets, ⅓ cup beans, and ½ tablespoon cheese).

Per serving: CALORIES 116; FAT 3.9g (sat 0.9g, mono 2.3g, poly 0.5g); PROTEIN 4.2g; CARB 18.5g; FIBER 5.5g; CHOL 3mg; IRON 2mg; SODIUM 171mg; CALC 63mg

Menu
PointsPlus value
per serving: 5

Green Bean, Roasted Beet,
and Feta Salad

3 thin sesame breadsticks
PointsPlus value
per serving: 2

Game Plan

1. While oven preheats:
   • Trim and cut beets.

2. While beets roast:
   • Trim and cook beans.
   • Slice red onion.

3. Prepare dressing.

4. Assemble salad.

Menu

PointsPlus value
per serving: 6

Marinated Bean Salad

12 baked tortilla chips
PointsPlus value
per serving: 3

Game Plan

1. Rinse and drain all beans.

2. Chop pepper, onion,
and celery.

3. Prepare vinegar mixture.

4. Assemble salad, and chill.

Marinated Bean Salad

prep: 12 minutes • **cook:** 2 minutes • **other:** 8 hours

PointsPlus value per serving: 3

 1 (15½-ounce) can dark red kidney beans, rinsed and drained
 1 (15¼-ounce) can lima beans, rinsed and drained
 1 (14½-ounce) can no-salt-added cut green beans, drained
 1 (14½-ounce) can cut wax beans, rinsed and drained
 1 cup chopped red or green bell pepper (about 1 large)
 1 cup chopped red onion (about ½ large)
 1 cup chopped celery (about 3 large stalks)
 1 cup cider vinegar
 ⅓ cup sugar
 ½ teaspoon garlic powder
 ¼ teaspoon salt
 ½ teaspoon freshly ground black pepper

1. Combine first 7 ingredients in a large bowl; set aside.

2. Combine vinegar and next 4 ingredients in a small saucepan; cook over medium-high heat until mixture comes to a boil and sugar dissolves, stirring occasionally. Pour hot vinegar mixture over bean mixture; toss gently to combine.

3. Cover and chill at least 8 hours, tossing occasionally. Serve with a slotted spoon.

Yield: 8 servings (serving size: 1 cup).

Per serving: CALORIES 109; FAT 0.3g (sat 0.1g, mono 0.1g, poly 0.1g); PROTEIN 4g; CARB 23.2g; FIBER 4.7g; CHOL 0mg; IRON 1.3mg; SODIUM 276mg; CALC 44mg

German Potato Salad

prep: 7 minutes • **cook:** 18 minutes   *PointsPlus* value per serving: 4

Traditionally, German potato salad has a tart bacon dressing and is served warm or at room temperature. Stir in 2 teaspoons mustard seed for a twist.

1	pound small red potatoes (about 10), cut into 1-inch pieces
4	bacon slices
½	cup finely chopped onion
¼	cup cider vinegar
2	tablespoons water
2	teaspoons sugar
¼	teaspoon salt
¼	teaspoon freshly ground black pepper

1. Cook potato in boiling water to cover 10 minutes or until very tender. Drain and keep warm.

2. Cook bacon in a large nonstick skillet over medium heat until crisp. Remove bacon from pan, reserving 2 teaspoons drippings in pan; crumble bacon. Add onion to drippings in pan; sauté 6 minutes. Remove from heat; stir in vinegar and next 4 ingredients. Pour dressing over potatoes; sprinkle with bacon, and stir, mashing potatoes slightly. Yield: 5 servings (serving size: ½ cup).

Per serving: CALORIES 160; FAT 8.3g (sat 2.7g, mono 3.6g, poly 1g); PROTEIN 4g; CARB 17.5g; FIBER 1.8g; CHOL 12mg; IRON 0.8mg; SODIUM 275mg; CALC 14mg

Menu
PointsPlus value per serving: 4

German Potato Salad

1 cup bell pepper slices and celery sticks
PointsPlus value per serving: 0

Game Plan

1. While water heats:
   - Wash and cut potatoes.
   - Chop onion.

2. While potato boils:
   - Prepare bacon.

3. Sauté onions, and prepare dressing.

4. Assemble salad.

Warm Gorgonzola Potato Salad

prep: 15 minutes • **cook:** 8 minutes   *PointsPlus* value per serving: 4

¼   cup water
32   baby red potatoes (1½ pounds), quartered
2   bacon slices, cooked and crumbled
¼   cup (1 ounce) crumbled Gorgonzola cheese
¼   cup light olive oil vinaigrette
⅛   teaspoon freshly ground black pepper
2   tablespoons sliced green onions (optional)

1. Combine ¼ cup water and potato in a large microwave-safe bowl. Cover with heavy-duty plastic wrap; vent. Microwave at HIGH 8 minutes or until tender, stirring after 4 minutes. Drain.

2. Combine potato, bacon, and next 3 ingredients; toss gently. Sprinkle with green onions, if desired. **Yield:** 6 servings (serving size: about ½ cup).

Per serving: CALORIES 132; FAT 4.9g (sat 2g, mono 2.4g, poly 0.5g); PROTEIN 4.4g; CARB 19.5g; FIBER 2.1g; CHOL 9mg; IRON 0.8mg; SODIUM 221mg; CALC 45mg

Grilled Potato and Arugula Salad

prep: 2 minutes • **cook:** 18 minutes   *PointsPlus* value per serving: 3

Cooking spray
2   pounds Yukon gold potatoes, cut into ¼-inch-thick slices
1   small red onion, cut into ¼-inch-thick slices
¼   cup creamy mustard blend
3   tablespoons white wine vinegar
¼   teaspoon freshly ground black pepper
1   (5-ounce) package arugula

1. Heat a nonstick grill pan over medium-high heat. Coat pan with cooking spray.

2. Cook potato and onion in pan, in batches, 3 minutes on each side or until tender.

3. Combine mustard blend, vinegar, and pepper in a large bowl, stirring with a whisk. Add grilled vegetables and arugula to dressing, tossing to coat.
Yield: 6 servings (serving size: 1 cup).

Per serving: CALORIES 140; FAT 0.3g (sat 0.1g, mono 0g, poly 0.1g); PROTEIN 3.9g; CARB 31.1g; FIBER 4.1g; CHOL 0mg; IRON 1.6mg; SODIUM 156mg; CALC 61mg

Sweet Lemon-Jicama Slaw

prep: 10 minutes   *PointsPlus* value per serving: 1

This crunchy, refreshing, citrusy slaw features jicama, a Mexican root vegetable with a texture similar to a water chestnut.

- 2 cups matchstick-cut peeled jicama
- ¼ cup thinly sliced red onion
- 2 jalapeño peppers, seeded and finely chopped
- 1 teaspoon grated fresh lemon rind
- 3 tablespoons fresh lemon juice
- 2 tablespoons sugar
- 2 tablespoons chopped fresh cilantro
- 1 teaspoon canola oil

1. Combine all ingredients in a medium bowl, and toss well. **Yield:** 5 servings (serving size: ½ cup).

Per serving: CALORIES 52; FAT 1g (sat 0.1g, mono 0.6g, poly 0.3g); PROTEIN 0.5g; CARB 11g; FIBER 2.7g; CHOL 0mg; Iron 0.4mg; SODIUM 2mg; Calc 9mg

Menu
PointsPlus value per serving: 5

Sweet Lemon-Jicama Slaw

5 toasted sesame crackers spread with 2 ounces whipped cream cheese
PointsPlus value per serving: 4

Game Plan

1. Rinse and cut all vegetables.

2. Grate rind, and juice lemon.

3. Prepare slaw, and serve with crackers.

Chunky Asian Slaw

prep: 14 minutes   *PointsPlus* value per serving: 1

Dark sesame oil is made from roasted or toasted sesame seeds and has a dark, rich flavor that lighter oils lack.

- 4 cups coarsely shredded napa (Chinese) cabbage
- 1 cup sugar snap peas, trimmed and halved
- ⅓ cup thinly sliced red bell pepper
- ¼ cup diagonally sliced green onions (about 2)
- 2 tablespoons rice vinegar
- 1 tablespoon hoisin sauce
- ½ teaspoon dark sesame oil
- 2 tablespoons chopped unsalted, dry-roasted peanuts

1. Combine first 4 ingredients in a large bowl.
2. Combine vinegar, hoisin sauce, and oil, stirring well. Pour vinegar mixture over cabbage mixture; toss well.
3. Serve immediately, or cover and chill. Sprinkle with peanuts just before serving. **Yield:** 5 servings (serving size: 1 cup).

Per serving: CALORIES 55; FAT 2.4g (sat 0.3g, mono 1.1g, poly 0.8g); PROTEIN 2.2g; CARB 5.7g; FIBER 1.9g; CHOL 0.1mg; IRON 0.5mg; SODIUM 63mg; CALC 45mg

Menu
PointsPlus value per serving: 4

Chunky Asian Slaw

15 brown rice crackers
PointsPlus value per serving: 3

Game Plan

1. Rinse cabbage and peas.

2. Rinse and cut bell pepper and green onions.

3. Prepare dressing.

4. Assemble slaw.

Bulgur and Pine Nut Salad

prep: 5 minutes • **cook:** 18 minutes • **other:** 10 minutes

PointsPlus value per serving: 4

Bulgur, a popular grain in Middle Eastern cuisine, has a great nutrition profile. In fact, it has fewer calories and less fat than brown rice, with more than twice the fiber.

Menu
PointsPlus value per serving: 7

Bulgur and Pine Nut Salad

1 (6-ounce) container fat-free Greek yogurt
PointsPlus value per serving: 3

Game Plan

1. While bulgur cooks:
- Juice lemon.
- Rinse and chop mint.
- Prepare dressing.

2. Toast pine nuts.

3. Assemble salad.

2 cups water
1 cup uncooked bulgur
½ teaspoon salt, divided
¼ cup fresh lemon juice
1 tablespoon extra-virgin olive oil
½ teaspoon Dijon mustard
½ teaspoon freshly ground black pepper
⅓ cup chopped fresh mint
⅓ cup golden raisins
⅓ cup dried cranberries
2 tablespoons pine nuts, toasted

1. Combine 2 cups water, bulgur, and ¼ teaspoon salt in a medium saucepan. Bring to a boil; cover, reduce heat, and simmer 12 to 15 minutes or until tender. Remove from heat, drain off excess liquid, and cool.

2. While bulgur cooks, combine ¼ teaspoon salt, lemon juice, and next 3 ingredients in a small bowl, stirring well with a whisk.

3. Combine cooled bulgur, mint, and next 3 ingredients. Drizzle dressing over salad; toss gently to mix. **Yield:** 7 servings (serving size: ½ cup).

Per serving: CALORIES 145; FAT 4g (sat 0.5g, mono 2g, poly 1.1g); PROTEIN 3.1g; CARB 26.3g; FIBER 4.5g; CHOL 0mg; IRON 0.9mg; SODIUM 179mg; CALC 15mg

Main Dishes

PointsPlus value per serving: 3
Lime-Marinated Grilled Sea Bass | page 106

PointsPlus value per serving: 4
Grouper à la Mango | page 107
Herb-Baked Trout | page 111
Pan-Seared Steaks with Balsamic–Pepper
   Jelly Sauce | page 137
Herbed Lamb Chops | page 138
Grilled Pork Teriyaki | page 139
Pork Medallions with Glazed Onions | page 140
Hot Peppered Pork | page 142

PointsPlus value per serving: 5
Spaghetti Squash with Tomatoes and Beans | page 104

PointsPlus value per serving: 6
Cheese-Stuffed Swordfish | page 108
Grilled Tilapia Tacos with Ranch Slaw | page 112
Beef Tenderloin with Horseradish
   Cream Sauce | page 136
Pork and Vegetables in Dijon Sauce | page 141
Apricot-Glazed Chicken | page 144

PointsPlus value per serving: 7
Pesto Pasta with Roasted Tomatoes
   and Walnuts | page 103
Sweet and Smoky Lemon-Broiled Salmon | page 110

Spaghetti Carbonara | page 131
Speedy Shepherd's Pie | page 133
Southwestern Fried Rice with Chicken | page 145
Hoisin–Five Spice Chicken Thighs | page 147

PointsPlus value per serving: 8
Linguine Verde | page 102
Salmon with Balsamic Reduction | page 109
Simple Roast Beef Stroganoff | page 132
Mexican Casserole | page 135
Ginger Chicken with Couscous | page 143
Chicken Breasts with Fig-Mustard Glaze | page 146
Chicken and Dumplings | page 148
Turkey Picadillo | page 149
Turkey-Spaghetti Casserole | page 150

PointsPlus value per serving: 9
Garlic Shrimp with Spinach and Vermicelli | page 130
Beef Tostadas | page 134
BBQ Chicken Pizza | page 144

PointsPlus value per serving: 10
Caramelized Onion Pizza | page 105
Linguine with Red Clam Sauce | page 129

PointsPlus value per serving: 11
Chutney Chicken Curry | page 147

pictured on page 46

Linguine Verde

prep: 10 minutes • **cook:** 14 minutes   *PointsPlus* value per serving: 8

Watercress is a green herb with a peppery taste. If you can't find fresh watercress, try substituting arugula, which shares a similar spicy flavor.

Menu
PointsPlus value per serving: 10

Linguine Verde

½ cup blood orange sorbet
PointsPlus value per serving: 2

Game Plan

1. While linguine cooks:
   • Rinse and chop vegetables.
   • Prepare vegetable mixture.

2. Add linguine, toss, and serve.

3. Scoop sorbet into serving bowls.

8   ounces uncooked linguine
3   cups loosely packed spinach leaves
2   cups trimmed watercress
2   large plum tomatoes, each cut into 8 wedges
¾   cup loosely packed sliced fresh basil leaves
2   teaspoons extra-virgin olive oil
¼   teaspoon salt
½   cup shredded Parmesan cheese
½   teaspoon freshly ground black pepper

1. Cook linguine according to package directions, omitting salt and fat. Set aside, and keep warm.

2. Combine spinach and next 5 ingredients in a large bowl; toss well. Add linguine to spinach mixture; sprinkle with Parmesan cheese and pepper, tossing well. Serve immediately. **Yield:** 4 servings (serving size: 2 cups).

Per serving: CALORIES 305; FAT 7.8g (sat 3.6g, mono 3g, poly 0.7g); PROTEIN 15.1g; CARB 46g; FIBER 3.3g; CHOL 15mg; IRON 2.8mg; SODIUM 443mg; CALC 242mg

Pesto Pasta with Roasted Tomatoes and Walnuts

prep: 8 minutes • **cook:** 10 minutes   *PointsPlus* value per serving: 7

Maximize the flavor of this dish by taking the extra time to toast the walnuts. Put them on a baking sheet, and bake at 350° for 7 minutes.

  4 cups grape tomatoes, halved lengthwise
Cooking spray
¼ teaspoon salt
¼ teaspoon freshly ground black pepper
  3 cups uncooked multigrain farfalle (bow tie pasta)
⅓ cup refrigerated reduced-fat pesto
½ cup walnuts, toasted
¼ cup grated fresh Parmesan cheese (optional)
Fresh basil leaves, torn (optional)

1. Preheat oven to 450°.

2. Place tomato halves on a baking sheet coated with cooking spray. Sprinkle tomato halves evenly with salt and pepper; coat with cooking spray, and toss gently. Bake at 450° for 10 minutes or until tender and lightly browned.

3. While tomato halves bake, cook pasta according to package directions, omitting salt and fat. Drain and return to pan.

4. Add roasted tomato halves, pesto, and walnuts to pasta; toss gently. If desired, sprinkle with cheese and basil before serving. **Yield:** 6 servings (serving size: about 1 cup).

Per serving: CALORIES 277; FAT 12.1g (sat 1.5g, mono 4.1g, poly 5.8g); PROTEIN 10.7g; CARB 32.9g; FIBER 5g; CHOL 3mg; IRON 2.5mg; SODIUM 239mg; CALC 77mg

Menu
PointsPlus value
per serving: 7

Pesto Pasta with Roasted
Tomatoes and Walnuts

1 cup steamed green beans
PointsPlus value
per serving: 0

Game Plan

1. Toast walnuts.

2. While oven preheats:
  • Rinse and cut tomatoes and basil.
  • Boil water.

3. While tomatoes bake:
  • Cook pasta.
  • Steam green beans.

4. Toss tomatoes, pesto, walnuts, and pasta.

Menu
PointsPlus value
per serving: 7

**Spaghetti Squash with
Tomatoes and Beans**

**1 cup baby spinach with
2 tablespoons fat-free
honey Dijon dressing**
PointsPlus value
per serving: 1

**1 (1-ounce) slice
toasted garlic bread**
PointsPlus value
per serving: 1

Game Plan

1. While oven preheats:
 • Wash, cut, and prepare
  squash.

2. While squash bakes:
 • Rinse and drain beans.
 • Rinse and mince cilantro.

3. Combine ingredients, and
 spoon into casserole.

4. While casserole bakes:
 • Toast garlic bread.
 • Prepare salad.

Spaghetti Squash with Tomatoes and Beans

prep: 19 minutes • **cook:** 1 hour   *PointsPlus* value per serving: 5

When cooked and removed from the shell, spaghetti squash resembles angle hair pasta. This nutrient-packed substitute is still hearty enough to stand up to a heavy sauce.

1 (2½-pound) spaghetti squash
Cooking spray
1 (15-ounce) can diced tomatoes with green chiles, undrained
1 (15-ounce) can black beans, rinsed and drained
¾ cup (3 ounces) shredded reduced-fat Monterey Jack cheese, divided
¼ cup minced fresh cilantro
1 teaspoon ground cumin
¼ teaspoon freshly ground black pepper
Fresh cilantro leaves (optional)

1. Preheat oven to 375°.
2. Wash squash; cut in half lengthwise. Remove and discard seeds. Place squash halves, cut sides down, in a 13 x 9–inch baking dish coated with cooking spray. Add water to a depth of ½ inch. Bake at 375° for 25 minutes or until squash is tender; cool slightly. Using a fork, remove spaghetti-like strands; discard shells.
3. Combine squash strands, diced tomatoes, beans, ½ cup cheese, ¼ cup cilantro, cumin, and black pepper in a large bowl, stirring well. Spoon into a 1½-quart casserole coated with cooking spray. Sprinkle with remaining ¼ cup cheese.
4. Reduce oven temperature to 350°; bake, uncovered, for 35 minutes or until thoroughly heated. Garnish with cilantro leaves, if desired. Serve immediately.
Yield: 4 servings (serving size: about 2 cups).

Per serving: CALORIES 220; FAT 5.9g (sat 2.8g, mono 1.2g, poly 0.5g); PROTEIN 12.4g; CARB 31.8g; FIBER 7.9g; CHOL 15.2mg; IRON 2.3mg; SODIUM 563mg; CALC 245mg

pictured on page 47

Caramelized Onion Pizza

prep: 19 minutes • **cook:** 35 minutes   *PointsPlus* value per serving: 10

Cooking spray
2   teaspoons olive oil, divided
2   medium red onions, thinly sliced (about 4 cups)
1   tablespoon brown sugar
⅛   teaspoon salt
½   cup water
1   tablespoon minced fresh rosemary
1   tablespoon balsamic vinegar
1   teaspoon cornmeal
1   (13.8-ounce) can refrigerated pizza crust dough
1   cup (4 ounces) shredded reduced-fat Jarlsberg cheese

1. Preheat oven to 450°.
2. Coat a large nonstick skillet with cooking spray; add 1 teaspoon oil. Place over medium heat until hot. Add onion, sugar, and salt; cook 10 minutes, stirring occasionally. Add ½ cup water; cook 5 minutes or until water evaporates and onion is tender, stirring often. Add rosemary and vinegar; cook 2 minutes or until vinegar evaporates.
3. Coat a large baking sheet with cooking spray; sprinkle with cornmeal. Unroll pizza dough into a 12 x 10–inch rectangle. Cut rectangle into 4 (6 x 5–inch rectangles. Brush edges of rectangles with remaining 1 teaspoon olive oil. Place rectangles on prepared baking sheet; top evenly with onion mixture, and sprinkle with cheese. Bake at 450° for 15 minutes or until golden. Cut each pizza in half diagonally. **Yield:** 4 servings (serving size: 2 wedges).

Per serving: CALORIES 400; FAT 8.7g (sat 3.2g, mono 2.5g, poly 0.4g); PROTEIN 18g; CARB 64.3g; FIBER 4.6g; CHOL 10.1mg; IRON 3.1mg; SODIUM 940mg; CALC 285mg

Menu
PointsPlus value
per serving: 10

Caramelized Onion Pizza

1 cup mixed greens with cherry tomatoes and 2 tablespoons fat-free vinaigrette
PointsPlus value
per serving: 0

Game Plan

1. While skillet heats:
• Slice onions.
• Mince rosemary.

2. While oven preheats:
• Sauté onions and other ingredients until vinegar evaporates.

3. While pizza bakes:
• Prepare salad.

Menu
PointsPlus value
per serving: 7

**Lime-Marinated
Grilled Sea Bass**

½ cup cooked orzo
PointsPlus value
per serving: 3

**1 cup baby arugula
with 1 tablespoon mixed
lemon juice and olive oil**
PointsPlus value
per serving: 1

Game Plan

1. While fish marinates:
• Preheat grill.
• Boil water for orzo.

2. While orzo cooks:
• Grill fish.
• Boil marinade.

3. Toss arugula with lemon
and olive oil.

Lime-Marinated Grilled Sea Bass

prep: 5 minutes • **cook:** 8 minutes • **other:** 30 minutes

PointsPlus value per serving: 3

Be careful not to let your fish marinate too long. The acid in the marinade can soften the outside of the fish before you get it to the grill.

¼ cup dry vermouth or dry white wine
2 tablespoons fresh lime juice
2 tablespoons minced fresh cilantro
1 tablespoon lower-sodium soy sauce
2 teaspoons olive oil
4 (6-ounce) sea bass fillets (1 inch thick)
Cooking spray

1. Preheat grill to high heat.
2. Combine first 5 ingredients in a heavy-duty zip-top plastic bag; add fillets. Seal bag, and shake gently to coat fillets. Marinate in refrigerator 30 minutes.
3. Remove fillets from marinade, reserving marinade. Place fillets on grill rack coated with cooking spray; grill, covered, 4 to 5 minutes on each side or until fish flakes easily when tested with a fork or until desired degree of doneness.
4. While fillets cook, place reserved marinade in a small saucepan, and bring to a boil; remove from heat. Spoon marinade over fish. **Yield:** 4 servings (serving size: 1 fillet and about 2 tablespoons marinade).

Per serving: CALORIES 152; FAT 4.6g (sat 0.9g, mono 2.1g, poly 1.1g); PROTEIN 22.3g; CARB 1.3g; FIBER 0g; CHOL 49mg; IRON 0.4mg; SODIUM 233mg; CALC 15mg

Grouper à la Mango

prep: 13 minutes • **cook:** 20 minutes   *PointsPlus* value per serving: 4

1½ cups finely chopped peeled ripe mango (about 2 mangoes)
½ cup finely chopped red bell pepper
⅓ cup finely chopped red onion
¼ cup chopped fresh cilantro
2 tablespoons fresh lime juice
½ teaspoon salt, divided
4 (6-ounce) grouper fillets
¼ teaspoon ground red pepper
Cooking spray
Cilantro sprigs (optional)

1. Preheat oven to 425°.
2. Combine mango, bell pepper, onion, chopped cilantro, lime juice, and ¼ teaspoon salt in a small bowl, tossing well to combine. Set aside, or chill, if desired.
3. Sprinkle fillets evenly with remaining ¼ teaspoon salt and ground red pepper; arrange in an 11 x 7–inch baking dish coated with cooking spray. Bake at 425° for 20 minutes or until fish flakes easily when tested with a fork or until desired degree of doneness. Serve with mango salsa. Garnish with cilantro sprigs, if desired. **Yield:** 4 servings (serving size: 1 fillet and ½ cup salsa).

Per serving: CALORIES 153; FAT 1.5g (sat 0.3g, mono 0.3g, poly 0.4g); PROTEIN 22.8g; CARB 12.1g; FIBER 1.6g; CHOL 42mg; IRON 1.2mg; SODIUM 344mg; CALC 32mg

---

Menu
PointsPlus value
per serving: 6

Grouper à la Mango

⅓ cup cooked yellow rice
PointsPlus value
per serving: 2

**1 cup steam-in-bag
green beans**
PointsPlus value
per serving: 0

Game Plan

1. While oven preheats:
  • Boil water for rice.
  • Rinse and chop mango, pepper, onion, and cilantro.
  • Prepare salsa.

2. While fish bakes:
  • Boil rice.
  • Prepare beans according to instructions on bag.

3. Serve fish with mango salsa.

Menu

PointsPlus value
per serving: 8

Cheese-Stuffed Swordfish

⅓ cup precooked brown rice
PointsPlus value
per serving: 2

**1 cup baby spinach
with 2 tablespoons fat-free
balsamic dressing**
PointsPlus value
per serving: 0

Game Plan

1. While grill preheats:
• Cut, stuff, and dredge fish.

2. While fish cooks:
• Heat rice.
• Prepare salad.

Cheese-Stuffed Swordfish

prep: 20 minutes • **cook:** 10 minutes   *PointsPlus* value per serving: 6

For a quick dinner, add precooked brown rice and a side salad to this fast and easy fish.

  3 tablespoons grated Parmesan cheese
  2 tablespoons dry breadcrumbs
  1 tablespoon drained capers, minced
  1 tablespoon minced fresh parsley
  ½ teaspoon freshly ground black pepper
  1 garlic clove, minced
  1 (1½-pound) swordfish fillet (about 2 inches thick)
  2 ounces part-skim mozzarella cheese, cut into 4 equal slices
Olive oil–flavored cooking spray

1. Preheat grill to medium-high heat.

2. Combine first 6 ingredients; mix well.

3. Cut swordfish fillet into 4 equal pieces; cut a pocket in each piece, cutting to, but not through, remaining 3 sides. Place cheese slices in fish pockets; secure openings with wooden picks. Coat fillets with cooking spray; dredge in breadcrumb mixture.

4. Place fish on grill rack coated with cooking spray; grill, covered, 5 minutes on each side or until fish flakes easily when tested with a fork or until desired degree of doneness. Serve immediately. Yield: 4 servings (serving size: 1 cheese-stuffed piece of fish).

Per serving: CALORIES 222; FAT 11.5g (sat 4.5g, mono 4.1g, poly 1.4g); PROTEIN 25.9g; CARB 3.6g; FIBER 0.3g; CHOL 80mg; IRON 0.7mg; SODIUM 379mg; CALC 183mg

Salmon with Balsamic Reduction

prep: 4 minutes • **cook:** 15 minutes   *PointsPlus* value per serving: 8

A few minutes is all it takes to turn tangy balsamic vinegar into a sweet, syrupy glaze for fish, chicken, and even vegetables.

    Cooking spray
  4 (6-ounce) salmon fillets (about 1 inch thick)
1½ teaspoons chopped fresh rosemary
 ½ teaspoon salt
 ¼ teaspoon freshly ground black pepper
  1 tablespoon olive oil
 ¾ cup balsamic vinegar

1. Preheat oven to 450°.
2. Line a baking sheet with foil; coat foil with cooking spray. Place fillets, skin sides down, on foil; sprinkle evenly with rosemary, salt, and pepper. Drizzle fillets with olive oil. Bake at 450° for 15 minutes or until fish flakes easily when tested with a fork or until desired degree of doneness.
3. While salmon cooks, bring vinegar to a boil in a small saucepan over medium-high heat. Cook, uncovered, 15 minutes or until vinegar is reduced to 2 tablespoons. Drizzle balsamic reduction evenly over salmon. **Yield:** 4 servings (serving size: 1 fillet and 1½ teaspoons balsamic reduction).

Per serving: CALORIES 345; FAT 16.4g (sat 3.6g, mono 8.1g, poly 3.5g); PROTEIN 36.4g; CARB 8.3g; FIBER 0.1g; CHOL 87mg; IRON 1mg; SODIUM 386mg; CALC 35mg

Menu
PointsPlus value per serving: 10

Salmon with Balsamic Reduction

Roasted Fennel, Carrots, and Shallots (page 154)
PointsPlus value per serving: 2

Game Plan

1. While oven preheats:
• Prepare Roasted Fennel, Carrots, and Shallots.

2. Fifteen minutes before vegetables are done baking:
• Add fish to oven.

3. While fish and vegetables finish baking:
• Prepare balsamic reduction.

Menu

PointsPlus value
per serving: 9

**Sweet and Smoky
Lemon-Broiled Salmon**

½ cup precooked brown rice
PointsPlus value
per serving: 2

1 cup steamed snow peas
PointsPlus value
per serving: 0

Game Plan

1. While broiler preheats:
  • Prepare spread for fish.

2. While fish broils:
  • Steam snow peas.
  • Heat rice.

Sweet and Smoky Lemon-Broiled Salmon

prep: 7 minutes • **cook:** 8 minutes   *PointsPlus* value per serving: 7

Combine smoked paprika with honey for a smoky flavor and a rich, red-colored glaze.

2 large lemons, divided
1 tablespoon smoked paprika
1 tablespoon honey
¾ teaspoon kosher salt
4 (6-ounce) salmon fillets (about 1 inch thick)

1. Preheat broiler.
2. Grate rind and squeeze juice from 1 lemon to measure 1 tablespoon each. Cut remaining lemon into 4 wedges.
3. Combine lemon rind, lemon juice, paprika, honey, and salt, stirring to form a paste. Spread lemon paste evenly over tops and sides of fillets.
4. Place fillets on a rack in a broiler pan. Broil 4 to 5 minutes on each side or until fish flakes easily when tested with a fork or until desired degree of doneness. Serve with lemon wedges. **Yield:** 4 servings (serving size: 1 fillet and 1 lemon wedge).

Per serving: CALORIES 296; FAT 13.2g (sat 3.1g, mono 5.7g, poly 3.2g); PROTEIN 36.4g; CARB 5.6g; FIBER 0.7g; CHOL 87mg; IRON 0.8mg; SODIUM 442mg; CALC 26mg

Herb-Baked Trout

prep: 8 minutes • **cook:** 13 minutes   *PointsPlus* value per serving: 4

Lemon slices hold up well during cooking, but for a fresh appearance you can replace the cooked slices on top of fish with fresh lemon slices.

¼ cup minced fresh basil
¼ cup fresh lemon juice
2 teaspoons olive oil
4 (6-ounce) rainbow trout fillets
Cooking spray
½ teaspoon freshly ground black pepper
¼ teaspoon salt
1 small lemon, thinly sliced

1. Preheat oven to 350°.
2. Combine first 3 ingredients in a 1-cup glass measure; set aside.
3. Place trout in a 13 x 9–inch baking dish coated with cooking spray. Sprinkle fillets with pepper and salt; top with lemon slices. Pour half of basil mixture over trout. Bake at 350° for 13 to 15 minutes or until fish flakes easily when tested with a fork or until desired degree of doneness. Spoon remaining basil mixture over fish, and serve immediately. **Yield:** 4 servings (serving size: 1 fillet and about 1 tablespoon basil mixture).

Per serving: CALORIES 160; FAT 7.4g (sat 1.7g, mono 3.2g, poly 1.8g); PROTEIN 20.2g; CARB 2.5g; FIBER 0.7g; CHOL 60mg; IRON 0.5mg; SODIUM 197mg; CALC 87mg

Menu
PointsPlus value per serving: 6

Herb-Baked Trout

½ cup angel hair pasta with parsley
PointsPlus value per serving: 2

1 cup mixed cucumbers, cherry tomatoes, and sliced red onions with red wine vinegar
PointsPlus value per serving: 0

Game Plan

1. While oven preheats:
• Season fish.
• Boil water for pasta.

2. While fish cooks:
• Boil pasta.
• Rinse and slice vegetables for salad.

pictured on page 48

Grilled Tilapia Tacos with Ranch Slaw

prep: 4 minutes • **cook:** 6 minutes   *PointsPlus* value per serving: 6

We loved the warm spiciness that chipotle sauce adds to this recipe, but leave it out if you'd like a milder version. If tilapia isn't your favorite catch of the day, then give catfish or grouper a try.

Cooking spray
¼ cup light ranch dressing
¾ teaspoon bottled chipotle sauce (optional)
2 cups packaged coleslaw
1 pound tilapia fillets
¼ teaspoon kosher salt
¼ teaspoon freshly ground black pepper
8 (6-inch) corn tortillas
Lime wedges (optional)

1. Heat a grill pan over medium-high heat for 2 minutes. Coat pan with cooking spray.
2. While pan heats, combine dressing and, if desired, chipotle sauce in a medium bowl, stirring with a whisk. Stir in coleslaw; set aside.
3. Sprinkle fish evenly with salt and pepper. Add to pan. Cook 3 to 4 minutes on each side or until fish flakes easily when tested with a fork or until desired degree of doneness.
4. Wrap tortillas in damp paper towels. Microwave at HIGH 30 seconds or until warm.
5. Flake fish into bite-sized pieces. Spoon fish evenly onto 1 side of each tortilla; top each with ½ cup coleslaw mixture. Fold tortillas over filling. Serve with lime wedges, if desired. **Yield:** 4 servings (serving size: 2 tacos).

Per serving: CALORIES 239; FAT 5g (sat 1g, mono 1.4g, poly 1.8g); PROTEIN 24.9g; CARB 22.5g; FIBER 2g; CHOL 59mg; IRON 0.6mg; SODIUM 418mg; CALC 35mg

Garlic Shrimp with Spinach
and Vermicelli | page 130

113

**Beef Tenderloin with
Horseradish Cream Sauce** | page 136

Ginger Chicken with Couscous | page 143

Pork Medallions with Glazed Onions | page 140

Mexican Casserole | page 135

117

BBQ Chicken Pizza | page 144

Chicken and Dumplings | page 148

**Roasted Broccoli with
Gremolata** | page 154

Grilled Corn, Red Peppers,
and Onions | page 157

Orzo with Basil, Orange, and Pine Nuts | page 158

Ginger-Caramelized Pineapple | page 160

123

Creamy Rosemary
Apples | page 160

**Grilled Rosemary
Flatbreads** | page 168

Parmesan-Prosciutto
Biscotti | page 167

Pecan Pie Squares | page 186

Chocolate-Raspberry-
Coconut Cake | page 179

Linguine with Red Clam Sauce

prep: 4 minutes • **cook:** 18 minutes   *PointsPlus* value per serving: 10

Be sure to purchase canned clams in water for this classic Italian-American recipe.

8   ounces uncooked linguine
Cooking spray
3   garlic cloves, minced
2   (14½-ounce) cans no-salt-added stewed tomatoes
¼   teaspoon crushed red pepper
3   (6½-ounce) cans clams, drained
⅓   cup grated Parmesan or Romano cheese

1. Cook pasta according to package directions, omitting salt and fat.

2. While pasta cooks, coat a large deep skillet with cooking spray, and place over medium heat. Add garlic; cook, stirring constantly, 2 minutes. Add tomatoes and red pepper to skillet. Bring mixture to a boil; reduce heat, and simmer, uncovered, 7 to 8 minutes.

3. Stir in clams; cook 8 minutes or until thoroughly heated.

4. Drain pasta, and arrange on plates. Top evenly with clam sauce, and sprinkle with cheese. **Yield:** 4 servings (serving size: about 1½ cups).

Per serving: CALORIES 382; FAT 4.6g (sat 2.4g, mono 1.1g, poly 0.6g); PROTEIN 26.3g; CARB 60.9g; FIBER 5.1g; CHOL 37mg; IRON 3.9mg; SODIUM 313mg; CALC 200mg

Menu
PointsPlus value
per serving: 10

Linguine with Red Clam Sauce

1 cup mixed baby greens with sliced red onion and 2 tablespoons fat-free balsamic vinegrette
PointsPlus value
per serving: 0

Game Plan

1. While pasta cooks:
   • Prepare clam sauce.
   • Prepare salad.

2. Top pasta with sauce.

pictured on page 113

Garlic Shrimp with Spinach and Vermicelli

prep: 7 minutes • **cook:** 6 minutes   *PointsPlus* value per serving: 9

The heat and moisture from cooked pasta will help wilt the fresh spinach. Be sure to have your spinach ready when the pasta is done boiling.

Menu
PointsPlus value
per serving: 9

**Garlic Shrimp with
Spinach and Vermicelli**

1 orange
PointsPlus value
per serving: 0

Game Plan

1. While pasta boils:
• Cook shrimp.

2. Add pasta and other
ingredients to shrimp
mixture.

3. Peel orange, and serve.

  5   ounces uncooked vermicelli
  1   (6-ounce) package fresh baby spinach
  ⅓   cup julienne-cut sun-dried tomatoes, packed without oil
1½   tablespoons butter, divided
1¼   pounds large shrimp, peeled and deveined
  3   large garlic cloves, minced
  ½   teaspoon kosher salt
  ¼   teaspoon freshly ground black pepper
  ⅓   cup dry white wine
  3   tablespoons fresh lemon juice
  ¼   cup (1 ounce) grated fresh Parmesan cheese

1. Break pasta in half. Cook pasta according to package directions, omitting salt and fat. Place spinach and tomatoes in a colander. Pour pasta and cooking liquid over spinach mixture in colander, turning with tongs until spinach wilts.
2. While pasta cooks, melt 1 tablespoon butter in a large nonstick skillet over medium heat; add shrimp and garlic. Sprinkle shrimp with salt and pepper. Sauté 4 minutes or just until shrimp turn pink. Stir in wine; cook 1 minute. Remove pan from heat.
3. Add pasta mixture, remaining 1½ teaspoons butter, and lemon juice to shrimp mixture; toss well. Sprinkle with Parmesan cheese. **Yield:** 4 servings (serving size: 1 cup).

Per derving: CALORIES 356; FAT 8.1g (sat 4.2g, mono 2g, poly 1g); PROTEIN 32.5g; CARB 36.1g; FIBER 3.8g; CHOL 227mg; IRON 6.3mg; SODIUM 711mg; CALC 197mg

Spaghetti Carbonara

prep: 2 minutes • **cook:** 12 minutes   *PointsPlus* value per serving: 7

Your family won't guess that this creamy dish with rich bacon flavor is light. Be sure to use pasteurized eggs because the eggs aren't fully cooked to make the sauce.

　3　large pasteurized eggs
　¾　cup (3 ounces) finely shredded fresh Parmesan cheese, divided
　¼　teaspoon freshly ground black pepper
　7　ounces uncooked whole-grain spaghetti
　10　center-cut bacon slices, cooked and crumbled
　1½　cups frozen petite green peas, cooked (optional)

1. Combine eggs, ½ cup cheese, and pepper in a large bowl, stirring with a whisk. Cook pasta according to package directions, omitting salt and fat. Drain, reserving 1 cup cooking liquid.
2. Add hot pasta, bacon, and, if desired, peas to egg mixture. Gradually add enough reserved cooking liquid to reach desired consistency, tossing well. Sprinkle with remaining ¼ cup cheese. Serve immediately. **Yield:** 6 servings (serving size: about 1 cup).

Per serving: CALORIES 253; FAT 10.8g (sat 5.5g, mono 3.6g, poly 1g); PROTEIN 17.3g; CARB 25.1g; FIBER 4g; CHOL 133mg; IRON 1.7mg; SODIUM 518mg; CALC 207mg

Menu
PointsPlus value per serving: 9

Spaghetti Carbonara

1 cup wilted spinach with 1 tablespoon toasted pine nuts
PointsPlus value per serving: 2

Game Plan

1. While pasta cooks:
　• Combine eggs, cheese, and pepper.
　• Wilt spinach.
　• Toast pine nuts.

2. Add cooked pasta, bacon, and desired amount of cooking liquid to egg mixture.

Menu

PointsPlus value
per serving: 8

Simple Roast Beef Stroganoff

1 cup steamed green beans
with shallots
PointsPlus value
per serving: 0

Game Plan

1. While pasta cooks:
- Sauté mushrooms.
- Microwave roast.
- Steam green beans and
  shallots.

2. Combine pasta,
mushrooms, roast, and
remaining ingredients.

Simple Roast Beef Stroganoff

prep: 6 minutes • **cook:** 9 minutes   *PointsPlus* value per serving: 8

**This version might be the fastest stroganoff you'll ever whip up.
It's ready in just about the time it takes to cook the noodles.**

3   cups uncooked medium egg noodles
Butter-flavored cooking spray
1   (8-ounce) package presliced mushrooms
1   (17-ounce) package fully-cooked beef pot roast au jus
1   (8-ounce) carton light sour cream
1   (10¾-ounce) can condensed reduced-fat, reduced-sodium cream of
    mushroom soup, undiluted
½   teaspoon freshly ground black pepper
½   cup chopped green onions (optional)
Freshly ground black pepper (optional)

1. Cook pasta according to package directions, omitting salt and fat.
2. While pasta cooks, heat a large nonstick skillet over medium-high heat. Coat
pan with cooking spray. Add mushrooms to pan; sauté 6 minutes or until tender.
3. While mushrooms cook, microwave roast according to package directions.
Strain roast, reserving ⅓ cup jus. Break roast into bite-sized chunks using a fork.
4. Drain pasta, return to pan, and immediately stir in sour cream and soup until
blended. Cook over medium heat 2 minutes or until thoroughly heated. Gently
stir in roast, reserved jus, mushrooms, and ½ teaspoon pepper. Garnish with
green onions and freshly ground black pepper, if desired; serve immediately.
Yield: 6 servings (serving size: about 1 cup).

Per serving: CALORIES 289; FAT 11.4g (sat 4g, mono 4.3g, poly 2.4g); PROTEIN 18.4g; CARB 28.8g; FIBER 2g; CHOL 73mg; IRON 1.5mg; SODIUM 534mg; CALC 84mg

Speedy Shepherd's Pie

prep: 8 minutes • **cook:** 15 minutes • **other:** 5 minutes

PointsPlus value per serving: 7

Using frozen cut russet potatoes in this recipe helps reduce cooking time and makes this simple dish a quick meal on a busy night.

½ (22-ounce) package frozen cut russet potatoes (about 3 cups)
1⅓ cups fat-free milk
1 pound 93% lean ground beef
1 cup fresh or frozen chopped onion
1 cup frozen peas and carrots
½ teaspoon freshly ground black pepper
1 (12-ounce) jar fat-free beef gravy
½ cup (2 ounces) shredded reduced-fat cheddar cheese

1. Preheat broiler.
2. Combine potatoes and milk in a microwave-safe bowl. Microwave at HIGH, uncovered, 8 minutes, stirring once. Mash to desired consistency; set aside.
3. While potatoes cook, cook beef and onion in a 10-inch ovenproof skillet over medium heat until meat is browned, stirring until meat crumbles. Add peas and carrots, pepper, and gravy. Cook over medium heat 3 minutes or until thoroughly heated, stirring often; remove from heat.
4. Spoon potatoes evenly over meat mixture, leaving a 1-inch border around edge of skillet. Broil 3 minutes or until bubbly. Sprinkle with cheese; let stand 5 minutes.
Yield: 6 servings (serving size: ⅙ of casserole).

Per serving: CALORIES 269; FAT 9.7g (sat 4.3g, mono 3.8g, poly 0.4g); PROTEIN 23.7g; CARB 21g; FIBER 2g; CHOL 56.5mg; IRON 2mg; SODIUM 687mg; CALC 211mg

Menu
PointsPlus value
per serving: 7

Speedy Shepherd's Pie

1 cup mixed greens with cherry tomatoes and 2 tablespoons fat-free vinaigrette
PointsPlus value
per serving: 0

Game Plan

1. While potatoes cook:
• Cook beef, onion, peas, carrots, pepper, and gravy.

2. While casserole broils:
• Mix salad, and serve in a side bowl.

Menu
PointsPlus value
per serving: 10

Beef Tostadas

1 cup shredded lettuce with
2 tablespoons pico de gallo
and 2 tablespoons fat-free
sour cream
PointsPlus value
per serving: 1

Game Plan

1. While oven preheats:
   • Coat tortillas with
   cooking spray.

2. While tortillas heat:
   • Microwave beef.

3. Assemble tacos and bake.

4. Serve with lettuce, pico
   de gallo, and sour cream
   toppings.

Beef Tostadas

prep: 6 minutes • **cook:** 13 minutes   *PointsPlus* value per serving: 9

Serve these tostadas with typical taco condiments, such as pico de gallo, light sour cream, and shredded lettuce.

    4 (6-inch) flour tortillas
    Cooking spray
    1 (17-ounce) package fully-cooked beef pot roast au jus
    1 (7-ounce) package refrigerated guacamole
    ¾ cup (3 ounces) preshredded reduced-fat 4-cheese Mexican blend cheese

1. Preheat oven to 400°.
2. Coat tortillas on both sides with cooking spray; place on a large baking sheet. Bake at 400° for 8 minutes or until crisp.
3. While tortillas cook, microwave roast according to package directions. Shred beef with 2 forks, discarding juices. Cover beef, and keep warm.
4. Spread tortillas evenly with guacamole; top evenly with beef and cheese.
5. Bake at 400° for 5 minutes or until cheese melts. Serve immediately.
Yield: 4 servings (serving size: 1 tostada).

Per serving: CALORIES 349; FAT 18.9g (sat 6.9g, mono 9.7g, poly 1.9g); PROTEIN 22.1g; CARB 22.5g; FIBER 4g; CHOL 50mg; IRON 1mg; SODIUM 747mg; CALC 339mg

pictured on page 117

Mexican Casserole

prep: 15 minutes • **cook:** 35 minutes • **other:** 8 hours

PointsPlus value per serving: 8

This cheesy casserole is one of our favorites. It can be prepared up to a day in advance so keep this recipe on hand if you have a busy week planned.

- 1 pound ground round
- ½ cup chopped onion (about ½ medium onion)
- 2 garlic cloves, minced
- 3 cups cooked rice (cooked without salt or fat)
- ¼ cup sliced ripe olives
- 2 tablespoons chopped fresh cilantro
- 1 (28-ounce) can whole tomatoes, undrained and chopped
- 1 (4.5-ounce) can chopped green chiles, undrained
- 1 (1.25-ounce) package 40%-less-sodium taco seasoning mix
- Cooking spray
- ¾ cup (3 ounces) reduced-fat Monterey Jack cheese
- Chopped fresh cilantro (optional)

1. Cook first 3 ingredients in a large skillet over medium-high heat until beef is browned, stirring until it crumbles; drain and return to skillet.

2. Stir in rice and next 5 ingredients. Bring to a boil; reduce heat, and simmer, uncovered, 10 minutes. Spoon mixture into a 2-quart baking dish coated with cooking spray. Cool completely; cover and chill 8 hours or overnight.

3. Preheat oven to 350°.

4. Bake casserole, uncovered, at 350° for 30 minutes or until thoroughly heated. Sprinkle with cheese, and bake an additional 5 minutes or until cheese melts. Garnish with cilantro, if desired. **Yield:** 6 servings (serving size: ⅙ of casserole).

Per serving: CALORIES 314; FAT 9.2g (sat 3.9g, mono 3.3g, poly 0.5g); PROTEIN 20.4g; CARB 33.7g; FIBER 2.2g; CHOL 47mg; IRON 4.1mg; SODIUM 779mg; CALC 155mg

---

Menu
PointsPlus value per serving: 8

Mexican Casserole

1 cup wilted greens with chopped green onions
PointsPlus value per serving: 0

Game Plan

1. Brown beef, onion, and garlic.

2. Prepare rice mixture, and let chill.

3. While casserole bakes:
 • Prepare greens.

---

pictured on page 114

Beef Tenderloin with Horseradish Cream Sauce

prep: 7 minutes • **cook:** 6 minutes • **other:** 8 hours

PointsPlus value per serving: 6

½ cup fat-free sour cream
2 tablespoons prepared horseradish
¾ teaspoon white wine Worcestershire sauce
⅛ teaspoon salt
⅛ teaspoon freshly ground black pepper
¼ cup red wine vinegar
1 teaspoon chopped fresh thyme (or ½ teaspoon dried thyme)
¼ teaspoon freshly ground black pepper
4 (4-ounce) beef tenderloin steaks, trimmed (about 1 inch thick)
Cooking spray
Thyme sprigs (optional)

1. Combine first 5 ingredients. Cover horseradish sauce, and chill 8 hours or overnight.

2. Combine vinegar, chopped thyme, and ¼ teaspoon pepper in a large heavy-duty zip-top plastic bag. Add steaks; seal bag, and shake until meat is well coated. Marinate steaks in refrigerator 8 hours or overnight, turning bag occasionally.

3. Preheat broiler.

4. Remove steaks from marinade, discarding marinade. Place steaks on rack of a broiler pan coated with cooking spray. Broil 3 to 4 minutes on each side or until desired degree of doneness.

5. Place steaks on plates; serve with horseradish sauce. Garnish with thyme sprigs, if desired. **Yield:** 4 servings (serving size: 1 steak and 2½ tablespoons sauce).

Per serving: CALORIES 238; FAT 7.5g (sat 2.8g, mono 3g, poly 0.3g); PROTEIN 34g; CARB 6.1g; FIBER 0.3g; CHOL 92mg; IRON 2mg; SODIUM 207mg; CALC 88mg

Menu

PointsPlus value per serving: 9

Beef Tenderloin with Horseradish Cream Sauce

1 cup mixed greens with cherry tomatoes and 2 tablespoons fat-free balsamic vinaigrette
PointsPlus value per serving: 0

½ cup microwavable prepared mashed potatoes
PointsPlus value per serving: 3

Game Plan

1. Prepare and chill horseradish sauce.

2. Prepare marinade, and chill steaks.

3. While broiler preheats:
• Prepare salad.

4. Broil steaks, and top steaks with sauce.

Pan-Seared Steaks with Balsamic–Pepper Jelly Sauce

prep: 2 minutes • **cook:** 8 minutes   *PointsPlus* value per serving: 4

Although this recipe uses only a handful of ingredients and takes just 10 minutes to make, it delivers steak-house flavor fine enough for guests.

- ½ teaspoon garlic powder
- ½ teaspoon freshly ground black pepper
- ¼ teaspoon salt
- 4 (4-ounce) beef tenderloin steaks, trimmed (1 inch thick)
- Cooking spray
- ¼ cup red pepper jelly
- 2 tablespoons water
- 2 tablespoons balsamic vinegar

1. Heat a large cast-iron or nonstick skillet over medium-high heat 1 minute or until very hot.

2. While skillet heats, rub garlic powder, black pepper, and salt evenly over both sides of steaks. Coat steaks with cooking spray; add to pan. Cook 3 minutes on each side or until desired degree of doneness.

3. Remove steaks from pan; keep warm. Combine jelly, 2 tablespoons water, and vinegar; add to pan. Cook, stirring frequently, 1 minute or until jelly melts and sauce is slightly thick. Spoon sauce over steaks. **Yield:** 4 servings (serving size: 1 steak and 1 tablespoon sauce).

Per serving: CALORIES 169; FAT 4g (sat 1.5g, mono 1.5g, poly 0g); PROTEIN 22.1g; CARB 11.8g; FIBER 0.1g; CHOL 60mg; IRON 2.8mg; SODIUM 250mg; CALC 4mg

Menu
PointsPlus value per serving: 9

Pan-Seared Steaks with Balsamic–Pepper Jelly Sauce

1 (6-ounce) baked sweet potato with 1 teaspoon light stick butter
PointsPlus value per serving: 5

1 cup steamed green beans
PointsPlus value per serving: 0

Game Plan

1. While sweet potato bakes:
- Steam green beans.
- Heat skillet.
- Season steaks.

2. Cook steaks, keeping warm once removed from heat.

3. Prepare balsamic–pepper jelly sauce, and serve over steaks.

Menu

PointsPlus value
per serving: 9

Herbed Lamb Chops

**1 (6-ounce) package
precooked mashed potatoes
with 1 tablespoon light
stick butter**
PointsPlus value
per serving: 5

**1 cup arugula with
2 tablespoons fat-free
balsamic vinaigrette**
PointsPlus value
per serving: 0

Game Plan

1. Marinate lamb chops.

2. While broiler preheats:
  • Prepare vinegar mixture.

3. While lamb broils:
  • Heat mashed potatoes
  according to directions.
  • Prepare arugula salad.

4. Spoon vinegar mixture
over chops to serve.

Herbed Lamb Chops

prep: 10 minutes • **cook:** 17 minutes • **other:** 1 hour

PointsPlus value per serving: 4

½   teaspoon dried rosemary, crushed
½   teaspoon freshly ground black pepper
¼   teaspoon salt
¼   teaspoon dried oregano
¼   teaspoon dried rubbed sage
1   garlic clove, minced
4   (5-ounce) lean lamb loin chops, trimmed (1 inch thick)
¼   cup balsamic vinegar
¼   cup lower-sodium beef broth
1   tablespoon sugar
1   teaspoon dried rosemary, crushed
Cooking spray

1. Combine first 6 ingredients in a small bowl; stir well. Press mixture evenly onto all sides of lamb chops; place chops on a plate. Cover and marinate in refrigerator 1 to 2 hours.

2. Preheat broiler.

3. Combine vinegar and next 3 ingredients in a small saucepan; bring to a boil over low heat. Cook 1 minute; remove from heat, and cool. Strain through a sieve, reserving liquid.

4. Arrange chops on the rack of a broiler pan coated with cooking spray. Broil 7 to 8 minutes on each side or until desired degree of doneness. Spoon vinegar mixture over lamb chops. **Yield:** 4 servings (serving size: 1 lamb chop).

Per serving: CALORIES 160; FAT 5.9g (sat 2.1g, mono 2.6g, poly 0.4g); PROTEIN 18.2g; CARB 6.7g; FIBER 0.3g; CHOL 57mg; IRON 1.5mg; SODIUM 237mg; CALC 26mg

Grilled Pork Teriyaki

prep: 5 minutes • **cook:** 25 minutes • **other:** 8 hours

PointsPlus value per serving: 4

For an Asian-inspired meal, try our Chunky Asian Slaw as a side dish.

  2 (¾-pound) pork tenderloins, trimmed
  ½ cup lower-sodium soy sauce
  ¼ cup unsweetened orange juice
  ¼ cup unsweetened pineapple juice
  2 tablespoons brown sugar
  1 tablespoon grated peeled fresh ginger
  2 garlic cloves, minced
     Cooking spray

1. Place tenderloins in a large heavy-duty zip-top plastic bag. Combine soy sauce and next 5 ingredients; pour over tenderloins. Seal bag; marinate in refrigerator 8 hours or overnight, turning bag occasionally.

2. Preheat grill to medium-high heat.

3. Remove tenderloins from marinade, discarding marinade. Place tenderloins on grill rack coated with cooking spray; grill, covered, 25 to 30 minutes or until a thermometer registers 160°, turning occasionally. **Yield:** 6 servings (about 4 ounces pork).

Per serving: CALORIES 158; FAT 4g (sat 1.3g, mono 1.5g, poly 0.6g); PROTEIN 24.2g; CARB 4.4g; FIBER 0g; CHOL 74mg; IRON 1.1mg; SODIUM 463mg; CALC 11mg

Menu

PointsPlus value
per serving: 7

Grilled Pork Teriyaki

Chunky Asian Slaw
(page 99)
PointsPlus value
per serving: 1

⅓ cup precooked brown rice
PointsPlus value
per serving: 2

Game Plan

1. Prepare and marinate pork.

2. While grill preheats:
  • Prepare slaw.
  • Warm rice.

3. Grill pork, being sure to check temperature.

pictured on page 116

Pork Medallions with Glazed Onions

Menu

PointsPlus value per serving: 4

Pork Medallions with Glazed Onions

1 cup steamed green beans
PointsPlus value per serving: 0

Game Plan

1. Trim and season pork.

2. While skillet heats:
• Cut onion.

3. While pork cooks:
• Lightly steam green beans.

4. Serve pork with glazed onions.

prep: 14 minutes • **cook:** 16 minutes   *PointsPlus* value per serving: 4

The easy, sophisticated balsamic and honey glaze in this recipe can be used to top a variety of other dishes.

1 (1-pound) pork tenderloin
½ teaspoon dried thyme
¼ teaspoon salt
¼ teaspoon freshly ground black pepper
Cooking spray
1 teaspoon olive oil
1 small red onion, thinly sliced and separated into rings
3 tablespoons balsamic vinegar
2 teaspoons honey
Thyme sprigs (optional)

1. Trim fat from pork. Cut pork into 1-inch-thick slices. Place slices between two sheets of heavy-duty plastic wrap, and flatten to ½-inch thickness using a meat mallet or small heavy skillet. Sprinkle with dried thyme, salt, and pepper.
2. Place a large nonstick skillet coated with cooking spray over medium heat until hot. Add pork; cook 3 minutes on each side or until browned. Remove from pan, and keep warm. Heat oil in pan over medium heat; add onion. Cook 8 to 10 minutes or until onion is tender, stirring often. Add vinegar and honey; cook, stirring constantly, 1 minute or until onion is glazed. Spoon glazed onion over pork. Garnish with thyme sprigs, if desired. **Yield:** 4 servings (serving size: about 4 ounces pork and 1 tablespoon onions).

Per serving: CALORIES 176; FAT 5.2g (sat 1.5g, mono 2.4g, poly 0.8g); PROTEIN 23.7g; CARB 6.7g; FIBER 0.4g; CHOL 74mg; IRON 1.4mg; SODIUM 210mg; CALC 17mg

Pork and Vegetables in Dijon Sauce

prep: 6 minutes • **cook:** 24 minutes   *PointsPlus* value per serving: 6

    2   (¾-pound) pork tenderloins
    Olive oil–flavored cooking spray
    1   teaspoon olive oil
    2   cups sliced carrot (about 8 medium)
    2   cups broccoli florets
    1   cup small green beans, trimmed
    1   (8-ounce) package presliced mushrooms
    2   cups fat-free milk
    3   tablespoons all-purpose flour
 1½   tablespoons Dijon mustard
    ½   teaspoon salt
    ¼   teaspoon freshly ground black pepper
    ¼   cup (1 ounce) grated Asiago or Parmesan cheese

1. Trim fat from tenderloins. Cut pork into ½-inch-thick slices. Coat a large non-stick skillet with cooking spray; place over medium-high heat until hot. Add pork slices; cook 2 minutes on each side or until browned; drain and set aside. Wipe drippings from pan with a paper towel.

2. Recoat pan with cooking spray, and add oil; place over medium-high heat until hot. Add carrot, broccoli, and green beans; cook 4 minutes, stirring often. Add mushrooms; cook 2 minutes or until tender, stirring often.

3. Combine milk and next 4 ingredients, stirring until smooth. Add to vegetables in pan. Add pork slices, and bring to a boil; reduce heat, and simmer, uncovered, 10 minutes. Add cheese, stirring until smooth. **Yield:** 6 servings (serving size: about 4 ounces pork and about 1 cup vegetable sauce).

Per serving: CALORIES 246; FAT 6.6g (sat 2.5g, mono 2.5g, poly 0.9g); PROTEIN 30.6g; CARB 15.6g; FIBER 2.5g; CHOL 80mg; IRON 1.9mg; SODIUM 504mg; CALC 201mg

Menu
PointsPlus value per serving: 10

Pork and Vegetables in Dijon Sauce

1 (6-ounce) baked potato with 1 tablespoon light stick butter
PointsPlus value per serving: 4

Game Plan

1. While skillet heats:
  • Trim pork.

2. While pork cooks:
  • Rinse and trim vegetables.

3. While pork, vegetables, and sauce simmer:
  • Cook potato in microwave.

Menu

PointsPlus value
per serving: 6

Hot Peppered Pork

½ cup couscous
PointsPlus value
per serving: 2

1 cup grilled zucchini
PointsPlus value
per serving: 0

Game Plan

1. Freeze and trim pork.

2. While skillet heats:
• Rinse and cut vegetables.
• Prepare couscous
according to directions.

3. While pork cooks:
• Preheat grill pan, and
cook zucchini.

Hot Peppered Pork

prep: 15 minutes • **cook:** 14 minutes • **other:** 5 minutes

PointsPlus value per serving: 4

**This dish isn't too spicy, but if you don't handle heat well, try
reducing the crushed red pepper to ¼ teaspoon.**

1 pound boneless pork loin
1 tablespoon lower-sodium soy sauce
Cooking spray
1 medium red bell pepper, thinly sliced
1 teaspoon canola oil
2 teaspoons grated peeled fresh ginger
½ teaspoon crushed red pepper
2 garlic cloves, minced
¼ cup canned beef broth
4 cups shredded napa (Chinese) cabbage

1. Partially freeze pork; trim fat. Slice pork into ¼-inch-thick strips; cut strips into
2-inch pieces. Combine pork and soy sauce in a large heavy-duty zip-top plastic
bag; seal bag, and turn to coat pork. Let stand 5 minutes.
2. Coat a large nonstick skillet with cooking spray, and place over medium-high
heat until hot. Add bell pepper; cook 3 minutes or until crisp-tender, stirring often.
Remove from pan, and set aside.
3. Add oil to pan; place over medium-high heat until hot. Add ginger, crushed red
pepper, and garlic; cook, stirring constantly, 30 seconds. Add pork to pan; cook
5 minutes or until pork is done, stirring often. Add bell pepper and broth to pan;
bring to a boil. Reduce heat, and simmer 2 to 3 minutes or until most of liquid is
evaporated.
4. Place cabbage on plates. Spoon pork mixture evenly over cabbage. Serve immediately. **Yield:** 4 servings (serving size: 1 cup pork mixture and 1 cup cabbage).

Per serving: CALORIES 167; FAT 4g (sat 1g, mono 1.2g, poly 1.2g); PROTEIN 25.6g; CARB 5.8g; FIBER 1.7g; CHOL 73.7mg; IRON 1.3mg; SODIUM 225mg; CALC 72mg

pictured on page 115

Ginger Chicken with Couscous

prep: 16 minutes • **cook:** 28 minutes   *PointsPlus* value per serving: 8

Cooking spray
2 teaspoons light stick butter
1 cup sliced green onions
1 cup sliced green and red bell pepper
8 (6-ounce) skinless, boneless chicken breast halves
½ cup fat-free, lower-sodium chicken broth
⅓ cup lower-sodium soy sauce
2 tablespoons chopped peeled fresh ginger
1 (9-ounce) jar mango chutney
4 cups cooked couscous (cooked without salt or fat)

1. Coat a large nonstick skillet with cooking spray; add butter. Place over medium-high heat until butter melts. Add green onions and bell pepper; cook 5 minutes or until tender, stirring often. Transfer bell pepper mixture to a small bowl; set aside.
2. Recoat pan with cooking spray; place over medium heat until hot. Add chicken, and cook 4 minutes on each side or until browned. Combine broth and next 3 ingredients; pour over chicken in skillet. Bring to a boil; cover, reduce heat, and simmer 10 minutes or until chicken is done, turning occasionally. Remove chicken from pan with a slotted spoon; set aside, and keep warm.
3. Add bell pepper mixture to pan; bring to a boil. Reduce heat, and simmer, uncovered, 5 minutes.
4. Place couscous on plates, and top with chicken. Spoon bell pepper mixture evenly over chicken. **Yield:** 8 servings (serving size: 1 chicken breast half, ½ cup couscous, and ¼ cup bell pepper mixture).

Per serving: CALORIES 339; FAT 2.3g (sat 1g, mono 0.6g, poly 0.4g); PROTEIN 30.1g; CARB 44.5g; FIBER 2g; CHOL 68mg; IRON 1.5mg; SODIUM 657mg; CALC 33mg

Menu
PointsPlus value per serving: 9

Ginger Chicken with Couscous

1 cup steamed broccoli with 1 tablespoon light stick butter
PointsPlus value per serving: 1

Game Plan
1. While skillet heats:
• Rinse and chop vegetables.
2. While chicken mixture cooks:
• Steam broccoli.

pictured on page 118

BBQ Chicken Pizza

prep: 5 minutes • **cook:** 20 minutes   *PointsPlus* value per serving: 9

Menu
PointsPlus value
per serving: 9

BBQ Chicken Pizza

**1 cup mixed cucumbers,
cherry tomatoes,
and sliced red onions
with red wine vinegar**
PointsPlus value
per serving: 0

Game Plan

1. While crust bakes:
• Prepare toppings.

2. While pizza bakes:
• Prepare salad.

  1 (16-ounce) refrigerated fresh pizza crust dough
  ½ cup barbecue sauce, divided
  ¾ cup shredded cooked chicken
  1¼ cups (5 ounces) shredded reduced-fat jalapeño cheddar cheese
     Fresh cilantro leaves (optional)

1. Preheat oven to 450°.
2. Roll dough into a 12-inch circle on a lightly floured surface. Place dough on a 12-inch pizza pan or a large baking sheet. Pierce dough with a fork in several places. Bake at 450° for 10 minutes.
3. Remove crust from oven. Spread ¼ cup barbecue sauce over crust. Combine remaining ¼ cup barbecue sauce and chicken in a bowl, stirring well. Spoon chicken mixture over crust; top evenly with cheese. Bake at 450° for 10 minutes or until cheese melts. Garnish with cilantro, if desired. Cut into 6 wedges. **Yield:** 6 servings (serving size: 1 wedge).

Per serving: CALORIES 321; FAT 6.1g (sat 2.6g, mono 0.1g, poly 1.4g); PROTEIN 18.3g; CARB 50.6g; FIBER 1.3g; CHOL 25mg; IRON 2.5mg; SODIUM 782mg; CALC 205mg

Apricot-Glazed Chicken

prep: 3 minutes • **cook:** 13 minutes   *PointsPlus* value per serving: 6

Menu
PointsPlus value
per serving: 8

Apricot-Glazed Chicken

1 cup grilled zucchini
PointsPlus value
per serving: 0

½ cup cooked couscous
PointsPlus value
per serving: 2

Game Plan

1. While grill preheats:
• Prepare couscous
according to directions.
• Microwave glaze.

2. While chicken cooks:
• Grill zucchini.

  ½ cup low-sugar apricot preserves
  1 tablespoon lower-sodium soy sauce
  ½ teaspoon minced garlic
  4 (6-ounce) skinless, boneless chicken breast halves
  ¼ teaspoon salt
  ¼ teaspoon freshly ground black pepper
     Cooking spray

1. Preheat grill to high heat.
2. Combine first 3 ingredients in a small microwave-safe bowl. Microwave at HIGH 30 seconds or until preserves melt; whisk until smooth.
3. Sprinkle chicken evenly with salt and pepper. Place chicken on grill rack coated with cooking spray; grill 6 minutes. Turn chicken over; brush generously with apricot glaze. Grill an additional 6 minutes or until chicken is done. **Yield:** 4 servings (serving size: 1 chicken breast half).

Per serving: CALORIES 237; FAT 4.5g (sat 1g, mono 1.3g, poly 0.7g); PROTEIN 36.3g; CARB 9.8g; FIBER 0g; CHOL 109mg; IRON 0.6mg; SODIUM 463mg; CALC 9mg

Southwestern Fried Rice with Chicken

prep: 1 minute • **cook:** 5 minutes   *PointsPlus* value per serving: 7

Precooked rice gets put to ideal use in this easy stir-fried entrée. Add the rice straight from the package to a sizzling skillet.

    Cooking spray
  2 large garlic cloves, minced
1½ cups pulled cooked skinless, boneless chicken breast
  ½ teaspoon salt-free Southwest chipotle seasoning
  2 (8.5-ounce) packages Spanish-style precooked whole-grain rice medley
  ¼ cup water
  ¼ cup chopped fresh cilantro (optional)

1. Heat a large nonstick skillet over medium-high heat. Coat pan with cooking spray. Add garlic; sauté 30 seconds. Stir in chicken and seasoning. Sauté 1 minute. Add rice and ¼ cup water; cook, stirring constantly, 2 minutes or until thoroughly heated. Garnish with cilantro, if desired. **Yield:** 4 servings (serving size: 1 cup).

Per serving: CALORIES 273; FAT 4.4g (sat 0.5g, mono 2.3g, poly 1.5g); PROTEIN 22.2g; CARB 35.6g; FIBER 4.2g; CHOL 45mg; IRON 1.8mg; SODIUM 625mg; CALC 44mg

---

Menu
PointsPlus value
per serving: 7

**Southwestern Fried Rice
with Chicken**

**1 cup steamed
sugarsnap peas**
PointsPlus value
per serving: 0

Game Plan

1. While skillet heats:
- Mince garlic.
- Chop cilantro.

2. While chicken and rice cook:
- Steam peas.

Menu
PointsPlus value
per serving: 8

Chicken Breasts
with Fig-Mustard Glaze

1 cup sliced strawberries
with lemon juice and
2 tablespoons fat-free
whipped topping
PointsPlus value
per serving: 0

Game Plan

1. While skillet heats:
• Season chicken.

2. While chicken cooks:
• Microwave rice according
to directions.
• Rinse and slice
strawberries, and drizzle
with lemon juice.

3. Arrange chicken over rice,
and serve strawberries
in bowls topped with
whipped cream.

Chicken Breasts with Fig-Mustard Glaze

prep: 7 minutes • **cook:** 12 minutes   *PointsPlus* value per serving: 8

Frozen brown rice with broccoli and carrots makes this dish a complete meal. Try a light fruit dessert with fat-free whipped topping as an after-dinner treat.

Cooking spray
4 (6-ounce) skinless, boneless chicken breast halves
¼ teaspoon salt
¼ teaspoon freshly ground black pepper
½ cup fig preserves
2 tablespoons water
2 tablespoons stone-ground mustard
1 (10-ounce) package frozen brown and wild rice
with broccoli and carrots
Rosemary sprigs (optional)

1. Heat a large nonstick skillet over medium-high heat. Coat pan with cooking spray. Sprinkle chicken with salt and pepper; coat with cooking spray. Add chicken to pan; cook 4 minutes. Turn chicken over, and cook 3 minutes or until browned.
2. Combine fig preserves, 2 tablespoons water, and mustard; spoon over chicken in pan. Cover, reduce heat, and simmer 5 minutes or until chicken is done.
3. While chicken cooks, microwave rice according to package directions.
4. Cut each chicken breast into 5 slightly diagonal slices. Spoon rice evenly onto plates. Arrange chicken over rice, and spoon fig-mustard sauce over chicken. Garnish with rosemary sprigs, if desired. **Yield:** 4 servings (serving size: 1 chicken breast half, about ½ cup rice, and about 2 tablespoons sauce).

Per serving: CALORIES 346; FAT 2.8g (sat 0.6g, mono 0.9g, poly 0.7g); PROTEIN 41.1g; CARB 35.7g; FIBER 1.4g; CHOL 99mg; IRON 1.5mg; SODIUM 364mg; CALC 28mg

Chutney Chicken Curry

prep: 4 minutes • **cook:** 22 minutes   *PointsPlus* value per serving: 11

2 teaspoons light stick butter
1 cup chopped onion
2 teaspoons curry powder
1 (14½-ounce) can crushed tomatoes, undrained
⅓ cup mango chutney
3 tablespoons white wine vinegar
2 tablespoons honey
¾ pound skinless, boneless chicken breast halves, cut into 1-inch pieces
3 cups hot cooked rice (cooked without salt or fat)

1. Add butter to a large skillet; place skillet over medium-high heat until butter melts. Add onion, and cook 3 minutes or until tender, stirring often. Stir in curry powder; cook, stirring constantly, 1 minute.

2. Stir in tomatoes and next 3 ingredients; bring to a boil. Reduce heat, and simmer 5 minutes.

3. Stir in chicken. Bring to a boil; reduce heat, and simmer 8 to 10 minutes or until chicken is done. Serve over rice. **Yield:** 4 servings (serving size: about 1 cup chicken mixture and ¾ cup rice).

Per serving: CALORIES 421; FAT 4.6g (sat 1.8g, mono 1.3g, poly 0.5g); PROTEIN 23.5g; CARB 68.8g; FIBER 3.2g; CHOL 60mg; IRON 3.3mg; SODIUM 490mg; CALC 64mg

Menu
PointsPlus value per serving: 11

Chutney Chicken Curry

1 cup wilted spinach
PointsPlus value per serving: 0

Game Plan

1. Cook rice.

2. While skillet heats:
• Chop onion.
• Cut chicken.

3. While chicken cooks:
• Cook spinach.

Hoisin–Five Spice Chicken Thighs

prep: 2 minutes • **cook:** 15 minutes   *PointsPlus* value per serving: 7

1 tablespoon dark sesame oil
1½ pounds skinless, boneless chicken thighs (about 8 thighs)
⅓ cup hoisin sauce
½ teaspoon five-spice powder

1. Heat oil in a large nonstick skillet over medium-high heat. Add chicken; cook 6 minutes on each side or until browned.

2. Combine hoisin sauce and five-spice powder, and add to chicken in pan. Cook 2 minutes or until chicken reaches desired degree of doneness, stirring to coat. **Yield:** 4 servings (serving size: about 2 thighs).

Per serving: CALORIES 280; FAT 10.8g (sat 2.3g, mono 3.6g, poly 3.4g); PROTEIN 34.1g; CARB 9.6g; FIBER 0.6g; CHOL 142mg; IRON 2.2mg; SODIUM 487mg; CALC 27mg

Menu
PointsPlus value per serving: 10

Hoisin–Five Spice Chicken Thighs

1 cup mixed baby greens with 2 tablepoons fat-free sesame dressing
PointsPlus value per serving: 3

Game Plan

1. While skillet heats:
• Prepare salad.

2. While chicken browns:
• Prepare sauce.

pictured on page 119

Chicken and Dumplings

prep: 6 minutes • **cook:** 27 minutes   *PointsPlus* value per serving: 8

Celery, onion, and carrots are a classic combination of flavors. Simmering these vegetables in broth infuses these flavors through the entire dish.

Menu
PointsPlus value
per serving: 9

Chicken and Dumplings

1 cup mixed baby greens
with 2 tablespoons fat-free
honey Dijon dressing
PointsPlus value
per serving: 1

Game Plan

1. While vegetables simmer:
• Prepare baking mix.

2. Boil dumplings.

3. While dish simmers:
• Prepare salad.

4   (14¼-ounce) cans no-salt-added chicken broth
1   cup chopped celery (about 3 stalks)
1   cup chopped onion (about 1 medium)
1   cup chopped carrot (about 2 medium)
¼   teaspoon salt
¼   to ½ teaspoon freshly ground black pepper
2   cups low-fat baking mix
1   teaspoon dried parsley
¾   cup fat-free milk
3   cups chopped cooked chicken breast

1. Combine first 6 ingredients in a Dutch oven; bring to a boil. Cover, reduce heat to medium, and cook 5 minutes.
2. While vegetables simmer, combine baking mix and parsley. Add milk, stirring with a fork just until dry ingredients are moistened.
3. Return broth mixture to a boil. Drop dough by teaspoonfuls into boiling broth; reduce heat to medium. Cover and cook 10 minutes, stirring once.
4. Add chicken to broth mixture, stirring gently. Cook, uncovered, 5 minutes. Yield: 6 servings (serving size: about 2 cups).

Per serving: CALORIES 329; FAT 6.8g (sat 1.3g, mono 3.2g, poly 1.4g); PROTEIN 32g; CARB 33.9g; FIBER 2.3g; CHOL 88mg; IRON 2.4mg; SODIUM 773mg; CALC 271mg

Turkey Picadillo

prep: 6 minutes • **cook:** 23 minutes

PointsPlus value per serving: 8

2¾ cups water
1¼ cups uncooked long-grain rice
Cooking spray
1 pound ground turkey
1 cup chopped onion (about 1 medium)
1 cup chopped peeled cooking apple (about 1 medium)
¼ cup raisins
2 tablespoons sliced pimiento-stuffed olives
1 tablespoon canned diced jalapeño pepper
½ teaspoon salt
¼ teaspoon freshly ground black pepper
¼ teaspoon ground cinnamon
⅛ teaspoon ground cloves
1 (14.5-ounce) can no-salt-added diced tomatoes, undrained
1 (8-ounce) can tomato sauce

1. Bring 2¾ cups water to a boil in a medium saucepan over high heat. Add rice; stir well. Cover, reduce heat, and simmer 20 minutes or until liquid is absorbed and rice is tender.

2. While rice cooks, coat a large nonstick skillet with cooking spray; place pan over medium heat until hot. Add turkey and onion; cook, stirring constantly, until turkey is browned and onion is tender.

3. Add apple and next 9 ingredients to pan; cover and cook 15 minutes, stirring occasionally.

4. Place rice on plates, and top evenly with turkey mixture. **Yield:** 6 servings (serving size: ⅔ cup rice and about 1 cup turkey mixture).

Per serving: CALORIES 331; FAT 5.6g (sat 1.4g, mono 2g, poly 1.8g); PROTEIN 19.6g; CARB 49.6g; FIBER 2.5g; CHOL 43mg; IRON 3.5mg; SODIUM 549mg; CALC 35mg

---

Menu
PointsPlus value
per serving: 11

Turkey Picadillo

½ cup vanilla sorbet
PointsPlus value
per serving: 3

Game Plan

1. While water comes to a boil:
  • Rinse and prepare vegetables.

2. While rice cooks:
  • Cook turkey, onion, and additional ingredients.

3. Serve turkey mixture over rice.

4. Scoop sorbet into serving bowls.

Menu
PointsPlus value
per serving: 9

Turkey-Spaghetti Casserole

**1 cup mixed greens with
cherry tomatoes and
2 tablespoons fat-free
balsamic vinaigrette**
PointsPlus value
per serving: 0

**1 (1-ounce) slice toasted
whole-wheat bread**
PointsPlus value
per serving: 1

Game Plan

1. While pasta cooks:
 • Sauté vegetables.

2. Assemble casserole, and
chill.

3. Preheat oven.

4. While casserole cooks:
 • Prepare salad.
 • Toast bread.

Turkey-Spaghetti Casserole

prep: 20 minutes • **cook:** 35 minutes • **other:** 8 hours

PointsPlus value per serving: 8

    8   ounces uncooked spaghetti
Cooking spray
 ¾ cup chopped onion (about 1 small)
 ¾ cup chopped green bell pepper (about 1 small)
 ¾ cup fat-free milk
 ½ teaspoon freshly ground black pepper
 ¼ teaspoon salt
 1   (10¾-ounce) can condensed reduced-fat, reduced-sodium cream of chicken
     soup, undiluted
 2   cups chopped cooked turkey breast
 1   (4½-ounce) jar sliced mushrooms, drained
 1   (4-ounce) jar diced pimiento, drained
 1   cup (4 ounces) reduced-fat shredded sharp cheddar cheese

1. Cook spaghetti according to package directions, omitting salt and fat. Drain.
2. While spaghetti cooks, coat a Dutch oven with cooking spray; place over
medium heat until hot. Add onion and bell pepper; sauté 5 minutes or until tender.
3. Combine onion mixture, milk, and next 3 ingredients, stirring well. Combine
pasta, turkey, mushrooms, and pimiento; toss gently. Pour soup mixture over pasta
mixture; toss until pasta is well coated.
4. Spoon mixture into an 11 x 7–inch baking dish coated with cooking spray. Cover
and chill 8 hours or overnight.
5. Preheat oven to 375°.
6. Bake, uncovered, at 375° for 30 minutes. Sprinkle with cheese; bake, uncovered,
5 additional minutes or until cheese melts. **Yield:** 6 servings (serving size: ⅙ of
casserole).

Per serving: CALORIES 302; FAT 5.7g (sat 2.9g, mono 0.3g, poly 0.3g); PROTEIN 24g; CARB 39.5g; FIBER 2.7g; CHOL 49mg; IRON 2.4mg; SODIUM 548mg; CALC 334mg

Side Dishes

PointsPlus value per serving: 0
Roasted Broccoli with Gremolata | page 154

PointsPlus value per serving: 2
Grilled Zucchini with Mint and Oregano | page 152
Lemon-Sage Spaghetti Squash | page 153
Roasted Fennel, Carrots, and Shallots | page 154

PointsPlus value per serving: 3
Roasted Dill Potatoes | page 155
Collard Greens with Figs and Bacon Crumbles | page 156
Braised Brussels Sprouts with Cranberries and
    Bacon | page 156
Grilled Corn, Red Peppers, and Onions | page 157
Creamy Rosemary Apples | page 160
Ginger-Caramelized Pineapple | page 160

PointsPlus value per serving: 4
Mediterranean Couscous | page 157
Baked Onion Rings | page 159

PointsPlus value per serving: 5
Mustard Potatoes and Green Beans | page 155
Orzo with Basil, Orange, and Pine Nuts | page 158

Grocery List

☐ Balsamic vinegar

☐ Red wine vinegar

☐ 1 bunch fresh mint

☐ 1 bunch fresh oregano

☐ 6 zucchini

☐ Check staples: olive oil, salt, pepper, garlic, olive oil–flavored cooking spray

Grilled Zucchini with Mint and Oregano

prep: 10 minutes • **cook:** 6 minutes • **other:** 15 minutes

PointsPlus value per serving: 2

It's not unusual for a rich chocolate dessert to get a top rating at our taste-testing table. But when a vegetable receives our highest score, you can rest assured that it's one tasty side dish. And this recipe did just that, so put this one on your "must try" list.

2 tablespoons olive oil
1 tablespoon balsamic vinegar
1 tablespoon red wine vinegar
½ teaspoon salt
½ teaspoon freshly ground black pepper
3 garlic cloves, minced
¼ cup chopped fresh mint, divided
¼ cup chopped fresh oregano, divided
6 zucchini (about 1¾ pounds), cut diagonally into ½-inch-thick slices
Olive oil–flavored cooking spray

1. Preheat grill to medium-high heat.

2. Combine first 6 ingredients in a large bowl, stirring well with a whisk. Stir in 3 tablespoons mint and 3 tablespoons oregano.

3. Add zucchini slices to marinade, tossing gently to coat. Let stand at room temperature at least 15 minutes, stirring occasionally.

4. Remove zucchini from bowl, reserving marinade. Place zucchini slices on grill rack coated with cooking spray; cover and grill 3 minutes on each side or just until tender. Arrange zucchini on a platter; drizzle with reserved marinade, and sprinkle with remaining mint and oregano. Serve warm or at room temperature. **Yield:** 7 servings (serving size: about ½ cup).

Per serving: CALORIES 70; FAT 4.5g (sat 0.7g, mono 2.8g, poly 0.6g); PROTEIN 2.3g; CARB 6.6g; FIBER 1.6g; CHOL 0mg; IRON 0.7mg; SODIUM 183mg; CALC 43mg

Lemon-Sage Spaghetti Squash

prep: 6 minutes • **cook:** 16 minutes • **other:** 15 minutes

PointsPlus value per serving: 2

We gave this dish our Test Kitchen's highest rating. Similar in looks to spaghetti, this squash is good when it's seasoned like pasta—with butter, garlic, and cheese. Serve with chicken or fish in place of pasta or rice.

Grocery List

- ☐ 1 (2-pound) spaghetti squash
- ☐ 1 medium onion
- ☐ Parmesan cheese
- ☐ 1 bunch fresh sage
- ☐ 1 medium lemon
- ☐ 1 stick light butter
- ☐ Check staples: garlic, salt, pepper

1   (2-pound) spaghetti squash
⅓   cup water
2   tablespoons light stick butter
¼   cup chopped onion
2   garlic cloves, minced
2   tablespoons shredded fresh Parmesan cheese
2   teaspoons small fresh sage leaves
1   teaspoon grated fresh lemon rind
½   teaspoon salt
¼   teaspoon freshly ground black pepper

1. Pierce squash several times with a fork; place in an 11 x 7–inch microwave-safe baking dish. Microwave, uncovered, at HIGH 6 minutes. Cut in half lengthwise; discard seeds. Place squash, cut sides up, in baking dish; add ⅓ cup water. Cover tightly with heavy-duty plastic wrap, vent. Microwave at HIGH 5 minutes or until tender. Drain and cool 15 minutes.

2. While squash cools, melt butter in a large nonstick skillet over medium-high heat. Add onion and garlic; sauté 2 to 3 minutes or until onion is tender.

3. Using a fork, remove spaghetti-like strands from squash. Add strands (about 3 cups) to pan; cook 2 minutes or until thoroughly heated. Transfer to a bowl; add Parmesan cheese and remaining ingredients, and toss well. **Yield:** 6 servings (serving size: ½ cup).

Per serving: CALORIES 73; FAT 3.6g (sat 2.1g, mono 1g, poly 0.3g); PROTEIN 1.9g; CARB 9.5g; FIBER 2g; CHOL 7mg; IRON 0.5mg; SODIUM 275mg; CALC 60mg

pictured on page 120

Roasted Broccoli with Gremolata

prep: 4 minutes • **cook:** 18 minutes   *PointsPlus* value per serving: 0

Grocery List
- ☐ 1 (12-ounce) bag broccoli florets
- ☐ 1 small bunch fresh parsley
- ☐ 1 lemon
- ☐ Check staples: olive oil–flavored cooking spray, salt, garlic

3 cups refrigerated bagged prewashed broccoli florets
Olive oil–flavored cooking spray
¼ teaspoon salt
1 tablespoon chopped fresh parsley
2 teaspoons grated fresh lemon rind
1 teaspoon minced garlic

1. Preheat oven to 425°.
2. Place broccoli florets in a medium bowl. Coat broccoli generously with cooking spray, and sprinkle with salt; toss to coat. Place in a single layer on a large rimmed baking sheet.
3. Bake at 425° for 18 minutes or until crisp-tender and beginning to brown.
4. While broccoli bakes, combine parsley, lemon rind, and garlic in a small bowl. Sprinkle gremolata over broccoli before serving. **Yield:** 4 servings (serving size: about ¾ cup).

Per serving: CALORIES 20; FAT 0.3g (sat 0g, mono 0g, poly 0.1g); PROTEIN 1.6g; CARB 3.3g; FIBER 1.7g; CHOL 0mg; IRON 0.5mg; SODIUM 163mg; CALC 28mg

Roasted Fennel, Carrots, and Shallots

prep: 13 minutes • **cook:** 45 minutes   *PointsPlus* value per serving: 2

Grocery List
- ☐ 2 fennel bulbs
- ☐ 4 carrots
- ☐ 2 (3-ounce) bags shallots
- ☐ Check staples: butter-flavored cooking spray, salt, pepper

2 fennel bulbs (about 2 pounds), trimmed and cut into ½-inch-thick wedges
4 carrots, cut into 4 x ½–inch sticks
5 shallots (about ¼ pound), peeled and halved
Butter-flavored cooking spray
¼ teaspoon salt
¼ teaspoon freshly ground black pepper

1. Preheat oven to 450°.
2. Arrange fennel, carrot, and shallots in a single layer on a large rimmed baking sheet coated with cooking spray. Bake at 450° for 45 minutes (do not turn vegetables).
3. Transfer vegetables to a medium bowl; sprinkle with salt and pepper. **Yield:** 4 servings (serving size: 1 cup).

Per serving: CALORIES 82; FAT 0.6g (sat 0g, mono 0g, poly 0.1g); PROTEIN 3g; CARB 19.2g; FIBER 5.4g; CHOL 0mg; IRON 1.4mg; SODIUM 48mg; CALC 78mg

Roasted Dill Potatoes

prep: 3 minutes • **cook:** 17 minutes   *PointsPlus* **value per serving: 3**

These simply prepared potatoes won our Test Kitchen's highest rating for their bright flavor.

    1   tablespoon olive oil
    ½   teaspoon fine sea salt
    ½   teaspoon freshly ground black pepper
   32   baby Yukon gold and red potatoes (about 1½ pounds), quartered
    3   tablespoons chopped fresh dill
    2   tablespoons fresh lemon juice

1. Preheat oven to 450°.
2. Heat a large rimmed baking sheet in oven for 5 minutes. Combine first 4 ingredients in a large bowl, tossing to coat. Spread potato mixture in a single layer on hot pan.
3. Bake at 450° for 17 minutes or just until tender. Place potatoes in a bowl. Add dill and lemon juice; toss gently. **Yield:** 7 servings (serving size: ½ cup).

Per serving: CALORIES 99; FAT 1.9g (sat 0.3g, mono 1.4g, poly 0.2g); PROTEIN 2.3g; CARB 17.6g; FIBER 1.2g; CHOL 0mg; IRON 0.9mg; SODIUM 140mg; CALC 1mg

> ## Grocery List
> ☐ 1 (1½-pound) bag mixed baby Yukon gold and red potatoes
> ☐ 1 small bunch fresh dill
> ☐ 1 medium lemon
> ☐ Check staples: olive oil, fine sea salt, pepper

Mustard Potatoes and Green Beans

prep: 9 minutes • **cook:** 16 minutes   *PointsPlus* **value per serving: 5**

    6   small red potatoes, quartered
    1   pound green beans, trimmed
    2   tablespoons fat-free, lower-sodium chicken broth
    1   tablespoon stone-ground mustard
    2   teaspoons olive oil
    ½   teaspoon salt
    ½   teaspoon dried rosemary, crushed

1. Place potato quarters in a medium saucepan; add water to cover. Bring to a boil; cook 3 minutes. Add green beans; cover, reduce heat to medium, and cook 12 minutes or until potato and beans are tender. Drain.
2. Combine broth and remaining ingredients. Pour over potato mixture; toss gently to coat. **Yield:** 5 servings (serving size: 1 cup).

Per serving: CALORIES 197; FAT 2.9g (sat 0.5g, mono 1.5g, poly 0.3g); PROTEIN 6g; CARB 39.3g; FIBER 6.7g; CHOL 0mg; IRON 2.6mg; SODIUM 265mg; CALC 60mg

> ## Grocery List
> ☐ 6 small red potatoes
> ☐ 1 (1-pound) bag fresh green beans
> ☐ 1 (14.5-ounce) can fat-free, lower-sodium chicken broth
> ☐ 1 (4-ounce) jar stone-ground mustard
> ☐ 1 (1-ounce) bottle dried rosemary
> ☐ Check staples: olive oil, salt

Collard Greens with Figs and Bacon Crumbles

prep: 5 minutes • **cook:** 26 minutes   *PointsPlus* value per serving: 3

This updated Southern side has a perfect blend of sweet and salty flavors and is quick to assemble. Serve it with roasted or grilled pork.

2   bacon slices
1   (16-ounce) package chopped fresh collard greens
½   cup dried figs, chopped
⅓   cup water
2   teaspoons maple syrup

1. Cook bacon in a large nonstick skillet over medium heat until crisp. Crumble bacon, and return to pan. Add greens and remaining ingredients; cover and cook over medium heat 20 minutes or until greens are tender, stirring occasionally. **Yield:** 4 servings (serving size: 1 cup).

Per serving: CALORIES 119; FAT 3.5g (sat 1.2g, mono 1g, poly 0.5g); PROTEIN 4.4g; CARB 20.6g; FIBER 5.5g; CHOL 4.5mg; IRON 1.9mg; SODIUM 70mg; CALC 217mg

Braised Brussels Sprouts with Cranberries and Bacon

prep: 3 minutes • **cook:** 17 minutes   *PointsPlus* value per serving: 3

2   bacon slices
1   pound fresh Brussels sprouts, trimmed and halved lengthwise
½   cup water
¼   cup sweetened dried cranberries
⅛   teaspoon salt
¼   teaspoon freshly ground black pepper

1. Cook bacon in a large nonstick skillet over medium heat until crisp. Remove bacon from pan; crumble.
2. Add Brussels sprouts to drippings in pan, and sauté 4 minutes or until lightly browned. Stir in ½ cup water and next 3 ingredients. Cover and simmer 5 minutes or until sprouts are tender. Uncover and cook 2 minutes or until liquid evaporates; sprinkle with crumbled bacon. **Yield:** 4 servings (serving size: ¾ cup).

Per serving: CALORIES 126; FAT 5.4g (sat 1.8g, mono 2.3g, poly 0.7g); PROTEIN 5.2g; CARB 16.6g; FIBER 4.7g; CHOL 8mg; IRON 1.7mg; SODIUM 196mg; CALC 49mg

pictured on page 121

Grilled Corn, Red Peppers, and Onions

prep: 6 minutes • **cook:** 15 minutes   *PointsPlus* value per serving: 3

2 large ears shucked corn
1 large red bell pepper, cut in half and seeded
1 medium-sized red onion, cut into ½-inch-thick slices
Butter-flavored cooking spray
1 tablespoon olive oil
3 tablespoons chopped fresh cilantro
¼ teaspoon salt
¼ teaspoon freshly ground black pepper

1. Preheat grill to medium-high heat.
2. Coat first 3 ingredients heavily with cooking spray. Place vegetables on grill rack coated with cooking spray. Grill 15 minutes or until vegetables are tender.
3. Cut kernels from corn to yield 3 cups; place in a medium bowl. Cut pepper and onion into 1-inch pieces; add to corn. Add oil and remaining ingredients; toss well.
Yield: 4 servings (serving size: 1¼ cups).

Per serving: CALORIES 117; FAT 4.6g (sat 0.7g, mono 2.9g, poly 0.6g); PROTEIN 2.8g; CARB 18.3g; FIBER 2.6g; CHOL 0mg; IRON 0.7mg; SODIUM 164mg; CALC 21mg

Mediterranean Couscous

prep: 8 minutes • **cook:** 5 minutes   *PointsPlus* value per serving: 4

1 (5.8-ounce) package roasted garlic and olive oil couscous mix (with seasoning packet)
1 (14-ounce) can artichoke hearts, drained and chopped
1¼ cups chopped tomato (about 1 large tomato)
½ cup (2 ounces) crumbled feta cheese
¼ cup sliced ripe olives
1 tablespoon chopped fresh parsley
2 tablespoons fresh lemon juice
1 teaspoon dried oregano
¼ teaspoon freshly ground black pepper

1. Prepare couscous according to package directions, omitting fat and using 1 tablespoon seasoning from seasoning packet; discard remaining seasoning. Fluff couscous with a fork. Add chopped artichoke and remaining ingredients to couscous; toss gently. Serve warm or chilled. **Yield:** 7 servings (serving size: ¾ cup).

Per serving: CALORIES 139; FAT 3.2g (sat 1.2g, mono 1.1g, poly 0.3g); PROTEIN 6.7g; CARB 22.8g; FIBER 1.6g; CHOL 7mg; IRON 1.5mg; SODIUM 335mg; CALC 44mg

pictured on page 122

Orzo with Basil, Orange, and Pine Nuts

prep: 10 minutes • **cook:** 17 minutes   *PointsPlus* value per serving: 5

At first glance, this recipe may look like any other simple side dish, but the flavor is anything but simple. Orzo cooks in vegetable broth to boost the flavor before it's tossed with a garlic-infused orange-juice reduction and fresh basil. At the end of taste testing, there wasn't a piece of orzo left in the bowl, and the recipe received our highest rating.

2   (14-ounce) cans vegetable broth
1½ cups uncooked orzo (rice-shaped pasta)
2   tablespoons olive oil
1   tablespoon butter
1   tablespoon grated fresh orange rind
3   garlic cloves, minced
¾   cup fresh orange juice
⅓   cup chopped fresh basil
¾   cup shredded fresh Parmigiano-Reggiano cheese
2   tablespoons pine nuts, toasted
¼   teaspoon freshly ground black pepper

1. Bring broth to a boil in a medium saucepan. Add pasta; reduce heat to medium, and cook 9 to 12 minutes or until tender. Drain.

2. While pasta cooks, combine oil and next 3 ingredients in a medium saucepan; cook over medium-low heat 3 to 5 minutes or until butter melts and garlic is soft and fragrant, stirring often. Increase heat to medium-high. Add orange juice; cook 3 minutes or until juice reduces slightly, stirring often. Remove from heat; stir in basil. Add pasta to pan, tossing to coat. Stir in cheese, pine nuts, and pepper.

Note: Toast the pine nuts in a small skillet over medium heat for 1 minute until they are fragrant and begin to take on a golden hue; transfer to a plate to cool quickly. A grater works wonders to get the finest zest from the oranges; be sure to remove the zest before you juice them. **Yield:** 10 servings (serving size: ½ cup).

Per serving: CALORIES 189; FAT 7.1g (sat 2.4g, mono 3.1g, poly 1.2g); PROTEIN 7.3g; CARB 24.5g; FIBER 1.1g; CHOL 7.4mg; IRON 1.2mg; SODIUM 228mg; CALC 88mg

Baked Onion Rings

prep: 6 minutes • **cook:** 16 minutes   *PointsPlus* value per serving: 4

You can enjoy crunchy onion rings without all the fat. Serve them as an appetizer or alongside your favorite burger.

Grocery List

- [ ] 1 large sweet onion
- [ ] 1 (1.5-ounce) bottle ground red pepper
- [ ] 1 (8-ounce) box panko
- [ ] Check staples: cooking spray, flour, eggs, salt

  1   large Vidalia or other sweet onion, sliced and separated into rings
     Cooking spray
 1.1 ounces all-purpose flour (about ¼ cup)
  ¼ teaspoon ground red pepper
  3 large egg whites
  2 tablespoons water
1¾ cups panko (Japanese breadcrumbs)
  ¼ teaspoon salt

1. Preheat oven to 475°.

2. Place a large baking sheet in oven while it preheats. Coat onion rings with cooking spray. Combine flour and ground red pepper in a large heavy-duty zip-top plastic bag. Add onion; shake to coat.

3. Combine egg whites and 2 tablespoons water in a shallow bowl, stirring with a whisk. Place panko in a food processor; process into fine crumbs. Place crumbs in another shallow dish.

4. Dip onion rings in egg white mixture; dredge in crumbs. Remove hot baking sheet from oven; coat pan with cooking spray. Arrange onion rings in a single layer on pan. Coat onion rings with cooking spray.

5. Bake at 475° for 16 minutes or until browned and crisp. Sprinkle hot onion rings evenly with salt; serve immediately. **Yield:** 4 servings (serving size: ¼ of onion rings).

Per serving: CALORIES 176; FAT 1.1g (sat 0.1g, mono 0g, poly 0.1g); PROTEIN 8.1g; CARB 32.6g; FIBER 2.8g; CHOL 0mg; IRON 0.6mg; SODIUM 265mg; CALC 25mg

pictured on page 124

Creamy Rosemary Apples

prep: 4 minutes • **cook:** 15 minutes   *PointsPlus* value per serving: 3

These apples are a perfect match for pork. If you're unable to find crème fraîche, substitute sour cream.

Grocery List

☐ 3 Golden Delicious apples

☐ 1 small container fresh rosemary

☐ Crème fraîche

☐ Check staples: sugar, salt

    3   Golden Delicious apples (about 1½ pounds), peeled and cut into wedges
    1   tablespoon sugar
    2   teaspoons chopped fresh rosemary
    ⅛   teaspoon salt
    3   tablespoons crème fraîche

1. Preheat oven to 450°.
2. Place apple wedges in a large bowl. Combine sugar, rosemary, and salt in a small bowl; sprinkle over apple, and toss well. Spoon apple mixture into an 11 x 7–inch baking dish. Dollop crème fraîche, ½ tablespoon at a time, over apple wedges.
3. Bake at 450° for 15 minutes or until apple wedges are tender, stirring after 8 minutes. **Yield:** 5 servings (serving size: about ½ cup).

Per serving: CALORIES 114; FAT 3.5g (sat 2.1g, mono 0.9g, poly 0.2g); PROTEIN 0.4g; CARB 21.4g; FIBER 3.3g; CHOL 12mg; IRON 0.2mg; SODIUM 64mg; CALC 15mg

pictured on page 123

Ginger-Caramelized Pineapple

prep: 2 minutes • **cook:** 9 minutes   *PointsPlus* value per serving: 3

This delicious side dish won our Test Kitchen's highest rating. It's the perfect accompaniment for pork or chicken and especially dishes with Asian, Latin, or Caribbean flavors.

Grocery List

☐ 1 (1¼-pound) pineapple, cored

☐ 1 stick light butter

☐ 1 (3-ounce) jar honey

☐ 1 ounce crystallized ginger

☐ Check staples: cooking spray, salt

Cooking spray
    1   (1¼-pound) cored fresh pineapple, cut vertically into 12 spears
    2   tablespoons light stick butter, cut into pieces
    2   tablespoons honey
    1   tablespoon finely chopped crystallized ginger
    ⅛   teaspoon salt

1. Heat a large skillet over high heat. Coat pan with cooking spray; add pineapple. Add butter pieces, and quickly tilt pan in all directions so butter covers pan with a thin film. Cook pineapple 8 minutes or until browned, turning once. Add honey, ginger, and salt; cook 1 minute, tossing to coat with honey. **Yield:** 6 servings (serving size: 2 pineapple spears and 1 teaspoon syrup).

Per serving: CALORIES 90; FAT 2.1g (sat 1.2g, mono 0.5g, poly 0g); PROTEIN 0.5g; CARB 19.2g; FIBER 1.3g; CHOL 5mg; IRON 0.5mg; SODIUM 82mg; CALC 14mg

Breads

PointsPlus value per serving: 2
Parmesan-Prosciutto Biscotti | page 167

PointsPlus value per serving: 3
Rosemary Focaccia | page 162
Cream Cheese Biscuits | page 163
Pumpkin-Raisin Muffins | page 164

PointsPlus value per serving: 4
Apple Butter–Bran Muffins | page 163
Poppy Seed Quick Bread | page 166
Grilled Rosemary Flatbreads | page 168

PointsPlus value per serving: 5
Sticky Buns | page 165

Menu
PointsPlus value
per serving: 5

Rosemary Focaccia

1 cup sautéed asparagus
with ½ ounce shaved
Parmesan cheese
PointsPlus value
per serving: 2

Game Plan

1. While dough rises:
  • Preheat oven.
  • Chop rosemary.

2. Just before bread is done
baking:
  • Sauté asparagus in a
    nonstick skillet with salt
    and pepper.
  • Shave Parmesan cheese
    over warm asparagus.

3. Let bread cool before
cutting.

Rosemary Focaccia

prep: 15 minutes • **cook:** 15 minutes • **other:** 1 hour and 5 minutes

PointsPlus value per serving: 3

Be sure to check the temperature of your water before adding the yeast. If your water is too hot, the yeast may not react properly and can leave you with bread that doesn't rise to the occasion.

  1 package dry yeast
  ½ cup plus 2 tablespoons warm water (100° to 110°)
  7.9 ounces all-purpose flour (about 1¾ cups), divided
  ¾ teaspoon salt, divided
  Cooking spray
  2 tablespoons coarsely chopped fresh rosemary
  1 tablespoon olive oil
  ½ teaspoon freshly ground black pepper

1. Preheat oven to 450°.

2. Combine yeast and ½ cup plus 2 tablespoons warm water in a 2-cup glass measure; let stand 5 minutes. Lightly spoon flour into dry measuring cups; level with a knife. Combine 1½ cups flour, yeast mixture, and ¼ teaspoon salt in a large mixing bowl; beat with a mixer at medium speed until well blended.

3. Sprinkle remaining ¼ cup flour over work surface. Turn dough out onto floured surface; knead until smooth and elastic (about 5 minutes). Place in a bowl coated with cooking spray, turning to coat top. Cover and let rise in a warm place (85°), free from drafts, 1 hour or until doubled in size.

4. Punch dough down. Pat dough into an 8-inch circle (about ¼-inch-thick) on a baking sheet coated with cooking spray. Poke holes in dough at 1-inch intervals with handle of a wooden spoon. Sprinkle dough with remaining ½ teaspoon salt and rosemary. Drizzle with olive oil, and sprinkle with pepper. Bake at 450° for 15 to 17 minutes or until golden. Cut focaccia into 8 wedges. **Yield:** 8 servings (serving size: 1 wedge).

Per serving: CALORIES 119; FAT 2g (sat 0.3g, mono 1.3g, poly 0.3g); PROTEIN 3.2g; CARB 21.4g; FIBER 1.1g; CHOL 0mg; IRON 1.4mg; SODIUM 224mg; CALC 6.9mg

Cream Cheese Biscuits

prep: 10 minutes • **cook:** 10 minutes   *PointsPlus* value per serving: 3

    9   ounces self-rising flour (about 2 cups), divided
    1   teaspoon sugar
    ½   (8-ounce) block ⅓-less-fat cream cheese, cut into small pieces
    2   tablespoons light stick butter
    ¼   cup plus 3 tablespoons fat-free milk
    Cooking spray

1. Preheat oven to 450°.
2. Lightly spoon flour into dry measuring cups; level with a knife. Sprinkle 1 tablespoon flour over work surface. Combine remaining flour and sugar in a bowl; stir well. Cut in cream cheese with a pastry blender or 2 knives until mixture resembles coarse meal. Cut in butter until it forms small pieces. Add milk, stirring mixture just until moist.
3. Turn dough out onto prepared work surface. Knead 4 or 5 times. Pat dough to ½-inch thickness; cut into rounds with a 2-inch biscuit cutter. Place rounds on a baking sheet coated with cooking spray.
4. Bake at 450° for 10 minutes or until biscuits are lightly browned. **Yield:** 14 biscuits (serving size: 1 biscuit).

Per serving: CALORIES 100; FAT 3.1g (sat 1.8g, mono 0.8g, poly 0.2g); PROTEIN 2.8g; CARB 14.2g; FIBER 0.5g; CHOL 8mg; IRON 0.9mg; SODIUM 266mg; CALC 80mg

Menu
PointsPlus value per serving: 5

Cream Cheese Biscuits

1 tablespoon jam
PointsPlus value per serving: 1

1 cup mixed melon
PointsPlus value per serving: 1

Game Plan

1. While oven preheats:
• Prepare biscuits.
• Spray baking sheet with cooking spray.

2. While biscuits bake:
• Chop melon.

Apple Butter–Bran Muffins

prep: 5 minutes • **cook:** 10 minutes   *PointsPlus* value per serving: 4

    1   (7.4-ounce) package honey bran muffin mix
    ½   cup apple butter
    ⅓   cup chopped dates
    1   tablespoon fat-free milk
    1   large egg, lightly beaten
    Cooking spray

1. Preheat oven to 450°.
2. Combine first 5 ingredients, stirring just until moist. Spoon batter into muffin cups coated with cooking spray, filling three-fourths full.
3. Bake at 450° for 10 to 12 minutes or until lightly browned. Remove from pan immediately. **Yield:** 8 muffins (serving size: 1 muffin).

Per serving: CALORIES 160; FAT 2.8g (sat 0.7g, mono 0.7g, poly 1.3g); PROTEIN 3g; CARB 31.2g; FIBER 2.9g; CHOL 23mg; IRON 1.6mg; SODIUM 219mg; CALC 130mg

Menu
PointsPlus value per serving: 6

Apple Butter–Bran Muffins

1 medium orange
PointsPlus value per serving: 0

1 cup fat-free milk
PointsPlus value per serving: 2

Game Plan

1. While oven preheats:
• Prepare muffin batter.

2. Bake muffins.

Menu
PointsPlus value
per serving: 7

Pumpkin-Raisin Muffins

1 (6-ounce) carton fat-free
honey vanilla Greek yogurt
PointsPlus value
per serving: 4

Game Plan

1. While oven preheats:
• Prepare muffin mixture.

2. Bake muffins.

Pumpkin-Raisin Muffins

prep: 12 minutes • **cook:** 15 minutes   *PointsPlus* value per serving: 3

Pumpkin is a popular fall flavor, but these tasty pumpkin muffins are easy to make and delicious all year. Try pairing a muffin with a sweet Greek yogurt or a spiced Chai tea for a delicious afternoon treat.

6.75 ounces all-purpose flour (about 1½ cups)
⅓ cup firmly packed brown sugar
1 teaspoon baking powder
½ teaspoon baking soda
¼ teaspoon salt
1½ teaspoons pumpkin pie spice
⅓ cup raisins
1 large egg, lightly beaten
½ cup canned pumpkin
⅓ cup orange juice
1 tablespoon butter, melted
Cooking spray

1. Preheat oven to 400°.
2. Lightly spoon flour into dry measuring cups; level with a knife. Combine flour and next 5 ingredients in a large bowl; stir in raisins. Make a well in center of mixture. Combine egg and next 3 ingredients in a small bowl. Add to dry ingredients, stirring just until moist (batter will be very thick).
3. Spoon batter into muffin cups coated with cooking spray, filling two-thirds full. Bake at 400° for 15 minutes. **Yield:** 12 muffins (serving size: 1 muffin).

Per serving: CALORIES 117; FAT 1.6g (sat 0.8g, mono 0.4g, poly 0.2g); PROTEIN 2.5g; CARB 23.1g; FIBER 1.1g; CHOL 18mg; IRON 1.1mg; SODIUM 166mg; CALC 24mg

Sticky Buns

prep: 10 minutes • **cook:** 21 minutes • **other:** 1 minute

PointsPlus value per serving: 5

¼ cup firmly packed dark brown sugar
3 tablespoons light stick butter, divided
¼ cup apple juice
Cooking spray
2 tablespoons finely chopped pecans
2 tablespoons granulated sugar
½ teaspoon ground cinnamon
¼ cup currants
1 (10.8-ounce) can refrigerated reduced-calorie biscuits

1. Preheat oven to 375°.
2. Combine brown sugar, 2 tablespoons margarine, and apple juice in a small saucepan. Bring to a boil; reduce heat, and simmer, uncovered, 8 minutes or until slightly thickened. Pour syrup evenly into 8 muffin pans coated with cooking spray; sprinkle with pecans, and set aside.
3. Combine granulated sugar, cinnamon, and currants in a small bowl; toss well to coat currants. Set aside.
4. Roll biscuits on a lightly floured surface into a 12 x 9–inch rectangle. Spread dough with remaining 1 tablespoon butter, and sprinkle with currant mixture to within ¼ inch of edge. Beginning at short side, roll up dough, tightly, jelly-roll fashion. Pinch seam to seal (do not seal ends of roll). Cut dough into 8 slices. Place cut sides of slices on top of pecan mixture in muffin cups. Bake at 375° for 12 minutes or until golden. Invert buns onto a serving plate; let buns stand, covered with muffin cups, 1 minute. Remove from cups, scraping any remaining pecan mixture from cups onto buns. Serve warm. **Yield:** 8 buns (serving size: 1 bun).

Per serving: CALORIES 206; FAT 8.5g (sat 2.5g, mono 4.2g, poly 1.6g); PROTEIN 3g; CARB 30.3g; FIBER 1g; CHOL 0mg; IRON 1.2mg; SODIUM 432mg; CALC 26mg

Menu
PointsPlus value
per serving: 5

Sticky Buns

1 medium apple, sliced
PointsPlus value
per serving: 0

Game Plan

1. While syrup mixture heats:
• Prepare baking pan.

2. While oven preheats:
• Roll out dough.
• Assemble Sticky Buns.

2. While buns bake:
• Wash and slice apple.

Menu
PointsPlus value
per serving: 4

Poppy Seed Quick Bread

1 cup mixed strawberries
and blueberries
PointsPlus value
per serving: 0

Game Plan

1. While oven preheats:
• Prepare batter.
• Coat pan with cooking
spray.

2. While bread bakes:
• Prepare glaze.

3. While bread cools:
• Rinse and chop berries.

Poppy Seed Quick Bread

prep: 18 minutes • **cook:** 50 minutes • **other:** 10 minutes

PointsPlus value per serving: 4

Adding the two tablespoons of orange rind to this recipe intensifies the sweet citrus taste.

10.1	ounces all-purpose flour (about 2¼ cups)
1	teaspoon baking powder
½	teaspoon baking soda
¼	teaspoon salt
½	cup sugar
2	tablespoons grated fresh orange rind
1	tablespoon poppy seeds
½	cup fat-free milk
½	cup unsweetened orange juice
¼	cup egg substitute
2	tablespoons butter, melted
½	cup chopped walnuts
	Cooking spray
½	cup sifted powdered sugar
2	teaspoons orange juice

1. Preheat oven to 350°.

2. Lightly spoon flour into dry measuring cups; level with a knife. Combine flour and next 6 ingredients in a large bowl; mix well. Combine milk and next 3 ingredients; add to dry ingredients, stirring just until moist. Stir in walnuts.

3. Spoon batter in an 8½ x 4½–inch loaf pan coated with cooking spray. Bake at 350° for 50 to 55 minutes or until a wooden pick inserted in center comes out clean.

4. Combine powdered sugar and 2 teaspoons orange juice; stir well. Drizzle glaze over hot bread in pan. Cool in pan 10 minutes. Remove from pan, and cool completely on a wire rack. **Yield:** 16 servings (serving size: 1 slice).

Per serving: CALORIES 153; FAT 4.3g (sat 1.2g, mono 0.7g, poly 2.1g); PROTEIN 3.2g; CARB 25.8g; FIBER 0.9g; CHOL 4mg; IRON 1.1mg; SODIUM 135mg; CALC 35mg

pictured on page 126

Parmesan-Prosciutto Biscotti

prep: 19 minutes • **cook:** 1 hour and 8 minutes • **other:** 20 minutes

PointsPlus value per serving: 2

Biscotti are crisp Italian cookies made by first baking a loaf of bread, and then slicing it and baking the slices again. To get 18 slices from the loaf, discard the two end pieces.

- 7.9 ounces all-purpose flour (about 1¾ cups)
- ¼ cup grated fresh Parmesan cheese
- 1 teaspoon baking powder
- ½ teaspoon salt
- ⅛ teaspoon freshly ground black pepper
- ¼ cup 2% reduced-fat milk
- 2 large eggs
- 2 garlic cloves, crushed
- 2 ounces prosciutto, finely diced
  Cooking spray

1. Preheat oven to 350°.

2. Lightly spoon flour into dry measuring cups; level with a knife. Combine flour and next 4 ingredients in a large bowl, stirring well with a whisk. Combine milk, eggs, and garlic in a small bowl; stir with a whisk until smooth. Add milk mixture to flour mixture, stirring until well blended. Stir in prosciutto. Turn dough out onto a lightly floured surface, and knead lightly 8 times. Shape dough into a 12-inch-long roll. Place roll on a baking sheet coated with cooking spray; pat to 1-inch thickness.

3. Bake at 350° for 30 minutes or until top is lightly browned. Remove roll from baking sheet, and cool 20 minutes on a wire rack.

4. Reduce oven temperature to 325°.

5. Cut roll diagonally into 18 slices using a serrated knife. Place slices, cut sides down, on baking sheet. Bake at 325° for 20 minutes. Turn biscotti over; bake an additional 18 to 20 minutes or until lightly browned. Remove from baking sheet; cool completely on wire rack. **Yield:** 18 servings (serving size: 1 biscotto).

Per serving: CALORIES 68; FAT 1.5g (sat 0.6g, mono 0.4g, poly 0.2g); PROTEIN 3.7g; CARB 9.9g; FIBER 0.3g; CHOL 25mg; IRON 0.7mg; SODIUM 218mg; CALC 37mg

---

Menu
PointsPlus value per serving: 5

Parmesan-Prosciutto Biscotti

Fresh Herb Insalata (page 84)
PointsPlus value per serving: 3

Game Plan

1. While oven preheats:
- Prepare biscotti dough.
- Spray baking sheet with cooking spray.

2. Bake biscotti.

3. While biscotti cools completely:
- Prepare salad.

pictured on page 125

Grilled Rosemary Flatbreads

prep: 25 minutes • **cook:** 6 minutes per batch • **other:** 1 hour and 15 minutes

PointsPlus value per serving: 4

Simply seasoned with olive oil and rosemary, these rustic grilled flatbreads received our Test Kitchen's highest rating. Place leftover grilled flatbreads in an airtight container, and freeze for up to 1 month.

    1   package quick-rise yeast (about 2¼ teaspoons)
   1½   cups warm water (100° to 110°)
  16.9 ounces all-purpose flour (about 3¾ cups), divided
    1   tablespoon kosher salt, divided
    2   tablespoons chopped fresh rosemary, divided
         Cooking spray
    2   tablespoons olive oil

1. Dissolve yeast in 1½ cups warm water in a large bowl; let stand 5 minutes.
2. Lightly spoon flour into dry measuring cups, and level with a knife. Stir 1 cup flour into yeast mixture. Cover and let stand 30 minutes.
3. Add remaining 2¾ cups flour, 1 teaspoon salt, and 1 tablespoon rosemary to yeast mixture; stir until a soft dough forms. Turn dough out onto a lightly floured surface, and knead until smooth and elastic (about 6 minutes). Place dough in a large bowl coated with cooking spray, turning to coat top. Cover and let rise in a warm place (85°), free from drafts, 40 minutes or until doubled in size. (Gently press two fingers into dough. If indentation remains, dough has risen enough.)
4. Preheat grill to medium-high heat.
5. Punch dough down, and divide into 12 equal portions. Roll each portion into a 4½- to 5-inch circle on a lightly floured surface. Brush dough rounds with olive oil; sprinkle rounds evenly with remaining 2 teaspoons salt and 1 tablespoon rosemary.
6. Place dough rounds on grill rack coated with cooking spray; grill 3 to 4 minutes on each side or until puffed and golden. Yield: 12 servings (serving size: 1 round).

Per serving: CALORIES 165; FAT 2.7g (sat 0.4g, mono 1.7g, poly 0.4g); PROTEIN 4.3g; CARB 30.1g; FIBER 1.2g; CHOL 0mg; IRON 1.9mg; SODIUM 482mg; CALC 7mg

---

Menu
PointsPlus value per serving: 5

Grilled Rosemary Flatbreads

½ heart romaine lettuce, grilled with olive oil–flavored cooking spray and ½ ounce shaved Parmesan cheese
PointsPlus value per serving: 1

Game Plan

1. While yeast mixture is resting:
• Chop rosemary.

2. While dough is rising:
• Rinse and halve romaine hearts.
• Shave Parmesan.

3. While grill heats:
• Spray romaine with olive oil–flavored cooking spray.
• Prepare dough for grill.

4. Grill dough until puffed.

5. Grill romaine for 2 minutes, and top with shaved Parmesan; add salt and pepper to taste.

Desserts

PointsPlus value per serving: 1
Chewy Lemon-Almond Cookies | page 185

PointsPlus value per serving: 2
Triple Chocolate–Toffee Trifle | page 180

PointsPlus value per serving: 3
Melon Sorbet | page 170
Blackberry-Buttermilk Sherbet | page 183
Affogato | page 184
Mojito'd Melon Mix-Up | page 184
No-Bake Chocolate-Oat Drop Cookies | page 187

PointsPlus value per serving: 5
Chai Tea Latte Ice Cream | page 176
Quick Tiramisu | page 179

PointsPlus value per serving: 6
Raspberry-Chocolate Tortes | page 171
Arborio Rice Pudding with Saffron | page 172
Nectarine and Berry Crumble | page 173
Layered Amaretti–Ice Cream Loaf | page 177
Caramel-Praline Ice-Cream Cake | page 178
Mocha Mousse | page 182
Pecan Pie Squares | page 186
S'mores Slabs | page 187
Chocolate Malt Crème Brûlée | page 188

PointsPlus value per serving: 7
Peanut Butter–Chocolate Ice Cream | page 175
Chocolate-Raspberry-Coconut Cake | page 179
Lemon Cheesecake | page 181
Milk Chocolate–Hazelnut Mousse | page 183

PointsPlus value per serving: 8
Caramelized Pineapple Sundaes | page 174
Pumpkin Gingerbread Trifles | page 180
White Chocolate Mousse with Strawberries | page 182

PointsPlus value per serving: 10
Pear Crisp | page 174

Grocery List

- ☐ 1 small bottle sweet white wine
- ☐ 1 (0.3-ounce) package sugar-free peach gelatin
- ☐ 1 small cantaloupe
- ☐ 1 lemon
- ☐ Check staples: sugar

Melon Sorbet

prep: 15 minutes • **cook:** 4 minutes • **other:** 50 minutes

PointsPlus value per serving: 3

This refreshing sorbet can be served as a light dessert or as a palate cleanser between the starter and main course. Be sure to use ripe, sweet cantaloupe. Purchase the cantaloupe several days in advance, and leave it on your counter to ripen. You'll know it's ripe when you can smell it as you walk into your kitchen. Place the cantaloupe in the refrigerator the day before you plan to make the sorbet so it will be thoroughly chilled.

½   cup sweet white wine
1   (0.3-ounce) package sugar-free peach-flavored gelatin
¾   cup sugar
4   cups cubed peeled ripe cantaloupe (about 1 small), chilled
1   tablespoon fresh lemon juice

1. Combine first 3 ingredients in a small saucepan. Bring to a simmer over medium heat; cook 1 minute. Pour into a metal bowl, and freeze 10 to 12 minutes or until mixture reaches the consistency of egg whites, stirring frequently.

2. Place half of cantaloupe in a blender or food processor; process until puréed and very smooth. Transfer to a large bowl. Repeat with remaining cantaloupe. Stir in wine mixture and lemon juice.

3. Pour mixture into the freezer can of an ice-cream freezer; freeze according to manufacturer's instructions. **Yield:** 9 servings (serving size: about ½ cup).

Per serving: CALORIES 105; FAT 0.1g (sat 0g, mono 0g, poly 0.1g); PROTEIN 1.1g; CARB 0.6g; FIBER 0.6g; CHOL 0mg; IRON 0.2mg; SODIUM 40mg; CALC 7mg

Raspberry-Chocolate Tortes

prep: 13 minutes • **cook:** 10 minutes • **other:** 2 minutes

PointsPlus value per serving: 6

The cocoa in this recipe adds to the rich chocolate flavor, and it is also packed with nutrients that have been shown to lower cholesterol and blood pressure. Consider this dessert a treat for the taste buds and for your health.

Cooking spray
2   tablespoons unsweetened cocoa
¼   cup light stick butter
¼   cup seedless raspberry preserves
¼   cup fat-free half-and-half
½   cup unsweetened cocoa
¾   cup granulated sugar
¾   cup egg substitute
1.1 ounces all-purpose flour (about ¼ cup)
1   teaspoon vanilla extract
3   tablespoons sugar-free hot fudge topping
2½ tablespoons seedless raspberry preserves
1½ teaspoons water
1½ tablespoons powdered sugar

1. Preheat oven to 450°.

2. Coat 9 muffin cups with cooking spray, and dust with 2 tablespoons cocoa. Set aside.

3. Melt butter in a small saucepan over low heat. Add ¼ cup preserves and half-and-half, stirring with a whisk until preserves melt. Remove from heat; add ½ cup cocoa, stirring until smooth.

4. Combine granulated sugar and egg substitute in a medium bowl; beat with a mixer at high speed for 5 minutes. Gradually add chocolate mixture to egg substitute mixture, beating until smooth. Lightly spoon flour into a dry measuring cup; level with a knife. Add flour, beating until blended. Stir in vanilla.

5. Divide batter evenly among prepared muffin cups. Spoon 1 teaspoon fudge topping into center of each torte.

6. Bake at 450° for 8 to 10 minutes or until edges are set and center is soft. Cool 2 minutes. Run a thin, flexible knife around edge of each muffin cup. Carefully invert tortes onto a baking sheet; transfer to dessert plates.

7. Combine 2½ tablespoons preserves and 1½ teaspoons water in a microwave-safe bowl. Microwave at HIGH 20 seconds or until preserves melt; stir until smooth. Drizzle 1 teaspoon raspberry sauce over each torte; dust each with ½ teaspoon powdered sugar. **Yield:** 9 servings (serving size: 1 torte).

Per serving: CALORIES 196; FAT 4.3g (sat 2.2g, mono 1.2g, poly 0.1g); PROTEIN 4.3g; CARB 38.9g; FIBER 2.2g; CHOL 7mg; IRON 1.6mg; SODIUM 95mg; CALC 24mg

Grocery List

- ☐ 1 (10-ounce) jar seedless raspberry preserves
- ☐ 1 (8-ounce) carton fat-free half-and-half
- ☐ 1 (8-ounce) carton egg substitute
- ☐ 1 (11.75-ounce) jar sugar-free hot fudge topping
- ☐ Check staples: cooking spray, cocoa, granulated sugar, butter, flour, vanilla extract, powdered sugar

Arborio Rice Pudding with Saffron

prep: 3 minutes • **cook:** 37 minutes   *PointsPlus* value per serving: 6

Our staff gave this rice pudding our highest rating. Italian medium-grain rice creates a wonderfully creamy texture. Saffron lends an aromatic flavor and a rich, golden color to the dessert.

    6   cups 1% low-fat milk, divided
    1   cup uncooked Arborio rice
    ⅔   cup sugar
    ½   teaspoon salt
    ⅛   teaspoon saffron threads
    ¼   teaspoon ground cinnamon
    ½   cup golden raisins
    1   teaspoon vanilla extract
    Cinnamon sticks (optional)

1. Combine 3 cups milk, rice, sugar, salt, saffron, and ¼ teaspoon ground cinnamon in a large microwave-safe glass bowl. Microwave at HIGH 9 minutes.

2. Stir in remaining 3 cups milk. Microwave at HIGH 28 to 30 minutes or until rice is tender and pudding is creamy and slightly thick, stirring every few minutes to prevent mixture from bubbling over (pudding will continue to thicken after cooking as it stands).

3. Stir in raisins and vanilla. Serve warm or chilled. Garnish with cinnamon sticks, if desired. **Yield:** 9 servings (serving size: ½ cup).

Note: We tested with an 1,100-watt microwave. All microwaves cook differently, so use the texture of the rice and pudding as your guide to determine when it is done, not the exact time.

Per serving: CALORIES 232; FAT 1.8g (sat 1g, mono 0.5g, poly 0.1g); PROTEIN 7.5g; CARB 46.8g; FIBER 1.4g; CHOL 8mg; IRON 0.4mg; SODIUM 205mg; CALC 209mg

Nectarine and Berry Crumble

prep: 18 minutes • **cook:** 35 minutes • **other:** 10 minutes

PointsPlus value per serving: 6

This combination of succulent fruits and a crunchy-sweet topping received our Test Kitchen's highest rating. You'll need to buy 2 to 3 lemons to yield 1 tablespoon of grated fresh lemon rind.

4 nectarines (about 2¼ pounds), sliced
1 cup blackberries
1 cup blueberries
2 tablespoons all-purpose flour
1 tablespoon grated fresh lemon rind
Cooking spray
½ cup packed brown sugar
½ cup old-fashioned rolled oats
½ teaspoon ground cinnamon
2 tablespoons chilled light stick butter, cut into small pieces
¼ cup sliced almonds

1. Preheat oven to 350°.
2. Combine first 5 ingredients in a large bowl, and toss gently to combine. Place nectarine mixture in an 8-inch square baking dish coated with cooking spray. Set aside.
3. To prepare topping, combine brown sugar, oats, and cinnamon, stirring well. Cut in butter with a pastry blender or 2 knives until mixture resembles coarse meal. Stir in almonds. Sprinkle brown sugar mixture evenly over nectarine mixture. Bake at 350° for 35 minutes or until filling is bubbly. Let stand 10 minutes before serving. **Yield:** 6 servings (serving size: about 1 cup).

Per serving: CALORIES 226; FAT 6.8g (sat 2.7g, mono 2.5g, poly 1g); PROTEIN 3.2g; CARB 41.6g; FIBER 4.6g; CHOL 10mg; IRON 1.2mg; SODIUM 40mg; CALC 39mg

Grocery List
- [ ] 4 nectarines
- [ ] 1 pint blackberries
- [ ] 1 pint blueberries
- [ ] 2 to 3 lemons
- [ ] 1 (18-ounce) container old-fashioned rolled oats
- [ ] 1 (10-ounce) bag sliced almonds
- [ ] Check staples: flour, cooking spray, brown sugar, cinnamon, butter

Pear Crisp

Grocery List

- ☐ 4 (15-ounce) cans sliced pears in light syrup
- ☐ 1 (17.5-ounce) box oatmeal cookie mix
- ☐ 1 stick light butter
- ☐ Check staples: cooking spray, flour

prep: 8 minutes • **cook:** 18 minutes   *PointsPlus* value per serving: 10

Cooking spray
4   (15-ounce) cans sliced pears in light syrup, drained
2   teaspoons all-purpose flour
¼   cup cold light stick butter, cut into ¼-inch cubes
1½ cups oatmeal cookie mix

1. Preheat oven to 425°.

2. Coat an 8-inch square baking dish with cooking spray. Combine pear slices and flour in prepared dish, tossing to coat.

3. Combine butter and cookie mix in a bowl, rubbing with fingers until mixture resembles coarse meal; sprinkle over pears.

4. Bake at 425° for 18 minutes or until topping is golden. **Yield:** 6 servings (serving size: ½ cup).

Per serving: CALORIES 347; FAT 5.9g (sat 2.3g, mono 0g, poly 0.9g); PROTEIN 3.6g; CARB 76.6g; FIBER 5.9g; CHOL 10mg; IRON 1.4mg; SODIUM 217mg; CALC 14mg

Caramelized Pineapple Sundaes

Grocery List

- ☐ 1 pineapple
- ☐ 1 stick light butter
- ☐ 1 pint caramel light ice cream
- ☐ 1 (4.5-ounce) can toasted macadamia nuts
- ☐ Check staples: sugar

prep: 4 minutes • **cook:** 8 minutes   *PointsPlus* value per serving: 8

Cooking the pineapple over high heat caramelizes it quickly, but watch it closely so it doesn't burn. You may substitute vanilla light ice cream for the caramel, if desired.

1   cored fresh pineapple, cut lengthwise into 8 wedges
¼   cup sugar
1   tablespoon light stick butter
1   cup caramel light ice cream
¼   cup toasted macadamia nuts, chopped

1. Place pineapple in a large bowl; sprinkle with sugar, and toss to coat.

2. Melt butter in a large nonstick skillet over high heat. Add pineapple to pan. Cook, turning often, 8 minutes or until golden. Remove pineapple from pan, and place in shallow dishes. Top each with ice cream, and sprinkle with nuts. **Yield:** 4 servings (serving size: 2 pineapple wedges, ¼ cup ice cream, and 1 tablespoon nuts).

Per serving: CALORIES 298; FAT 9.3g (sat 2.2g, mono 6.2g, poly 0.1g); PROTEIN 3g; CARB 54.7g; FIBER 3.9g; CHOL 6.3mg; IRON 0.9mg; SODIUM 50.3mg; CALC 65mg

Peanut Butter–Chocolate Ice Cream

prep: 6 minutes • **cook:** 16 minutes • **other:** 3 hours and 30 minutes

PointsPlus value per serving: 7

1⅓ cups sugar
⅓ cup cocoa
2½ cups 2% reduced-fat milk, divided
3 large egg yolks, lightly beaten
½ cup fat-free half-and-half
½ cup reduced-fat creamy peanut butter

1. Combine sugar and cocoa in a medium saucepan; add 1 cup milk, stirring with a whisk. Cook over medium heat 4 minutes or until hot. Gradually add about one-fourth hot milk mixture to eggs, stirring constantly with whisk. Add egg mixture to remaining hot milk mixture, stirring constantly.
2. Add remaining 1½ cups milk, half-and-half, and peanut butter to hot milk mixture in pan, stirring with a whisk until smooth. Cook 12 minutes over medium heat or until mixture reaches 160°, stirring constantly with whisk. Transfer mixture to a bowl. Cover and chill at least 1 hour, stirring occasionally.
3. Pour mixture into the freezer can of a 4-quart ice-cream freezer, and freeze according to manufacturer's instructions. Spoon ice cream into a freezer-safe container. Cover and freeze 2 hours or until firm. **Yield:** 9 servings (serving size: ½ cup).

Per serving: CALORIES 273; FAT 8.5g (sat 2.5g, mono 3.5g, poly 1.7g); PROTEIN 7.7g; CARB 43g; FIBER 1.5g; CHOL 67mg; IRON 0.9mg; SODIUM 157mg; CALC 107mg

Grocery List

- ☐ 1 (8-ounce) carton fat-free half-and-half
- ☐ 1 (12-ounce) or smaller jar reduced-fat creamy peanut butter
- ☐ Check staples: sugar, cocoa, 2% reduced fat milk, eggs

Chai Tea Latte Ice Cream

prep: 2 minutes • **cook:** 3 minutes • **other:** 1 hour and 55 minutes

PointsPlus value per serving: 5

If you're a fan of the chai lattes at your local coffeehouse, you're going to love this ice cream. It's ultra-creamy and fragrantly spiced and is the perfect ending to a spicy Indian- or Thai-style meal.

Grocery List

- ☐ 1 (20-count) box chai tea
- ☐ 1 vanilla bean
- ☐ 1 (12-ounce) can evaporated fat-free milk
- ☐ 1 (1-ounce) jar ground ginger
- ☐ 1 (1-ounce) jar ground cardamom
- ☐ 1 (1-ounce) jar ground nutmeg
- ☐ 1 (1-ounce) jar ground cloves
- ☐ Check staples: 2% reduced-fat milk, sugar, cornstarch, cinnamon, salt, pepper, eggs

2 cups 2% reduced-fat milk
8 chai tea bags
1 (3-inch) piece vanilla bean, split lengthwise
1 (12-ounce) can evaporated fat-free milk
⅔ cup sugar
2 tablespoons cornstarch
¼ teaspoon ground ginger
¼ teaspoon ground cinnamon
⅛ teaspoon salt
⅛ teaspoon ground cardamom
⅛ teaspoon ground nutmeg
⅛ teaspoon ground cloves
Dash of black pepper
2 large egg yolks

1. Cook 2% milk over medium-high heat in a heavy saucepan to 180° or until tiny bubbles form around edge (do not boil). Remove from heat. Add tea bags and vanilla bean; let stand 15 minutes. Remove and discard tea bags, pressing liquid out of bags. Remove vanilla bean; scrape seeds from bean into milk mixture, and discard bean. Add evaporated milk, stirring with a whisk.

2. Combine sugar and next 9 ingredients in a medium bowl. Gradually add milk mixture to sugar mixture, stirring constantly with whisk. Return milk mixture to pan. Cook over medium heat until mixture thickens and coats the back of a spoon, stirring constantly. Transfer mixture to a bowl. Place over an ice bath, and cool completely, stirring occasionally.

3. Pour milk mixture into the freezer can of a 2- to 3-quart ice-cream freezer, and freeze according to manufacturer's instructions. Spoon ice cream into a freezer-safe container. Cover and freeze 1 hour or until firm. Yield: 7 servings (serving size: about ½ cup).

Per serving: CALORIES 171; FAT 2.7g (sat 1.4g, mono 1g, poly 0.3g); PROTEIN 6.1g; CARB 31.9g; FIBER 0.1g; CHOL 58mg; IRON 0.2mg; SODIUM 123mg; CALC 211mg

Layered Amaretti–Ice Cream Loaf

prep: 10 minutes • **cook:** 2 minutes • **other:** 8 hours

PointsPlus value per serving: 6

Our Test Kitchen staff raved over this layered ice cream dessert, and your guests will, too.

⅓ cup sliced almonds, toasted
2 cups French chocolate fat-free ice cream, softened
1 cup crushed amaretti cookies, divided (about 14 cookies)
2 cups caramel-praline frozen yogurt, softened
2 cups coffee light ice cream, softened
10 tablespoons sugar-free hot fudge topping

1. Line an 8 x 4–inch loaf pan with plastic wrap, letting plastic wrap extend over sides of pan. Sprinkle toasted almonds evenly in pan. Carefully spoon chocolate ice cream over almonds, and spread evenly. Top chocolate ice cream with ½ cup crushed cookies. Spoon frozen yogurt over cookies, and spread. Top frozen yogurt evenly with remaining ½ cup cookies. Spoon coffee ice cream over cookies, and spread evenly.

2. Cover with plastic wrap, and freeze 8 hours or until firm.

3. Invert pan onto a serving plate, and remove plastic wrap. Cut into vertical slices; serve with fudge topping. **Yield:** 10 servings (serving size: 1 slice dessert and 1 tablespoon topping).

Per serving: CALORIES 264; FAT 6.3g (sat 2.5g, mono 1.5g, poly 0.5g); PROTEIN 5.9g; CARB 47.7g; FIBER 2.7g; CHOL 30mg; IRON 1.2mg; SODIUM 113mg; CALC 168mg

Grocery List

- ☐ 1 (10-ounce) bag sliced almonds
- ☐ 1 (1.5-quart) French chocolate fat-free ice cream
- ☐ 1 (7-ounce) bag amaretti cookies
- ☐ 1 (1.5-quart) caramel-praline frozen yogurt
- ☐ 1 (1.5-quart) coffee light ice cream
- ☐ 1 (11.75-ounce) jar sugar-free hot fudge topping

Caramel-Praline Ice-Cream Cake

prep: 4 minutes • **cook:** 10 minutes • **other:** 3 hours and 2 minutes

PointsPlus value per serving: 6

A homemade praline adds extra flavor and crunch to caramel ice cream in this highly rated dessert. Swirl each bite of cake into the ice cream as it melts to soak up the "cream."

Cooking spray
¼ cup sugar
 2 tablespoons water
¼ cup chopped pecans, toasted
Dash of salt
½ (15-ounce) loaf angel food cake, cut into ¾-inch-thick slices
 4 cups caramel light ice cream, softened

1. Line a baking sheet with parchment paper; coat with cooking spray. Combine sugar and water in a small nonstick skillet. Cook over medium-high heat 5 minutes or until edges are golden. Stir in pecans and salt; remove from heat, and quickly spread on prepared pan. Place in freezer to cool for 2 minutes. Carefully peel parchment from praline. Place praline in a heavy-duty zip-top plastic bag. Coarsely crush praline with a rolling pin.

2. While praline cooks, line a 9 x 5–inch loaf pan with foil allowing foil to extend over edge of pan.

3. Place half of cake slices in a single layer in bottom of prepared pan. Spread 2 cups ice cream over cake. Sprinkle ice cream with praline. Layer remaining 2 cups ice cream over praline, and top with remaining cake. Cover and freeze 3 hours or until firm. Lift cake out of pan; peel off foil. Cut into 8 slices. **Yield:** 8 servings (serving size: 1 slice).

Per serving: CALORIES 230; FAT 4.6g (sat 1.7g, mono 1.4g, poly 0.7g); PROTEIN 3.8g; CARB 44.6g; FIBER 0.3g; CHOL 5mg; IRON 0.1mg; SODIUM 179mg; CALC 62mg

pictured on page 128

Chocolate-Raspberry-Coconut Cake

prep: 5 minutes • **other:** 10 minutes   *PointsPlus* value per serving: 7

1	(11-ounce) frozen organic chocolate cake
¼	cup low-sugar red raspberry preserves
1⅔	cups frozen reduced-calorie whipped topping, thawed
½	cup flaked sweetened coconut

1. Remove cake from freezer. Unwrap and let stand 10 minutes at room temperature to thaw slightly for easier cutting. Cut cake horizontally into 3 equal layers. Place bottom layer on a serving plate. Spread 2 tablespoons preserves over cake layer. Top with center cake layer, and spread with remaining 2 tablespoons preserves. Replace top of cake.
2. Spread whipped topping over top and sides of cake; press coconut into topping. Serve immediately, or cover and freeze at least 1 hour. **Yield:** 6 servings (serving size: 1 slice).

Per serving: CALORIES 260; FAT 10.6g (sat 5g, mono 4.2g, poly 0.7g); PROTEIN 2.1g; CARB 39.8g; FIBER 1.3g; CHOL 0mg; IRON 1.2mg; SODIUM 143mg; CALC 1mg

Grocery List
- [ ] 1 (11-ounce) frozen organic chocolate cake
- [ ] 1 (10.25-ounce) jar low-sugar red raspberry preserves
- [ ] 1 (8-ounce) carton frozen reduced-calorie whipped topping
- [ ] 1 (7-ounce) bag flaked sweetened coconut

Quick Tiramisu

prep: 13 minutes   *PointsPlus* value per serving: 5

1	cup ready-to-eat classic cheesecake filling
¾	cup coffee-flavored liqueur, divided
1½	cups frozen fat-free whipped topping, thawed
2	(3-ounce) packages cake-style ladyfingers
¼	teaspoon unsweetened cocoa (optional)

1. Combine cheesecake filling and 1 tablespoon liqueur in a bowl, stirring until blended. Fold in whipped topping.
2. Split ladyfingers in half lengthwise. Arrange 24 ladyfinger halves in a single layer in an 11 x 7–inch baking dish. Drizzle half of remaining liqueur over ladyfingers. Spread half of cheesecake mixture over ladyfingers. Repeat procedure with remaining ladyfingers, liqueur, and cheesecake mixture. Sprinkle with cocoa, if desired. Serve immediately, or cover and chill. **Yield:** 10 servings (serving size: 1/10 of tiramisu).

Per serving: CALORIES 177; FAT 6.4g (sat 3.8g, mono 1.9g, poly 0.3g); PROTEIN 2.5g; CARB 25.4g; FIBER 0.2g; CHOL 52.7mg; IRON 0.4mg; SODIUM 216mg; CALC 46mg

Grocery List
- [ ] 1 (24.3-ounce) container ready-to-eat classic cheesecake filling
- [ ] Coffee-flavored liqueur
- [ ] 1 (8-ounce) carton frozen fat-free whipped topping
- [ ] 2 (3-ounce) packages ladyfingers
- [ ] Check staples: cocoa (optional)

Pumpkin Gingerbread Trifles

prep: 10 minutes • **cook:** 10 minutes • **other:** 6 minutes

PointsPlus value per serving: 8

Cooking spray
1½   cups gingerbread mix
⅔   cup water
1   large egg white
1   (15-ounce) can pumpkin
2   cups frozen reduced-calorie whipped topping, thawed and divided

1. Preheat oven to 350°.
2. Coat an 8-inch square baking pan with cooking spray. Combine gingerbread mix, ⅔ cup water, and egg white in a medium bowl, whisking until smooth. Pour batter into prepared pan.
3. Bake at 350° for 10 to 12 minutes or until a wooden pick inserted in center comes out clean. Cool in pan 2 minutes; remove from pan, and cool 4 minutes on a wire rack.
4. Place pumpkin in a medium bowl; fold in 1½ cups whipped topping.
5. Cut gingerbread evenly into 36 (1-inch) squares. Place 3 gingerbread squares in each of 6 (6-ounce) glasses. Top with about ¼ cup pumpkin mixture. Repeat layers. Top trifles evenly with remaining ½ cup whipped topping. Cover and chill until ready to serve. **Yield:** 6 servings (serving size: 1 trifle and 4 teaspoons topping).

Per serving: CALORIES 293; FAT 8.5g (sat 4.1g, mono 3.1g, poly 0.7g); PROTEIN 3.7g; CARB 52g; FIBER 6.5g; CHOL 0.5mg; IRON 2.5mg; SODIUM 415mg; CALC 79mg

Grocery List

- ☐ 1 (14.5-ounce) box gingerbread mix
- ☐ 1 (15-ounce) can pumpkin
- ☐ 1 (8-ounce) carton frozen reduced-calorie whipped topping
- ☐ Check staples: cooking spray, eggs

Triple Chocolate–Toffee Trifle

prep: 14 minutes

PointsPlus value per serving: 2

1   (11-ounce) frozen organic chocolate cake
1½   cups prepared chocolate pudding
1½   cups frozen fat-free whipped topping, thawed and divided
½   cup almond brickle chips, divided
8   ounces dark chocolate pudding

1. Remove cake from freezer. Unwrap and let stand 10 minutes at room temperature to thaw slightly for easier cutting. Cut cake into ½-inch-thick slices; cut slices into ½-inch cubes. Place half of cake cubes in a 2-quart trifle bowl.
2. Spoon 1½ cups chocolate pudding and ¾ cup whipped topping over cake cubes in bowl. Sprinkle with ¼ cup brickle chips. Top with remaining cake cubes. Top with dark chocolate pudding. Spoon remaining ¾ cup whipped topping over pudding. Sprinkle with remaining ¼ cup brickle chips. Cover and chill until ready to serve. **Yield:** 14 servings (serving size: ½ cup).

Per serving: CALORIES 125; FAT 4.6g (sat 2g, mono 0.5g, poly 0.1g); PROTEIN 1.7g; CARB 18.8g; FIBER 0.8g; CHOL 6.8mg; IRON 0.5mg; SODIUM 126mg; CALC 36mg

Grocery List

- ☐ 1 (11-ounce) frozen organic chocolate cake
- ☐ 1 (22-ounce) container prepared chocolate pudding
- ☐ 1 (8-ounce) carton frozen fat-free whipped topping
- ☐ 1 (8-ounce) bag almond brickle chips
- ☐ Dark chocolate pudding cups

Lemon Cheesecake

prep: 22 minutes • **cook:** 1 hour • **other:** 9 hours

PointsPlus value per serving: 7

The gingersnap cookie crust adds a delightful spice flavor to the otherwise sweet and tart cheesecake filling.

Grocery List

- ☐ 1 (8-ounce) bag gingersnap cookies
- ☐ 1 (16-ounce) carton 1% low-fat cottage cheese
- ☐ 1 (8-ounce) package light process cream cheese
- ☐ 3 lemons
- ☐ Check staples: butter, cooking spray, sugar, flour, eggs

- 1 cup gingersnap cookie crumbs
- 3 tablespoons light stick butter, melted
- Cooking spray
- 2 cups 1% low-fat cottage cheese
- 1 (8-ounce) package light process cream cheese
- 1 cup sugar, divided
- 4.5 ounces all-purpose flour (about 1 cup), divided
- 1 large egg
- 2 large egg whites
- 1 tablespoon plus 1 teaspoon grated fresh lemon rind, divided
- 2 tablespoons fresh lemon juice, divided
- 1 tablespoon light stick butter, softened

1. Preheat oven to 325°.

2. Combine gingersnap crumbs and 3 tablespoons butter. Press on bottom of an 8-inch springform pan coated with cooking spray.

3. Place cottage cheese and cream cheese in a blender or food processor; cover and process 1½ minutes or until smooth, stopping once to scrape down sides. Add ¾ cup sugar, ¼ cup flour, egg, egg whites, 1 tablespoon lemon rind, and 1 tablespoon lemon juice; process until blended. Pour into prepared pan.

4. Bake at 325° for 45 minutes (center will be soft). Combine remaining ¼ cup sugar, ¾ cup flour, 1 teaspoon lemon rind, 1 tablespoon lemon juice, and 1 tablespoon butter in a small bowl, stirring until mixture resembles coarse meal. Without moving cheesecake, sprinkle flour mixture carefully over cheesecake. Bake an additional 15 minutes. Turn off oven; partially open oven door. Leave cheesecake in oven 1 hour. Remove from oven; cool on a wire rack. Cover and chill 8 hours. **Yield:** 12 servings (serving size: 1 slice).

Per serving: CALORIES 244; FAT 9.6g (sat 5.4g, mono 2.5g, poly 0.5g); PROTEIN 8.9g; CARB 30.8g; FIBER 0.4g; CHOL 41mg; IRON 1.3mg; SODIUM 286mg; CALC 55mg

White Chocolate Mousse with Strawberries

prep: 3 minutes • **cook:** 1 minute • **other:** 17 minutes

PointsPlus value per serving: 8

8   ounces premium white baking chocolate, chopped
3   tablespoons fat-free half-and-half
1   (8-ounce) carton frozen fat-free whipped topping, thawed
1   (10-ounce) package frozen strawberry halves in light syrup, thawed

1. Place chocolate and half-and-half in a medium-sized microwave-safe bowl. Microwave at HIGH 1 minute. Stir until chocolate melts. Freeze 5 minutes.
2. Gently fold whipped topping into chocolate mixture. Spoon ½ cup chocolate mixture into each of 6 serving dishes. Cover and freeze 12 minutes. Remove from freezer, and refrigerate until ready to serve. Spoon strawberries in syrup evenly over desserts. **Yield:** 6 servings (serving size: ½ cup mousse and 3 tablespoons strawberries in syrup).
Note: Mousse may be refrigerated for 2 hours instead of freezing for 12 minutes.

Per serving: CALORIES 309; FAT 12.2g (sat 7.3g, mono 3.5g, poly 0.4g); PROTEIN 2.5g; CARB 45.7g; FIBER 1g; CHOL 8mg; IRON 0.3mg; SODIUM 63mg; CALC 86mg

Mocha Mousse

prep: 5 minutes • **cook:** 2 minutes • **other:** 1 hour and 30 minutes

PointsPlus value per serving: 6

Be sure to cook your milk only until small bubbles appear around the edge of the pan. Scalding your milk can leave you with an overcooked taste and a mousse that does not set up correctly.

¼   cup fat-free milk
2   tablespoons instant coffee granules
4   ounces bittersweet chocolate, chopped
2   cups frozen fat-free whipped topping, thawed

1. Cook milk in a small heavy saucepan over medium-high heat until tiny bubbles form around edge (do not boil). Remove from heat; add coffee and chocolate, stirring until chocolate melts. Cool to room temperature.
2. Fold whipped topping into chocolate mixture. Cover and chill until ready to serve. **Yield:** 4 servings (serving size: ½ cup).

Per serving: CALORIES 211; FAT 12.2g (sat 6.1g, mono 3g, poly 0.3g); PROTEIN 2.7g; CARB 27.6g; FIBER 2g; CHOL 0.3mg; IRON 0.8mg; SODIUM 27mg; CALC 21mg

Milk Chocolate–Hazelnut Mousse

prep: 14 minutes • **cook:** 1 minute • **other:** 6 minutes

PointsPlus **value per serving: 7**

½   cup chocolate-hazelnut spread
3   large pasteurized egg yolks
3   large pasteurized egg whites
1½ cups frozen reduced-calorie whipped topping, thawed
¼   cup coarsely chopped hazelnuts, toasted

1. Place chocolate-hazelnut spread in a medium-sized microwave-safe bowl. Microwave at HIGH 40 seconds or until melted, stirring after 20 seconds. Let cool 1 minute; add egg yolks, stirring with a whisk until smooth.
2. Place egg whites in a medium bowl; beat with a mixer at high speed until stiff peaks form. Gently fold egg whites into egg yolk mixture; fold in whipped topping.
3. Divide mousse evenly among 6 (6-ounce) custard cups. Sprinkle with hazelnuts. Freeze 5 minutes before serving. **Yield:** 6 servings (serving size: ½ cup).

Per serving: CALORIES 241; FAT 15.2g (sat 10.1g, mono 3.3g, poly 0.8g); PROTEIN 5.8g; CARB 20.8g; FIBER 1.8g; CHOL 106mg; IRON 1.8mg; SODIUM 59mg; CALC 59mg

Grocery List

☐ 1 (13-ounce) or smaller jar chocolate-hazelnut spread
☐ 1 (8-ounce) carton frozen reduced-calorie whipped topping
☐ 2 ounces hazelnuts
☐ Check staples: eggs

Blackberry-Buttermilk Sherbet

prep: 8 minutes • **cook:** 5 minutes • **other:** 3 hour and 30 minutes

PointsPlus **value per serving: 3**

¾   cup superfine sugar, divided
3   cups blackberries
1   tablespoon water
2   cups low-fat buttermilk

1. Combine ¼ cup sugar, blackberries, and 1 tablespoon water in a medium saucepan. Bring to a boil; boil 4 minutes or until sugar dissolves, stirring occasionally. Pour blackberry mixture through a sieve into a bowl, pressing with back of a spoon to remove as much liquid as possible; discard solids. Cool juice mixture completely. Cover and chill 2 hours.
2. Combine juice mixture, remaining ½ cup sugar, and buttermilk. Pour mixture into the freezer can of an ice-cream freezer; prepare according to manufacturer's instructions. Spoon ice cream into a freezer-safe container; cover and freeze 1 hour or until firm. **Yield:** 8 servings (serving size: ½ cup).

Per serving: CALORIES 124; FAT 0.9g (sat 0.4g, mono 0.2g, poly 0.2g); PROTEIN 3g; CARB 27.3g; FIBER 0g; CHOL 3.8mg; IRON 0.3mg; SODIUM 68mg; CALC 78mg

Grocery List

☐ 2 pints blackberries
☐ 1 pint low-fat buttermilk
☐ Check staples: superfine sugar

Affogato

prep: 5 minutes • **cook:** 5 minutes **PointsPlus** value per serving: 3

Grocery List

- [ ] 1 (2-ounce) jar instant espresso granules
- [ ] 1 pint chocolate or vanilla bean light ice cream
- [ ] 1 (8-ounce) carton frozen reduced-calorie whipped topping
- [ ] 1 small bag (1 tablespoon) dark chocolate–covered espresso beans

1 cup boiling water
2 tablespoons instant espresso granules
2 cups chocolate or vanilla bean light ice cream
¼ cup frozen reduced-calorie whipped topping, thawed
1 tablespoon dark chocolate–covered espresso beans, crushed

1. Combine boiling water and espresso granules, stirring with a whisk until espresso dissolves.
2. Spoon ice cream into 4 glasses; drizzle each with hot espresso, and top with whipped topping. Sprinkle each serving with crushed espresso beans. Serve immediately. **Yield:** 4 servings (serving size: ½ cup ice cream, ¼ cup hot espresso, 1 tablespoon whipped topping, and about 1 teaspoon crushed espresso beans).

Per serving: CALORIES 134; FAT 4.8g (sat 3g, mono 1.1g, poly 0.1g); PROTEIN 3.3g; CARB 18.7g; FIBER 1.1g; CHOL 20.3mg; IRON 0.1mg; SODIUM 49mg; CALC 65mg

Mojito'd Melon Mix-Up

prep: 7 minutes

PointsPlus value per serving: 3

Grocery List

- [ ] 1 small watermelon
- [ ] 12 large limes
- [ ] 1 small bunch mint
- [ ] 1 (8-ounce) bottle diet tonic water
- [ ] Light rum or vodka
- [ ] Check staples: "measures-like-sugar" calorie-free sweetener

The classic ingredients of the Cuban mojito cocktail are poured over watermelon cubes for a quick and refreshing dessert that earned our Test Kitchen's highest rating.

4 cups cubed seeded watermelon
1 teaspoon grated fresh lime rind
6 tablespoons fresh lime juice
¼ cup light rum or vodka
¼ cup "measures-like-sugar" calorie-free sweetener
¼ cup chopped fresh mint
1 cup diet tonic water, chilled

1. Combine first 6 ingredients in a large bowl; toss gently. Cover and chill until ready to serve.
2. Spoon watermelon mixture evenly into small serving dishes or parfait glasses. Pour tonic water over each serving. Serve immediately. **Yield:** 4 servings (serving size: 1 cup watermelon cubes, about 2½ tablespoons rum mixture, and ¼ cup tonic water).

Per serving: CALORIES 91; FAT 0.3g (sat 0g, mono 0.1g, poly 0.1g); PROTEIN 1.1g; CARB 15.2g; FIBER 0.9g; CHOL 0mg; IRON 0.5mg; SODIUM 11mg; CALC 18mg

Chewy Lemon-Almond Cookies

prep: 5 minutes • **cook:** 15 minutes

PointsPlus value per serving: 1

Grocery List

☐ 1 (7-ounce) tube almond paste

☐ 1 lemon

☐ Check staples: sugar, eggs

The sweet flavor of almond paste, made from sugar and ground almonds, is offset by the lemon rind in these cookies. Try serving these as an afternoon snack or with a warm cup of tea to end a meal.

   1   (7-ounce) tube almond paste
   1   cup sugar
   2   large egg whites
1½   teaspoons grated fresh lemon rind

1. Preheat oven to 300°.

2. Line 2 large baking sheets with parchment paper. Pulse almond paste and sugar in a blender or food processor 15 times or until paste is crumbly. Add egg whites and lemon rind; process 10 seconds or until smooth.

3. Spoon batter, 1½ teaspoons at a time, 1 inch apart onto prepared baking sheets. Bake at 300° for 8 minutes, placing 1 pan on middle oven rack and other on lower oven rack. Switch pans, and bake an additional 7 minutes or until puffed and golden.

4. Cool cookies on pans 1 minute. Remove cookies from pans, and cool completely on a wire rack. **Yield:** 40 servings (serving size: 1 cookie).

Per serving: CALORIES 41; FAT 0.9g (sat 0g, mono 0.8g, poly 0g); PROTEIN 0.6g; CARB 8g; FIBER 0.3g; CHOL 0mg; IRON 0.1mg; SODIUM 3mg; CALC 6mg

pictured on page 127

Pecan Pie Squares

prep: 10 minutes • **cook:** 53 minutes

PointsPlus value per serving: 6

Take this bar-cookie version of pecan pie to your next holiday gathering. These squares have a rich, buttery crust and a sweet nutty filling that earned them our Test Kitchen's highest rating. But they have only one-third the calories and 75% less fat than a slice of traditional pecan pie.

Grocery List

- ☐ 1 (16-ounce) bottle light-colored corn syrup
- ☐ 1 (8-ounce) bag chopped pecans
- ☐ Check staples: flour, sugar, salt, butter, cooking spray, brown sugar, eggs, vanilla extract

- 4.5 ounces all-purpose flour (about 1 cup)
- ¼ cup granulated sugar
- ⅛ teaspoon salt
- ¼ cup light stick butter, cut into small pieces
- Cooking spray
- ¾ cup packed brown sugar
- 1 cup light-colored corn syrup
- 1 large egg
- 4 large egg whites
- ¾ cup finely chopped pecans
- 1 teaspoon vanilla extract

1. Preheat oven to 350°.

2. Lightly spoon flour into a dry measuring cup; level with a knife. Combine flour, granulated sugar, and salt in a medium bowl. Cut in butter with a pastry blender or 2 knives until mixture resembles coarse meal. Press flour mixture evenly into bottom of an 8-inch square baking pan coated with cooking spray using a piece of plastic wrap to press mixture firmly into pan. Remove plastic wrap. Bake at 350° for 20 minutes or until lightly browned.

3. Combine brown sugar and corn syrup in a medium saucepan; bring to a boil over medium heat, stirring gently.

4. Combine egg and egg whites in a medium bowl. Stir one-fourth of warm syrup mixture into eggs; add to remaining warm syrup mixture. Stir in pecans and vanilla. Pour mixture into crust.

5. Bake at 350° for 30 minutes or until set (the filling will puff up as it bakes but will deflate as it becomes set). Remove from oven; cool completely in pan on a wire rack. Cut into squares. **Yield:** 16 servings (serving size: 1 square).

Per serving: CALORIES 213; FAT 7g (sat 2.2g, mono 3g, poly 1.3g); PROTEIN 2.6g; CARB 37g; FIBER 0.7g; CHOL 19mg; IRON 0.6mg; SODIUM 79mg; CALC 19mg

S'mores Slabs

prep: 6 minutes • **cook:** 4 minutes • **other:** 2 hours

PointsPlus value per serving: 6

Cooking spray
⅔ cup semisweet chocolate chips
⅓ cup light stick butter
¼ cup water
3 cups graham cracker crumbs (about 14 sheets), divided
1½ cups miniature marshmallows

1. Line an 8 x 4–inch loaf pan with parchment paper allowing paper to extend over edge of pan. Coat parchment with cooking spray.
2. Combine chocolate, butter, and ¼ cup water in a medium saucepan. Cook over medium heat 4 minutes or until chocolate melts and mixture is smooth, stirring occasionally.
3. While chocolate mixture cooks, place 2½ cups graham cracker crumbs and marshmallows in a large bowl. Stir hot chocolate mixture into graham cracker mixture. Stir in remaining ½ cup crumbs. Press chocolate mixture into prepared pan. Cover and chill 2 hours or until set.
4. Remove loaf from pan; peel off parchment, and cut into 12 slices. **Yield:** 12 servings (serving size: 1 slice).

Per serving: CALORIES 230; FAT 4.6g (sat 1.7g, mono 1.4g, poly 0.7g); PROTEIN 3.8g; CARB 44.6g; FIBER 0.3g; CHOL 5mg; IRON 0.1mg; SODIUM 62.5mg; CALC 179mg

Grocery List

- ☐ 1 (8-ounce) bag semisweet chocolate chips
- ☐ 1 (14.4-ounce) box graham crackers
- ☐ 1 (10.5-ounce) bag miniature marshmallows
- ☐ Check staples: cooking spray, butter

No-Bake Chocolate-Oat Drop Cookies

prep: 5 minutes • **cook:** 5 minutes   *PointsPlus* value per serving: 3

3 cups old-fashioned rolled oats
2 cups sugar
½ cup 1% chocolate low-fat milk
⅓ cup chocolate-hazelnut spread

1. Line a large baking sheet with wax paper. Place oats in a large bowl.
2. Bring sugar, chocolate milk, and hazelnut spread to a boil in a medium saucepan over high heat, stirring constantly with a whisk; boil 1½ minutes, stirring constantly with a whisk. Remove from heat; pour chocolate mixture over oats, stirring to coat. Working quickly, drop oat mixture by tablespoonfuls, 1 inch apart, onto prepared baking sheet. Cool completely. **Yield:** 24 servings (serving size: 1 cookie).

Per serving: CALORIES 128; FAT 2g (sat 1.3g, mono 0.3g, poly 0.3g); PROTEIN 1.6g; CARB 27.7g; FIBER 1.2g; CHOL 0.2mg; IRON 0.6mg; SODIUM 6.2mg; CALC 10.8mg

Grocery List

- ☐ 1 (18-ounce) container old-fashioned rolled oats
- ☐ 1 pint 1% chocolate low-fat milk
- ☐ 1 (13-ounce) jar or smaller chocolate-hazelnut spread
- ☐ Check staples: sugar

Chocolate Malt Crème Brûlée

prep: 18 minutes • **cook:** 1 hour and 16 minutes • **other:** 4 hours

PointsPlus value per serving: 6

This version of crème brûlée—French for "burnt cream"—uses malted milk powder to give the smooth, creamy custard a rich flavor. This dessert earned our Test Kitchen's highest rating.

    2   cups 1% chocolate low-fat milk
    ¼   cup chocolate malted milk powder
    ½   teaspoon vanilla extract
    3   ounces milk chocolate, chopped
    4   large egg yolks
    Cooking spray
    6   teaspoons sugar

1. Preheat oven to 300°.
2. Combine first 3 ingredients in a medium saucepan, and cook mixture over medium heat 5 to 6 minutes or until tiny bubbles form around edge (do not boil). Remove from heat, and add chocolate, stirring until chocolate melts.
3. Place egg yolks in a large bowl, stirring with a whisk. Gradually add hot milk mixture to yolks, stirring with a whisk until well blended.
4. Pour chocolate mixture evenly into 6 (4-ounce) ramekins or custard cups coated with cooking spray. Place ramekins in a 13 x 9–inch baking dish; add hot water to pan to a depth of 1 inch. Bake, uncovered, at 300° for 1 hour and 5 minutes or until center barely moves when ramekin is touched. Remove ramekins from pan; cool completely on a wire rack. Cover and chill at least 4 hours or overnight.
5. Sprinkle 1 teaspoon sugar evenly over each custard. Holding a kitchen blowtorch about 2 inches from the top of 1 custard, heat the sugar, moving the torch back and forth, until sugar is completely melted and caramelized (about 1 minute). Repeat procedure with remaining custards. Serve immediately or within 1 hour.
Yield: 6 servings (serving size: 1 crème brûlée).
Note: If you don't have a kitchen blowtorch, you can prepare the sugar topping on the stove top. Cook the sugar in a small saucepan over medium heat 5 to 8 minutes or until golden. Don't stir while the sugar is cooking; this will allow the sugar to caramelize. Working quickly, evenly drizzle the sugar mixture over the cold custards, and spread into a thin layer using a rubber spatula. The caramel will harden quickly.

Per serving: CALORIES 241; FAT 9.3g (sat 5.2g, mono 2.9g, poly 0.9g); PROTEIN 7.3g; CARB 31.7g; FIBER 0.8g; CHOL 133mg; IRON 0.8mg; SODIUM 126mg; CALC 180mg

Index

Almond Cookies, Chewy Lemon-, 185
Almond Oatmeal, Raisin and, 57
Appetizers
  Bacon-Chile-Cheese Crescents, 11
  Black Bean Cakes, 22
  Caponata, Italian Vegetable, 23
  Crostini
    Cherry, Goat Cheese, and Pistachio
      Crostini, Honey-Drizzled, 13
    Goat Cheese–Green Olive Tapenade
      Crostini, 14
    Manchego and Honeyed Orange Relish,
      Crostini with, 15
    Red Pepper Pesto Crostini, 12
  Croustades, Smoked Salmon, 18
  Dips
    Dill Feta Dip, Lemony, 8
    Hummus, Roasted Red Pepper and
      Chipotle, 9
    White Bean Dip, 8
  Marinated Goat Cheese, 17
  Pear and Swiss Triangles, 16
  Pork Sliders with Sweet Chipotle-Peach
    Sauce, Spicy, 20
  Pot Stickers with Spicy Dipping Sauce,
    Turkey, 21
  Spanakopita Bites, 16
  Spread, Chicken-Pesto, 10
  Tuna Rounds, Black Pepper and
    Sesame–Crusted, 19
Apple-Pecan Chicken Salad, 89
Apples, Creamy Rosemary, 160
Apricot-Glazed Chicken, 144
Artichokes
  Couscous, Mediterranean, 157
  Eggs with Tomatoes and Artichokes,
    Baked, 53
Asparagus Frittata, Leek and, 54
Avocados
  Dressing, Grilled Tuna Salad with
    Avocado-Wasabi, 93
  Greens with Grapefruit, Hearts of Palm,
    Avocado, and Queso Fresco, Mixed, 82
  Sandwiches, Fried Egg and Avocado Bagel, 70
  Soup, Avocado and Cucumber, 61

Bacon
  Collard Greens with Figs and Bacon
    Crumbles, 156

Crescents, Bacon-Chile-Cheese, 11
  Sandwiches with Basil Mayonnaise,
    Bacon and Egg, 55
  Spaghetti Carbonara, 131
  Spiced Bacon, 57
Banana-Oatmeal Bread, 30
BBQ Chicken Pizza, 144
Beans
  Black Bean Cakes, 22
  Falafel Sandwiches with Tahini
    Sauce, 72
  Green Bean, Roasted Beet, and Feta
    Salad, 95
  Green Beans, Mustard Potatoes
    and, 155
  Hummus, Roasted Red Pepper and
    Chipotle, 9
  Salad, Marinated Bean, 96
  Soup, Tuscan Squash and Bean, 65
  Spaghetti Squash with Tomatoes and
    Beans, 104
  White Bean Dip, 8
Beef. *See also* Beef, Ground.
  Roast Beef Stroganoff, Simple, 132
  Steaks
    Pan-Seared Steaks with Balsamic–Pepper
      Jelly Sauce, 137
    Salad with Figs, Warm Beef, 87
    Sandwiches with Horseradish Mayonnaise,
      Steak, 78
    Tenderloin with Horseradish Cream Sauce,
      Beef, 136
    Tostadas, Beef, 134
Beef, Ground
  Casserole, Mexican, 135
  Shepherd's Pie, Speedy, 133
Beet, and Feta Salad, Green Bean, Roasted, 95
Beverages
  Alcoholic
    Punch, Barbados, 24
    Sangria, Fruity White, 25
  Fizz, Pomegranate-Ginger, 24
  Hot Spiced Chocolate, 26
  Milk Shakes, Strawberry–Piña Colada, 25
  Slush, Strawberry-Cherry, 26
  Tea, Lemonade-Mint Iced, 12
  Tea, Sparkling Cranberry–Citrus Green, 14
Biscuits, Cream Cheese, 163
Biscuits, Orange, 28

Blackberry Buttermilk Sherbet, 183
Blueberries and Pecans, Hot Quinoa Cereal
  with, 56
Blueberry-Yogurt Muffins, 29
Bran Muffins, Apple Butter–, 163
Breads. *See also* Biscuits, Pancakes, Waffles.
  Biscotti, Parmesan-Prosciutto, 167
  Buns, Sticky, 165
  Crescents, Bacon-Chile-Cheese, 11
  Quick Bread, Poppy Seed, 166
  Yeast
    Flatbreads, Grilled Rosemary, 168
    Focaccia, Rosemary, 162
Broccoli with Gremolata, Roasted, 154
Brussels Sprouts with Cranberries and Bacon,
  Braised, 156
Bulgur and Pine Nut Salad, 100

Cakes
  Cheesecake, Lemon, 181
  Chocolate-Raspberry-Coconut Cake, 179
  Raspberry-Chocolate Tortes, 171
Caramel-Praline Ice Cream Cake, 178
Carrot Cake Pancakes with Cream Cheese
  Sauce, 49
Carrots, and Shallots, Roasted Fennel, 154
Casserole, Mexican, 135
Casserole, Turkey-Spaghetti, 150
Cereal with Blueberries and Pecans, Hot
  Quinoa, 56
Cheese. *See also* Appetizers.
  Biscotti, Parmesan-Prosciutto, 167
  Biscuits, Cream Cheese, 163
  Omelet with Goat Cheese, Garden, 52
  Salad, Date and Goat Cheese, 81
  Salad, Sun-Dried Tomato and Goat Cheese, 85
  Sauce, Cream Cheese, 49
  Swordfish, Cheese-Stuffed, 108
Cherries
  Crostini, Honey-Drizzled Cherry, Goat Cheese,
    and Pistachio, 13
  Sauce, Dark Cherry, 50
  Slush, Strawberry-Cherry, 26
Chicken
  Apricot-Glazed Chicken, 144
  Chowder, Poblano-Chicken, 68
  Curry, Chutney Chicken, 147
  Dumplings, Chicken and, 148
  Fig-Mustard Glaze, Chicken Breasts with, 146

Chicken *(continued)*

Ginger Chicken with Couscous, 143
Hoisin–Five Spice Chicken Thighs, 147
Panini, Grilled Chicken Caesar, 74
Pizza, BBQ Chicken, 144
Salads
Apple-Pecan Chicken Salad, 89
Curry Chicken Salad, 88
Green Goddess Chicken Salad, 89
Spicy Chicken Finger Salad, 90
Sandwiches, Cranberry-Chicken, 74
Soup, Southwestern Chicken and Rice, 69
Southwestern Fried Rice with Chicken, 145
Spread, Chicken Pesto, 10
Chocolate
Cookies, No-Bake Chocolate-Oat Drop, 187
Cake, Chocolate-Raspberry-Coconut, 179
Crème Brûlée, Chocolate Malt, 188
Hot Spiced Chocolate, 26
Ice Cream Loaf, Layered Amaretti–, 177
Ice Cream, Peanut Butter–Chocolate, 175
Mousse, Milk Chocolate–Hazelnut, 183
Mousse, Mocha, 182
Mousse with Strawberries, White
Chocolate, 182
S'mores Slabs, 187
Tortes, Raspberry-Chocolate, 171
Trifle, Triple Chocolate–Toffee, 180
Waffles with Dark Cherry Sauce,
Chocolate, 50
Chowder, Poblano-Chicken, 68
Clam Sauce, Linguine with Red, 129
Coconut Cake, Chocolate-Raspberry-, 179
Cookies
Lemon-Almond Cookies, Chewy, 185
No-Bake Chocolate-Oat Drop Cookies, 187
Pecan Pie Squares, 186
Corn, Red Peppers, and Onions, Grilled, 157
Couscous, Ginger Chicken with, 143
Couscous, Mediterranean, 157
Crab Cakes over Mixed Greens with Lemon
Dressing, 94
Cranberries
Brussels Sprouts with Cranberries and Bacon,
Braised, 156
Sandwiches, Cranberry-Chicken, 74
Tea, Sparkling Cranberry–Citrus Green, 14
Cucumbers
Gazpacho, Blender, 62
Soup, Avocado and Cucumber, 61
Curry, Chutney Chicken, 147

Date and Goat Cheese Salad, 81
Desserts. *See also* Cakes, Cookies, Mousse, Pies
and Pastries, Pudding.
Crème Brûlée, Chocolate Malt, 188

Frozen
Affogato, 184
Ice-Cream Cake, Caramel-Praline, 178
Ice Cream, Chai Tea Latte, 176
Ice Cream Loaf, Layered Amaretti–, 177
Ice Cream, Peanut Butter–Chocolate, 175
Sherbet, Blackberry Buttermilk, 183
Sorbet, Melon, 170
Melon Mix-Up, Mojito'd, 184
S'mores Slabs, 187
Sundaes, Caramelized Pineapple, 174
Tiramisu, Quick, 179
Trifles, Pumpkin Gingerbread, 180
Trifle, Triple Chocolate–Toffee, 180
Dumplings, Chicken and, 148

Eggs
Baked Eggs with Tomatoes and
Artichokes, 53
Fried Egg and Avocado Bagel Sandwiches, 70
Frittata, Leek and Asparagus, 54
Omelet with Goat Cheese, Garden, 52
Sandwiches with Basil Mayonnaise, Bacon
and Egg, 55
Spaghetti Carbonara, 131

Falafel Sandwiches with Tahini Sauce, 72
Fennel, Carrots, and Shallots, Roasted, 154
Fennel Slaw, Turkey Dogs with, 75
Figs
Collard Greens with Figs and Bacon
Crumbles, 156
Glaze, Chicken Breasts with Fig-Mustard, 146
Salad, Fig, Arugula, and Mint, 81
Salad with Figs, Warm Beef, 87
Fish. *See also* Clam, Crab, Salmon, Shrimp, Tuna.
Catfish Sandwiches with Tartar Sauce, 71
Grouper à la Mango, 107
Sea Bass, Lime-Marinated Grilled, 106
Swordfish, Cheese-Stuffed, 108
Tilapia Tacos with Ranch Slaw, Grilled, 112
Trout, Herb-Baked, 111
Frittata, Leek and Asparagus, 54
Fruit. *See also* specific types.
Beverages
Punch, Barbados, 24
Sangria, Fruity White, 25
Crumble, Nectarine and Berry, 173
Parfaits with Mixed Berries, Honey, and
Mint, Yogurt, 56

Garlic Shrimp with Spinach and Vermicelli, 130
Gingerbread Trifles, Pumpkin, 180
Glaze, Chicken Breasts with Fig-Mustard, 146
Grapefruit, Broiled, 42

Grapefruit, Hearts of Palm, Avocado, and Queso
Fresco, Mixed Greens with, 82
Grape Salad, Pear and, 58
Greens with Figs and Bacon Crumbles,
Collard, 156
Gremolata, Roasted Broccoli with, 154
Grilled
Fish
Sea Bass, Lime-Marinated Grilled, 106
Swordfish, Cheese-Stuffed, 108
Tuna Salad with Avocado-Wasabi Dressing,
Grilled, 93
Flatbreads, Grilled Rosemary, 168
Hot Balsamic Slaw Dogs, 75
Pork Teriyaki, Grilled, 139
Vegetables
Corn, Red Peppers, and Onions,
Grilled, 157
Zucchini with Mint and Oregano,
Grilled, 152

Ham
Prosciutto Biscotti, Parmesan-, 167
Soup with Ham, Smoky Lentil, 64
Hearts of Palm, Avocado, and Queso Fresco,
Mixed Greens with Grapefruit, 82
Hot Dogs
Balsamic Slaw Dogs, Hot, 75
Turkey Dogs with Fennel Slaw, 75
Hummus, Roasted Red Pepper and Chipotle, 9

Jicama Slaw, Sweet Lemon-, 99

Lamb Chops, Herbed, 138
Leek and Asparagus Frittata, 54
Lemon
Cheesecake, Lemon, 181
Cookies, Chewy Lemon-Almond, 185
Dip, Lemony Dill Feta, 8
Dressing, Crab Cakes over Mixed Greens with
Lemon, 94
Salmon, Sweet and Smoky Lemon-Broiled, 110
Slaw, Sweet Lemon-Jicama, 99
Spaghetti Squash, Lemon-Sage, 153
Tea, Lemonade-Mint Iced, 12
Lentil Soup with Ham, Smoky, 64
Lime-Marinated Grilled Sea Bass, 106
Lime Vinaigrette and Berries, Spring Greens with
Sweet, 83
Linguine Verde, 102
Linguine with Red Clam Sauce, 129

Mangoes
Grouper à la Mango, 107
Salad, Smoked Turkey–Mango, 91

Salsa, Strawberry-Mango, 10
Soup, Chilled Mango, 60
Mayonnaise, Bacon and Egg Sandwiches with Basil, 55
Mayonnaise, Steak Sandwiches with Horseradish, 78
Melon Mix-Up, Mojito'd, 184
Melon, Sorbet, 170
Microwave
  Appetizer
    Sliders with Sweet Chipotle-Peach Sauce, Spicy Pork, 20
  Desserts
    Mousse, Milk Chocolate–Hazelnut, 183
    Mousse with Strawberries, White Chocolate, 182
    Pudding with Saffron, Arborio Rice, 172
    Tortes, Raspberry-Chocolate, 171
  Main Dishes
    Chicken, Apricot-Glazed, 144
    Chicken Breasts with Fig-Mustard Glaze, 146
    Oatmeal, Raisin and Almond, 57
    Spaghetti Squash, Lemon-Sage, 153
Mousse. *See also* Pudding.
  Milk Chocolate–Hazelnut Mousse, 183
  Mocha Mousse, 182
  White Chocolate Mousse with Strawberries, 182
Muffins
  Apple Butter–Bran Muffins, 163
  Blueberry-Yogurt Muffins, 29
  Pumpkin-Raisin Muffins, 164
Mushrooms
  Portobello Paninis, 73

Nectarine and Berry Crumble, 173
Noodles
  Roast Beef Stroganoff, Simple, 132

Oats
  Bread, Banana-Oatmeal, 30
  Cookies, No-Bake Chocolate-Oat Drop, 187
  Oatmeal, Raisin and Almond, 57
Olives
  Couscous, Mediterranean, 157
  Tapenade Crostini, Goat Cheese–Green Olive, 14
Omelet with Goat Cheese, Garden, 52
Onions
  Caramelized Onion Pizza, 105
  Glazed Onions, Pork Medallions with, 140
  Grilled Corn, Red Peppers, and Onions, 157
  Rings, Baked Onion, 159

Oranges
  Biscuits, Orange, 28
  Relish, Crostini with Manchego and Honeyed Orange, 15
  Salad, Fresh Orange and Spring Greens, 80
Orzo with Basil, Orange, and Pine Nuts, 158

Pancakes
  Buttermilk Pancakes, 32
  Carrot Cake Pancakes with Cream Cheese Sauce, 49
  Potato Pancake with Smoked Salmon, Herbed, 31
Pasta. *See also* Couscous, Linguine, Orzo, Spaghetti, Vermicelli.
  Pesto Pasta with Roasted Tomatoes and Walnuts, 103
  Vermicelli, Garlic Shrimp with Spinach and, 130
Peach Sauce, Spicy Pork Sliders with Sweet Chipotle-, 20
Peanut Butter–Chocolate Ice Cream, 175
Pears
  Crisp, Pear, 174
  Salad, Pear and Grape, 58
  Triangles, Pear and Swiss, 16
Pea Salad, Minted, 84
Pea Soup with Spicy Sausage, Yellow Split, 66
Pecans
  Quinoa Cereal with Blueberries and Pecans, Hot, 56
  Salad, Apple-Pecan Chicken, 89
  Squares, Pecan Pie, 186
  Waffles, Pecan, 51
Peppers
  Chile
    Chipotle-Peach Sauce, Spicy Pork Sliders with Sweet, 20
    Crescents, Bacon-Chile-Cheese, 11
    Poblano-Chicken Chowder, 68
  Red
    Grilled Corn, Red Peppers, and Onions, 157
    Pesto Crostini, Red Pepper, 12
    Pork, Hot Peppered, 142
    Soup with Basil, Rustic Italian Tomato and Red Pepper, 63
    Roasted Red Pepper and Chipotle Hummus, 9
Pesto Crostini, Red Pepper, 12
Pesto Spread, Chicken-, 10
Picadillo, Turkey, 149
Pies and Pastries
  Nectarine and Berry Crumble, 173
  Pear Crisp, 174
  Shepherd's Pie, Speedy, 133
  Spanakopita Bites, 16

Pineapple, Ginger-Caramelized, 160
Pineapple Sundaes, Caramelized, 174
Pistachio Crostini, Honey-Drizzled Cherry, Goat Cheese, and, 13
Pizza, BBQ Chicken, 144
Pizza, Caramelized Onion, 105
Pomegranate-Ginger Fizz, 24
Pork. *See also* Ham.
  Hot Peppered Pork, 142
  Salad, Spicy Thai Pork, 92
  Tenderloin
    Dijon Sauce, Pork and Vegetables in, 141
    Grilled Pork Teriyaki, 139
    Medallions with Glazed Onions, Pork, 140
    Moo Shu Pork Wraps, 76
    Sliders with Sweet Chipotle-Peach Sauce, Spicy Pork, 20
Potatoes
  Mustard Potatoes and Green Beans, 155
  Pancake with Smoked Salmon, Herbed Potato, 31
  Roasted Dill Potatoes, 155
  Salads
    German Potato Salad, 97
    Grilled Potato and Arugula Salad, 98
    Warm Gorgonzola Potato Salad, 98
  Shepherd's Pie, Speedy, 133
Pudding. *See also* Mousse.
  Arborio Rice Pudding with Saffron, 172
Pumpkin
  Muffins, Pumpkin-Raisin, 164
  Soup, Thai Pumpkin, 64
  Trifles, Pumpkin Gingerbread, 180

Quinoa Cereal with Blueberries and Pecans, Hot, 56

Raspberry-Chocolate Tortes, 171
Raspberry-Coconut Cake, Chocolate-, 179
Relish, Crostini with Manchego and Honeyed Orange, 15
Rice
  Arborio Rice Pudding with Saffron, 172
  Casserole, Mexican, 135
  Fried Rice with Chicken, Southwestern, 145
  Soup, Southwestern Chicken and Rice, 69

Salads
  Bean Salad, Marinated, 96
  Beef Salad with Figs, Warm, 87
  Bulgur and Pine Nut Salad, 100
  Chicken
    Apple-Pecan Chicken Salad, 89
    Curry Chicken Salad, 88
    Green Goddess Chicken Salad, 89

10 Simple Side Dishes

Vegetable	Servings	Preparation	Cooking Instructions
Asparagus	3 to 4 per pound	Snap off tough ends. Remove scales, if desired.	To steam: Cook, covered, on a rack above boiling water 2 to 3 minutes. To boil: Cook, covered, in a small amount of boiling water 2 to 3 minutes or until crisp-tender.
Broccoli	3 to 4 per pound	Remove outer leaves and tough ends of lower stalks. Wash; cut into spears.	To steam: Cook, covered, on a rack above boiling water 5 to 7 minutes or until crisp-tender.
Carrots	4 per pound	Scrape; remove ends, and rinse. Leave tiny carrots whole; slice large carrots.	To steam: Cook, covered, on a rack above boiling water 8 to 10 minutes or until crisp-tender. To boil: Cook, covered, in a small amount of boiling water 8 to 10 minutes or until crisp-tender.
Cauliflower	4 per medium head	Remove outer leaves and stalk. Wash. Break into florets.	To steam: Cook, covered, on a rack above boiling water 5 to 7 minutes or until crisp-tender.
Corn	4 per 4 large ears	Remove husks and silks. Leave corn on the cob, or cut off kernels.	Cook, covered, in boiling water to cover 8 to 10 minutes (on cob) or in a small amount of boiling water 4 to 6 minutes (kernels).
Green beans	4 per pound	Wash; trim ends, and remove strings. Cut into 1½-inch pieces.	To steam: Cook, covered, on a rack above boiling water 5 to 7 minutes. To boil: Cook, covered, in a small amount of boiling water 5 to 7 minutes or until crisp-tender.
Potatoes	3 to 4 per pound	Scrub; peel, if desired. Leave whole, slice, or cut into chunks.	To boil: Cook, covered, in boiling water to cover 30 to 40 minutes (whole) or 15 to 20 minutes (slices or chunks). To bake: Bake at 400° for 1 hour or until done.
Snow peas	4 per pound	Wash; trim ends, and remove tough strings.	To steam: Cook, covered, on a rack above boiling water 2 to 3 minutes. Or sauté in cooking spray or 1 teaspoon oil over medium-high heat 3 to 4 minutes or until crisp-tender.
Squash, summer	3 to 4 per pound	Wash; trim ends, and slice or chop.	To steam: Cook, covered, on a rack above boiling water 6 to 8 minutes. To boil: Cook, covered, in a small amount of boiling water 6 to 8 minutes or until crisp-tender.
Squash, winter (including acorn, butternut, and buttercup)	2 per pound	Rinse; cut in half, and remove all seeds. Leave in halves to bake, or peel and cube to boil.	To boil: Cook cubes, covered, in boiling water 20 to 25 minutes. To bake: Place halves, cut sides down, in a shallow baking dish; add ½ inch water. Bake, uncovered, at 375° for 30 minutes. Turn and season, or fill; bake an additional 20 to 30 minutes or until tender.